OUTLINES

OF

NEW TESTAMENT HISTORY

BY

REV. FRANCIS E. GIGOT, D.D.,

*Mooney Professor of the Sacred Scriptures in St. Joseph's Seminary,
Dunwoodie, New York.*

PREFACE.

THE present is a companion volume to the " Outlines of Jewish History " published some months ago. It deals with the historical data supplied by the inspired writings of the New Testament, in exactly the same manner as the preceding work did with the various events recorded in the sacred books of the Old Testament. In both volumes the writer has pursued the same purpose and followed the same methods.

Both works have been prepared for the special use of theological students, not, however, without the hope that they may prove serviceable to a much larger number of readers, such as teachers of Bible history in Sunday-schools, colleges, academies, and the like. In neither volume has it been the aim of the writer to supply a substitute for the Bible itself, but rather a help towards a more careful perusal of the inspired record. With this purpose in view, he has set forth such results of modern investigation as may render the sacred narrative more intelligible and attractive. Many of the difficulties which are daily being raised on historical grounds are also touched upon, and the biblical student is supplied with constant references to further sources of information.

Like the historical writings of the New Testament, the present volume contains two distinct, though very closely connected parts. The first part, gathered from the four narratives of our canonical gospels, describes the life and times of Our Lord ; the second, based mainly on the book of the Acts, presents a brief sketch of the labors of Peter, Paul, James, and John, the leading apostles of Christ. The first part, under the title of "The Gospel History," takes up the sacred narrative at the point where it was left in the "Outlines of Jewish History," and deals with the three-and-thirty years of Our Lord's mortal life ; the second, entitled "The Apostolic History," narrates the principal events connected with the planting and early spread of Christianity in the Roman Empire down to the year 98 A.D.

As an additional help to the student, two maps—one of Palestine in the Time of Our Lord, the other of the Roman Empire in the Apostolic Times—have been especially prepared, and will be found at the end of the volume, together with a Chronological Table established on the now commonly admitted fact that the birth of Our Lord took place some years before what is called the Christian era.

July 16, 1898.

NOTE TO THE SECOND EDITION.

THIS second edition is not a recast of the first which appeared some years ago. Much critical and historical work has indeed been done meantime by students of the New Testament Literature. It does not seem, however, that the results so far reached require a re-writing of the present work. The few changes introduced into this second edition are therefore of comparatively little importance and consist chiefly in verbal modifications.

November 4, 1902.

CONTENTS.

PART FIRST.

THE GOSPEL HISTORY.

First Period: Before Our Lord's Public Ministry.

Second Period: Our Lord's Public Ministry.

CHAPTER XVI.

Third Period: The Passion and Resurrection.

CHAPTER XVII.

CHAPTER XVIII.

CHAPTER XIX.

CHAPTER XX.

PART SECOND.

THE APOSTOLIC HISTORY.

CHAPTER XXI.

CHAPTER XXII.

CHAPTER XXIII.

CHAPTER XXIV.

CHAPTER XXV.

CHAPTER XXVI.

PART FIRST.

THE GOSPEL HISTORY.

OR

The Life and Times of Christ.

SYNOPSIS OF CHAPTER I.

GEOGRAPHY OF PALESTINE IN THE TIME OF CHRIST.

I. VARIOUS NAMES : Palestine : the most common · origin.

II. SITE AND SIZE :
1. Site: Latitude and Longitude.—Boundaries.—Admirable situation.
2. Size: Length.—Breadth.—Total area.

III. GENERAL ASPECT AND DIVISIONS.

IV. PHYSICAL DESCRIPTION OF

1. Eastern Palestine :
The high table-land beyond Jordan.
Rivers and mountains.

2. Western Palestine :
Three long Parallel Tracts:
Sea-coast.
The hilly country.
The Jordan valley.
Mountains (begin in the south and proceed northward).
Lowlands (three principal).
Rivers: Only one; streams or torrents besides.
Lakes.

FIRST PERIOD:

BEFORE OUR LORD'S PUBLIC MINISTRY.

CHAPTER I.

GEOGRAPHY OF PALESTINE IN THE TIME OF CHRIST.

1. Various Names. Palestine, the scene of Gospel history, has in different ages been designated by the following names: (1) the land of **Chanaan**; (2) the land of **Promise**; (3) the land of **Israel**; (4) the land of **Juda** or **Judæa**; (5) the **Holy** Land; (6) **Palestine**. This last, by far the most common name, was originally applied by the Hebrews merely to the strip of maritime plain inhabited by their encroaching neighbors, the Philistines, hence the name; but ultimately it became the usual appellation for the whole country of the Jews.

2. Site and Size. Palestine lies between the 31° and 33° 20′ of north latitude, and between the 34° 20′ and 36° 20′ of east longitude. In the time of Christ it was limited on the west by Phenicia and the Great or Mediterranean Sea; on the south by the Brook of Egypt, the Negeb, the south end of the Dead Sea, and the Arnon river; on the east by Arabia; on the north by Anti-Lebanon, Lebanon, and Phenicia. Its situation in the temperate zone, in the centre of the ancient world, has often been admired : it combined, with a sufficient isolation from heathen influences, a position well suited to the preservation and spread of the true religion among mankind.

Like many regions which have played a great part in the world's history, Palestine is a very small country. Its average length is about 150 miles, and its average breadth west of the Jordan a little more than 40 miles, east of the Jordan a little less than 40 miles. The total area between the Jordan and the Great Sea is about 6600 square miles ; the portion east of the Jordan has an area of about 5000 or perhaps 6000 square miles,—making the whole area of Palestine 12,000 or 13,000 square miles, or about equal to the two States of Massachusetts and Connecticut together.

3. **General Aspect and Divisions.**   A single glance at a physical map of the Holy Land is quite sufficient to make us realize that its general aspect is that of a mountainous country.   It owes this hilly appearance to the great Lebanon range, whose eastern branch (the Anti-Lebanon) is prolonged through Palestine by two distinct chains of mountains, the one on the west side, with the exception of one broad depression (the plain of Esdraelon), extending as far as the desert of Sinai, the other, on the east of the Jordan, reaching as far as the mountains of Arabia Petræa. To the west of each one of its mountain-chains Palestine has a large plain, namely, the valley of the Jordan and the sea-coast, so that the Holy Land is naturally divided into four parallel tracts extending north and south.   Three of these parallel tracts are almost entirely situated to the west of the Jordan and are usually designated under the name of **Western** Palestine, while the track altogether east of the Jordan is known as **Eastern** Palestine or the **Transjordanic** region.

In the time of Christ Eastern Palestine comprised several great tracts of country, the exact limits of which cannot be defined at the present day. These regions were (1) **Peræa Proper,** which lay chiefly between the rivers Arnon and Jabbok; (2) **Galaaditis** (Galaad); (3) **Batanea** (Basan); (4) **Gaulanitis** (Golan); (5) **Ituræa**; (6) **Trachonitis**; (7) **Abilene**; (8) and finally, the **Decapolis,** which lay partly west of the Jordan.

The country west of the Jordan included only three great regions, viz., **Judæa, Samaria,** and **Galilee.** Of these regions Judæa was the most famous. It extended along the coast of the Mediterranean Sea almost as far north as Mount Carmel, but on the northeast its limit did not extend quite as far as Sichem. Its southern part formed a portion of **Idumæa,** and it extended westward from the Dead Sea to the Mediterranean. It was about 40 miles wide, and was divided into eleven districts whose metropolis was Jerusalem. North of Judæa lay **Samaria,** which derived its name from the ancient capital of the kingdom of Israel, and whose central position in Western Palestine gave it great political importance. Finally, north of Samaria was **Galilee,** 50 miles long by 20 to 25 miles wide. It was divided into **Upper** or **Northern,** and **Lower** or **Southern,** Galilee.

4. Physical Description of Eastern and Western Palestine. The country beyond Jordan consists in a table-land whose length is about 150 miles from the Anti-Lebanon on the north to the Arnon river on the south, and whose breadth varies from 30 to 80 miles from the edge of the Jordan valley to the edge of the Arabian desert. Its surface, which is tolerably uniform, has an average elevation of about 2000 feet above the level of the sea, and while its western edge is broken by deep ravines running into the valley of the Jordan, its eastern edge melts away into the desert.

Eastern Palestine has three natural divisions, marked by the three rivers which cut it at right angles to the Jordan—

the **Arnon,** the **Jabbok,** and the **Yarmuk.** Across the northernmost of these divisions, which extends from Anti-Lebanon to the Yarmuk, "the limestone which forms the basis of the country is covered by volcanic deposits. The stone is basalt, the soil is rich, red loam resting on beds of ash, and there are vast 'harras' or eruptions of lava, suddenly cooled and split open into the most tortuous shapes. Down the edge of the Jordan valley and down the border of the desert run rows of extinct volcanoes. The centre of this northern province is a great plain, perhaps 50 miles long by 20 miles broad, scarcely broken by a hill, and almost absolutely without trees. To the west of this, above the Jordan, is the hilly and once well-wooded district of Jaulan (Golan of Scripture); to the east the 'harras' and extinct volcanoes already noticed ; and in the southeast, the high range of Jebel Hauran. All beyond is desert draining to the Euphrates." *

In the second division of Eastern Palestine, which extends from the Yarmuk to the Jabbok, the volcanic elements almost entirely disappear and the limestone comes into view again. The surface of the country is generally made up of high ridges covered with forests and furnishing rich pasturage ; eastward, there are plains covered with luxuriant herbage.

The third division of the Transjordanic region lies between the Jabbok and the Arnon rivers. In it " the ridges and forests alike diminish, till by the north of the Dead Sea, the country assumes the form of an absolutely treeless plateau, in winter bleak, in summer breezy and fragrant. This plateau is broken only by deep, wide, warm valleys like the Arnon, across which it rolls southward ; eastward it is separated from the desert by low, rolling hills." †

The country west of the Jordan, or Western Palestine,

* G. A. SMITH, The Historical Geography of the Holy Land, 1897, p. 534.
† G. A. SMITH, ibid., p. 535.

by far the most important in Gospel history, is naturally divided into three long parallel tracts extending north and south :

(1) **Sea-coast.** This tract is a plain, the main portion of which extends without a break from the desert below Gaza to the ridge of Mount Carmel. A great part of this plain is flat and naturally fertile. It is intersected by deep gullies which have high earthen banks, and through some of which flow perennial streams. The neighborhood of these streams is marshy, especially towards the north. This main portion of the maritime plain is some 80 miles long and from 100 to 200 feet above the sea, with low cliffs near the Mediterranean ; towards the north it is 8 miles, and near Gaza 20 miles, broad. North of the headland of Carmel, which comes within 200 yards of the sea, is the second and narrower portion of the maritime plain extending to Phenicia through the territory of Acre ; very near this town the plain has an average width of about 5 miles and is remarkably fertile.

(2) **The Hilly Country.** Next to the coast-plain eastward comes the high table-land, which gives to Western Palestine the aspect of a hilly region. This tract is about 25 miles wide, and its eastern slopes are extremely steep and rugged. The fertility of this highland region improves gradually as one goes northward.

The southern district below Hebron is mostly made up of barren uplands. Passing a little farther north into **Judæa,** we find the central and northern parts of the hilly country scarcely more fertile, for the soil is poor and scanty, and springs are very rare ; its western and north-western parts, being reached by sea-breezes, offer a better vegetation, olives abound, and some thickets of pine and laurel are to be noticed ; the eastern part is an uninhabitable tract known as the wilderness of Judæa.

Proceeding northward from Judæa to **Samaria,** the

central section of Western Palestine, the country gradually opens and is more inviting. Its rich plains become gradually larger; the valleys are tillable and possess springs; there are orange-groves and orchards; the mountains are still bare of wood; northwest of Nablous, however, the slopes are dotted with fields of corn and tracts of wood.

Proceeding still northward, we reach **Galilee**, the northernmost division of Western Palestine, where we find the plain of Esdrælon, 15 square miles in extent. The vegetation is more luxuriant here than elsewhere west of the Jordan, and springs are abundant. The hills are richly wooded with oaks, maples, poplars; covered with wild flowers, rich herbage, etc. East of these hills is the rounded mass of Mount Thabor, covered with oaks and contrasting with the bare slopes of the Little Hermon about 4 miles distant to the southwest. North of Thabor is the plain El Buttauf, of a similar nature to that of Esdrælon, but much more elevated.

(3) **The Jordan Valley.** This valley extends from the base of Mount Hermon to the southern shore of the Dead Sea. Its width varies from half a mile to 5 miles; at some points it is 12 miles broad. At the foot of Mount Hermon this valley is about 1000 feet above the sea; 12 miles below, it is upon the sea-level; 10 miles farther south it is lower by 692 feet; and 65 miles farther, at the Dead Sea, it is 1292 feet below the level of the Mediterranean. The mountains on either side reach a great altitude, some points being 4000 feet high. These heights, combined with the deep depression of the valley, afford a great variety of temperature, and bring into close proximity productions usually found widely apart.

Mountains, Lowlands, Rivers, and Lakes of Western Palestine. Along the coast the only mountain of importance is the ridge of Carmel, the highest point of which is about 1750 feet. In the hilly region, the best-known points of elevation are: Hebron, 3000 feet; Mount Olivet, 2600 feet; Mounts Hebal and Garizim, 3000 feet; Little Hermon and Thabor, 1900 feet.

The three principal lowlands are: (1) the maritime plain subdivided into Philistia, the plain of Saron, and the plain of Acre; (2) the plain of Esdrælon; (3) the valley of the Jordan.

The most important river of Palestine is the **Jordan.** At the junction of its three principal sources it is 45 feet wide and flows in a channel from 10 to 20 feet below the level of the plain. It traverses successively the lakes of Merom and Genesareth, and empties itself into the Dead Sea after an actual course of 260 miles, although the distance between its source and the Dead Sea is not more than 136 miles in a straight line. Its width varies from 45 to 185 feet, and its depth from 3 to 12 feet.

Three things are chiefly noticeable in connection with this river, namely: (1) its enormous fall of nearly 3000 feet; (2) its endless windings; (3) the absence of towns on its banks. The other streams of Western Palestine worthy of mention are the **Leontes,** the **Belus,** the **Cison,** and the **Zerka.**

The three principal lakes are the lake of **Merom,** the lake of **Genesareth,** and the **Dead Sea.**

SYNOPSIS OF CHAPTER II.

"IN THE DAYS OF KING HEROD."

I. **HEROD,** **KING OF JUDÆA.**	1. Origin and Early Life. 2. Accession to the Jewish Throne. 3. Consolidation of his Power.
II. **PUBLIC WORKS IN**	1. Jerusalem: Theatre; Palace; Temple. 2. Palestine and Foreign Countries.
III. **SOCIAL LIFE IN** **JERUSALEM.**	1. The Court and the Upper Classes. 2. The People and their Hatred of Herod.
IV. **RELIGIOUS CONDITION** **OF THE JEWS.**	1. Jerusalem the Religious Centre of the Jewish World. 2. Heathenism Widespread in Palestine. 3. The Messianic Expectation.
V. **LAST PERIOD OF** **HEROD'S REIGN.**	1. Domestic Affairs of Herod. 2. Condition of Palestine at Herod's Death.

20

CHAPTER II.

§ 1. *Herod, king of Judæa.*

1. **Origin and Early Life.** Herod, whose last years of reign mark the beginning of New Testament history, did not, as was claimed by his partisans, descend from one of the noble Jewish families which returned from Babylon, but belonged to the despised children of Edom, whom the valiant John Hyrcanus had formerly conquered and forcibly converted to the Jewish faith. He was the second son of the shrewd Antipater, who during the rule of the weak Machabean prince Hyrcanus II. gradually became the real master of Judæa under the title of *procurator* conferred upon him by Julius Cæsar, and who profited by this fulness of power to appoint Herod, then only twenty-five years old, to the government of Galilee.

In that province Herod soon displayed the energy which ever characterized him. He crushed a guerrilla warfare, and put to death Ezechias, its leader, and nearly all his associates. This aroused the indignation of the patriots of Jerusalem, and Herod, as professing the Jewish religion, was summoned to appear before the great Sanhedrim for having arrogated to himself the power of life and death. He appeared, but escaped condemnation through the interference of Hyrcanus II., and took refuge near Sextus Cæsar, the president of Syria.

On the murder of Julius Cæsar (B.C. 44), and the possession of Syria by Cassius, Antipater and Herod changed sides, and in return for substantial services Herod was recognized as governor of Cœle-Syria, that is, of the fertile valley between Lebanon and Anti-Lebanon. When the battle of Philippi (B.C. 41) placed the Roman world in the hands of Antony and Octavius, the former obtained Asia. Once more Herod knew how to gain the new ruler, and he became *tetrarch* of Judæa, with the promise of the crown if all went well.*

2. Accession to the Jewish Throne. Forced the following year, by an irruption of the Parthians, who had espoused the cause of his rival Antigonus (the son of Aristobulus II.), to abandon Jerusalem, Herod first betook himself to Egypt, and then to Rome. There, owing chiefly to the influence of Antony, he was declared king of Judæa by the Roman senate, and, preceded by the consuls and the magistrates, he walked in procession between Antony and Octavius to the capitol, where the usual sacrifices were offered and the decree formally laid up in the archives.

After an absence of barely three months, Herod was again in Palestine, where, at the head of an army, he soon made himself master of Galilee. He next set himself at work to take the Holy City. But before investing it—which he did in the early spring of B.C. 37—he repaired to Samaria to wed the unfortunate Machabean princess, Mariamne, betrothed to him five years before. The uncle of that ill-fated queen was Antigonus, whom Herod now besieged in Jerusalem. After a siege of six months Jerusalem fell, and a fearful scene of carnage ensued. At length Herod, by rich presents, induced the Romans to leave the Holy City, carrying Antigonus with them (June, B.C. 37).† Herod, the Idumæan, now ascended the throne of Judæa and inaugurated his long reign of 37 years.

---

* JOSEPHUS, Antiquities of the Jews, book XIV., chaps. viii.-xiii., § 2.
† Cf. JOSEPHUS, *ibid.*, book XIV., chaps. xiv.-xvi.

3. **Consolidation of His Power.** The first part of Herod's reign (B.C. 37–25) was spent in bloody endeavors to consolidate his power. Antigonus was executed, together with forty-five of his more prominent partisans. The aged Hyrcanus II., who had taken refuge among the Parthians, was induced by the most solemn promises of protection to return to Jerusalem, and was then assassinated (B.C. 30). Aristobulus III., the grandson and successor of Hyrcanus in the priesthood, was drowned at Jericho by the orders of the king, and even Mariamne—the only wife for whom Herod ever bore a real affection—fell a victim to her husband's blind jealousy. The next victim whom the tyrant suspected of plotting against his throne was Alexandra, his mother-in-law. And when, at length, he discovered, concealed with his brother-in-law, the sons of Babas, distant relatives of the Machabean family, whom he had long sought for in vain, he had them put to death together with their protector. Only then did he feel sure that no Asmonean would endanger his possession of the Jewish throne.

Meanwhile, and also with a view to consolidate his power, Herod neglected nothing to keep up friendly relations with Rome. To please his then all-powerful patron, Antony, he gave up to Cleopatra—who exercised a controlling influence over Antony—a valuable part of his dominions, the fertile district of Jericho. Upon the fall of Antony at Actium (B.C. 31) he succeeded in making a friend of Octavius on the island of Rhodes. Not only did this new patron confirm him in his kingdom, but he greatly enlarged it. When Herod sent his two sons by Mariamne, Alexander and Aristobulus, to Rome for their education, he received from Octavius a new increase of territory, and afterwards was appointed procurator of the province of Syria, and with such authority that his colleagues in command could take no step without his concurrence.

§ 2. *Public Works.*

1. In Jerusalem. To establish himself still more in the favor of Augustus, Herod imitated him in great works of peace. He erected a theatre within the Holy City, and without the walls an amphitheatre in which he held games in honor of the emperor with horse and chariot races and the bloody fights of gladiators and wild beasts. He not only embellished the old residence of the Asmoneans which stood at the end of the bridge between the southern part of the Temple and the upper city, but built for himself in the upper city a royal palace with wide porticoes, rows of pillars and baths, and for the adornment of which he spared neither marble nor gold. Contiguous to that new palace arose three towers of great size and magnificence to which he gave the names of Hippicus, after one of his friends, Phasælus, after his brother, and Mariamne, after his beloved wife. He restored and enlarged the citadel, which he named Antonia, after his former patron. Finally, the most magnificent of all his buildings in Jerusalem was the Temple, which in its former condition was out of keeping with the beautiful recent structures in the Holy City, and which after its rebuilding by Herod became justly the greatest national glory of the Jews.

2. In Palestine and Foreign Countries. Herod's love of building naturally extended to other places within his dominions. Samaria, already raised from its ruins by Gabinius, was now reconstructed in a magnificent style, fortified, and adorned with a temple in honor of Augustus ; hence its new name of *Sebaste* (Augusta). Jericho received among other embellishments a theatre, amphitheatre, and hippodrome. In place of the ancient Capharsaba, Herod founded the city of Antipatris, thus named from his father; the new city of Phasælis arose north of Jericho ; to one of the many strongholds which he built in various directions

he gave the name of Herodium, and he took care that it
should be supplied with rooms splendidly fitted up for his
own use ; other fortresses, like that of Machœrus, were restored and adorned with royal palaces.   No less than twelve
years of work were spent in raising a maritime city on the
site of Straton's tower, and which received the name of
Cæsarea in honor of the emperor.   Its exposed anchorage
was slowly transformed into a safe harbor by a strong break-
water, which was carried far out into the Mediterranean,
and from the quays which lined its harbor the stately city
arose in the form of an amphitheatre.   In its centre was a
hill, on which Herod built a temple dedicated to Augustus,
with two colossal statues, one of Rome, and the other of
the emperor.

This munificence of the Jewish monarch was not, however, limited to his own dominions. " For the Rhodians he
built at his own cost the Pythian temple.   He aided in the
construction of most of the public buildings of the city of
Nicopolis, which Augustus had founded near Actium.   In
Antioch he caused colonnades to be erected along both
sides of the principal street. . . .   Tyre and Sidon, Byblus
and Berytus, Tripolis, Ptolemais and Damascus were also
graced with memorials to the glory of Herod's name.   And
even as far as Athens and Sparta proofs of his liberality
were to be found." *

§ 3. *Social Life in Jerusalem.*

1. **The Court and the Upper Classes.**   In his great
desire to please Augustus and appear a liberal and cultured
prince, Herod held a court whose splendor and general tone
resembled in many ways that of the emperor.   Like the
Roman ruler, the king of Judæa surrounded himself with

* Schürer, The Jewish People in the Time of Jesus Christ, division I., vol. i., p. 437,
Eng. Transl.

men accomplished in Greek literature and art, and many among them were placed in offices of trust or honor. Prominent among them was the historian, Nicholas of Damascus, on whom Herod relied implicitly, and to whom he intrusted all important and difficult diplomatic missions. Another Greek, a certain Ptolemy, was at the head of the royal finances, while other Greeks or half-Greeks acted as tutors or travelling companions to his sons. Foreign mercenaries surrounded his person, and in so far contributed to give to his court a non-Jewish aspect. Again, the personal example of the king, who had himself submitted to receive lessons from Nicholas of Damascus in philosophy, rhetoric, and history, contributed powerfully to make his various officers reach a wider and higher culture than that which had ever been witnessed at the court of the Asmoneans. Unfortunately the Jewish monarch ever remained a barbarian at heart, and his practice of polygamy, together with his suspicious temperament, greatly interfered with the peace and happiness of those immediately connected with him.

Under Herod the upper classes lost much of their hereditary power, and endeavored to make up for it by a life of luxury and enjoyment; yet the high priests continued to form an influential aristocracy.

2. **The People and their Hatred of Herod.** Amid all his power and glory, Herod himself realized how far he was from enjoying the good-will of his subjects at large. He knew that they murmured at his introduction of foreign and heathen practices, his arbitrary setting up and deposition of the high priests, his prodigal expenditure, and his terrible severity against his opponents. Hence he several times attempted to pacify the people by truly generous and liberal deeds; but their gratitude did not last long, and time and again serious conspiracies endangered his life.

§ 4. *Religious Condition of the Jews.*

1. Jerusalem the Religious Centre of the Jewish World. In consequence of such popular opposition to his rule, as to that of a hated Idumæan and of a direct representative of the foreign and pagan authority of Rome, Herod carefully refrained from interfering with all that the worship of Jehovah in His own sanctuary required in the eyes of the Jews of Palestine and of the Dispersion. Under him, therefore, as under his predecessors, Jerusalem remained the great metropolis of Judaism. It was at the Holy City that the dispersed Jews regularly congregated in hundreds of thousands, bearing their yearly tribute and anxious to worship the God of their ancestors within the sacred precincts of His Temple. It was in the Holy City that each important section of the Hellenistic Jews had contributed to erect a beautiful synagogue, where those of the same tongue and country and interests could hold meetings of their own, and welcome their fellow-countrymen at the time of the annual festivals. It was in Jerusalem that the great masters of Israel, looked up to by the whole Jewish world, expounded the Law and the traditions of the elders, and from the Holy City that all the parts of the Eastern and Western Dispersion * received the teachings of their fathers, the regulations for the feast-days, etc. All this had besides the advantage to secure for the capital of Judæa a commerce, an influence, a prestige which it would never have possessed otherwise, and, as long as he was able to control it by the free appointment or removal of the head of the Jewish hierarchy, Herod had no direct interest to interfere with it.

2. Heathenism Widespread in Palestine. That this conduct of the Jewish king was simply the result of

* For details concerning the Jews of the Dispersion, see Outlines of Jewish History chap. xxx.

expediency is made plain by his manner of action wherever he felt himself free to encourage heathenism. Not only far away, in Phenicia, Syria, Asia Minor, and Greece, he made himself the ostentatious patron of everything pagan, rearing temples, theatres, porticoes, gymnasia, etc., but also around the central district of Palestine, and even to some extent within its limits, he started or encouraged idolatry. Gaza, Ascalon, Dor, Cæsarea, Joppe, Samaria, Panias were desecrated by heathen temples, altars, idols, and priests. Even "in the Temple of Jerusalem the Grecian style of architecture was freely adopted. It is true that in the Temple proper Herod could not venture to forsake the traditional forms ; but in the building of the inner fore-courts we see the influence of Greek models."* Indeed the king went so far as to place within its sacred precincts a number of trophies, and to display over its main entrance a golden eagle, the symbol of pagan Rome.

3. **The Messianic Expectation.** It is easy to understand how such unholy changes, forced upon the Jewish patriots and believers by the iron hand of the royal Idumæan, made them long ardently for the reign of the Messias, which their sacred books represented as a future kingdom of righteousness, and which their apocryphal literature—such writings, for instance, as the **Sibylline Books**, the **Book of Enoch,** and the **Psalter of Solomon**—described chiefly under the attractive images of material prosperity. False Messiahs made their appear·ance at the very moment of Our Lord's stay in Egypt, and the message of John the Baptist, a little later, gave a new impulse to the general belief that the Messias was at hand. Not only the New Testament is full of references to such an expectation,† but even pagan writers bear witness to it.‡

---

* SCHÜRER, division II., vol. i., p. 35.

† MATT xi. 3 ; LUKE i. 39 ; ii. 25 ; JOHN vii. 26, 59, etc.

‡ TACITUS, Hist. v. 13 ; SUETONIUS, Vespas. 4 ; cf. also JOSEPHUS, Wars of the Jews, book VI., chap. v., § 4.

The full frame of mind of Our Lord's contemporaries regarding the person and work of the Messias will be gradually unfolded in the course of the present work ; yet, even from now, it may be useful to set forth the general belief of the time. According to the popular ideal, the Messias was to be primarily a political leader, a mighty deliverer of His people from the tyranny of its pagan oppressors, and also a restorer of the Jewish institutions in their primitive purity. Issued from David's race and born in Judæa, He was expected to start a world-wide empire, of which Jerusalem would be the capital, and in which the sons of Abraham would be superior in things temporal as well as spiritual to the rest of the world. To be admitted into this Messianic kingdom it would be sufficient to observe the enactments of the Mosaic law, to which the Messias would Himself be subjected. Finally, a large number of Jews believed that if the nation was once engaged in such an extreme conflict with the Romans as to threaten Jerusalem and its Temple with destruction, the Messias must needs appear.

We shall see later on how Our Lord gradually modified these expectations.

§ 5. *Last Period of Herod's Reign.*

1. **Domestic Affairs of Herod.** The last period of Herod's rule (B.C. 15–4) was disgraced by scenes of bloodshed still more awful than those which darkened its first years, and the history of his domestic affairs is that of a long succession of intrigues and murders. Antipater, his eldest son by his former wife Doris, accused his step-brothers Alexander and Aristobulus of wishing to avenge upon Herod the death of Mariamne, their mother. Antipater was believed, as well as the court people whom the accuser had won over, and who were constantly inventing

new reports. Accusations and reconciliations now alter-
nated with each other ; but the calumnies did not cease in
the king's palace till Alexander and Aristobulus were
strangled by his order at Sebaste (B.C. 7). A multitude of
Pharisees, with some of the courtiers who had conspired
against Herod in favor of Pheroras, his brother, were put
to death. Upon further inquiry, the death of Pheroras
brought to light the whole secret history of years. He
had died by taking poison sent by Antipater to dispatch
Herod. Even the second Mariamne—the daughter of
Simon the high priest—was proved to have been privy to
the plot, and her son Philip was, on this account, blotted
out of his father's will (B.C. 5). Antipater, now unmasked,
was handed over for trial to the Syrian propraetor. Easily
convicted, he was led away in chains. At last the strong
nature of Herod gave way under such revelations, a deadly
illness seized him, and soon word ran through Jerusalem
that he was no more. At once riots took place ; but the
troops were turned out and the unarmed rioters scattered ;
many who had been seized were put to death.

Antipater was executed only five days before his father's
demise. Herod died in the seventieth year of his age
(750 U.C.).

2. Condition of Palestine at Herod's Death. At
the news of the tyrant's death frightful anarchy prevailed
in Palestine. The popular voice, backed up by tumult and
riot, clamored for the redress of grievances, such as the
diminution of public burdens, the release of the prisoners
with whom Herod had crowded the dungeons, the abandon-
ment of onerous taxes, etc. Very soon, in fact, Archelaus,
to whom Herod had left by his last will the government of
Judæa, Idumæa, and Samaria, saw himself compelled to
send a large body of troops against the rioters, 3000 of
whom were slain.

A little later the Roman officials seized upon the treasures of the late king, and insurrection upon insurrection broke out against them. Even the troops of Herod wandered about in bands, plundering as they pleased, and false Messiahs appeared who assumed the diadem and gathered troops of bandits. Finally, a large number of the Jews had been so disgusted with the Herodian rule that they sent 500 of their number to Augustus to ask him not to ratify the will of the deceased monarch, and to suppress the royal authority in Judæa.

SYNOPSIS OF CHAPTER III.

THE INCARNATION AND NATIVITY.

I. THE INCARNATION.

1. The Annunciation
   - to Zachary: Conception and circumcision of the precursor.
   - to Mary: Place; Gabriel's message; "the Word made Flesh."

2. The Visitation.
   - Departure of Mary.
   - Scene on arrival (the Magnificat).

3. The Marriage of Our Blessed Lady.
   - Marriage Ceremonies in the East.
   - St. Joseph's anxious misgivings removed.
   - The marriage itself.

II. THE NATIVITY.

1. Not in Nazareth.
   - The enrolment
     - Nature and extent.
     - Connection with Cyrinus.
   - The two genealogies (general features—theories).
   - Date of birth (approximative).

2. But in Bethlehem.
   - The town: situation and description.
   - The inn: An Eastern khan described.
   - The manger (cave, ox, and ass, etc.).

3. The Adoration of the Shepherds (Luke ii. 8–20).

32

CHAPTER III.

THE INCARNATION AND NATIVITY.

§ 1. *The Incarnation.*

1. The Annunciation. Herod was still living* when the birth of the precursor of Christ was foretold (October, 6 B.C.; 748 U.C.).† Elizabeth, his mother, and Zachary, his father, both of priestly race, after having long prayed for a son, had now lost all hope to see this, their most ardent desire, fulfilled; but their request, we are told by the sacred narrative, was finally granted.

When the days of the ministration of the priestly course of Abia, to which Zachary belonged, had come, he repaired to the Temple of Jerusalem to carry out whatever duties might be assigned to him by lot. To burn incense on the golden altar in the Holy Place was the most honorable of the functions of the simple priests, and this office now fell to Zachary. During this ceremony the people waited in the Court of Israel, praying in silence till the priest should reappear; and, as a rule, he never tarried in the Holy Place longer than was absolutely necessary. On that day the people waited long for Zachary, and when he came out he was speechless; hence, all understood that something extraordinary had happened. He had had a vision, which is recorded in St. Luke (i. 11–20), and during which he was told

---

* LUKE i. 5.

† It will be remembered that the dates throughout the present work are based on the now commonly admitted fact that the birth of Christ took place some years before what is called the Christian era.

by the angel Gabriel that Elizabeth should bear him a son whom he should call **John,** and who would be the holy pre-cursor of the Messias.

The unbelief of Zachary at the voice of the angel had been punished by a temporary dumbness; and at the end of his week's service he departed to his own house.*

In due time a child was born to Elizabeth, and on the eighth day after his birth he underwent the rite of the cir-cumcision, in which he received the name of John, as fore-told by the angel.† It was on the day of the circumcision of his son that Zachary recovered his power of speech, and uttered a beautiful canticle known as the " **Benedictus,**" from its first word in the Latin Vulgate. It is essentially a Messianic hymn, Hebraic in its language and conceptions. In the first part ‡ Zachary, speaking as a *priest,* praises God for the realization of all the Messianic hopes created by the prophets of the Old Testament; in the second part,§ speaking as a *father,* he addresses his son as destined to exercise a preparatory ministry to the Lord.

Six months after his appearance to Zachary, the angel Gabriel was sent from God to Nazareth, a humble village unknown and unnamed in the Old Testament, and hidden away among the hills of Galilee. It is there that, far from their ancestral seat, Joseph and Mary lived, who were both of the tribe of Juda and the house of David; and it is to Mary, " a virgin espoused to Joseph," that the angel was directed. The precise place where he visited her is not indicated in the Gospel; but the Latin tradition, which affirms that he found Mary in a grotto over which stood the house which was ultimately carried by angels into Italy, agrees with the expression used in the inspired record: " And the angel be-ing *come in.*"‖

* LUKE i. 21-23.   † LUKE i. 24-26, 39-45, 57-63.   ‡ LUKE i. 68-75.
§ LUKE i. 76-79.   ‖ LUKE i. 26-28 *a.*

See also VIGOUROUX, Dictionnaire de la Bible, art. Annonciation ; ANDREWS, Life of Our Lord upon the Earth, pp. 67, 68.

What follows in the sacred narrative * is as simple and un-
pretentious as a legend of Oriental imagination would have
been gorgeous and hyperbolical. The angel appeared probably under the form of a man, † and saluted Mary with
these remarkable words: " Hail, full of grace,"—a translation objected to by Protestant writers, chiefly because of erroneous dogmatic views,—" the Lord is with thee, blessed art
thou among women." At these words Mary was troubled;
but after bidding her not to fear, Gabriel delivered his
wonderful message, which summarized the principal Messianic predictions of the Old Testament, and by means of
which Mary easily understood she was to be the mother of
the Messias. Whereupon she humbly inquired, " How
shall this be done, because I know not man ? " ‡ The
angel told her that by His omnipotence, the Lord would
make of her the virgin-mother of the Son of God. To this
he added a suitable sign: the pregnancy of her cousin
Elizabeth. Mary then believed in the infinite power of
God, and submitted humbly to His eternal designs in these
simple words: " Behold the handmaid of the Lord; be it
done to me according to Thy word." Then was it also that
" the Word was made flesh and dwelt among us " and became for us all a permanent source of grace and the Medi-
ator of the new and eternal Covenant.§

2. The Visitation (March–April, 749, 5 B.C.). From
St. Luke's statement (i. 39) that " Mary went into the
hill country with haste," it may be inferred that she at
once began her journey, even before she informed St.
Joseph of the incomparable honor bestowed upon her.
She wished to congratulate Elizabeth on her pregnancy

---

* LUKE i. 28–38.   † Cfr. DANIEL ix. 21.

‡ These words suggest a difficulty in the mind of Mary, which Christian writers,
after St. Augustine, have commonly taken as implying a pledge of virginity.—Dr.
Swete (The Apostles' Creed) has clearly shown that the doctrine of the miraculous
conception of Jesus was, from the earliest times, part of the Creed.

§ JOHN i. 1–18.

revealed by the angel, and unite with her in praising God. It is beyond doubt that Joseph did not accompany Mary on her journey, but it is not unlikely that she was accompanied by some of her friends, or a body of neighbors going up to the Pasch, now near at hand.

She went to the "*house of Zachary*," * in the hill country of Juda.   As the name of the town where Zachary resided is not indicated in the sacred text, several places are mentioned as having possibly given birth to the holy precursor: (1) **Hebron,** a very ancient city situated in the hill country, and pointed out by a Jewish tradition as St. John's birthplace; (2) **Yuttah,** a town about 4 or 5 miles south of Hebron, a priestly town also, but without tradition connecting it with the birth of St. John; (3) **Ain Karin,** 4 miles west of Jerusalem, which Greek and Latin traditions concur in marking as the home of Zachary.†

As the distance from Nazareth to Jerusalem is about 80 miles, if Zachary lived at Hebron, about 20 miles farther south, the whole journey would take up four or five days.

The scene on Mary's arrival is very beautiful.   It bears the impress of the holiest joy : Mary salutes first her cousin Elizabeth, and at once the yet unborn John leaps for joy and is sanctified in the womb of his mother ; while Elizabeth herself, filled with enthusiasm, proclaims blessed the mother of her Lord.‡   All this is manifestly the result of

* LUKE i. 40.

† See ANDREWS, Life of Our Lord, p. 54 sq.; FOUARD, Life of Jesus, p. 18 and footnote.

‡ The words of Elizabeth exhibit the characteristics of Hebrew poetry in a marked degree, and may be divided into two stanzas of four lines each, as follows:

> Blessed art thou among women,
>   And blessed is the fruit of thy womb.
> And whence is this to me
>   That the mother of my Lord should come to me?

> For behold as soon as the voice of thy salutation sounded in my ears,
>   The infant in my womb leaped for joy.
> And blessed art thou that hast believed, because those things shall be accomplished
>   That were spoken to thee by the Lord.

(See St. LUKE, in International Critical Commentary, p. 27.)

the presence of Our Lord, unseen, but inspiring all. Again, there is a great contrast between the excited enthusiasm of Elizabeth, who " *cried out with a loud voice,*" and Mary's canticle, which breathes a sentiment of deep and inward repose, in harmony with her more complete and more constant dependence on the Holy Spirit.*

The **Magnificat** is made up of three stanzas, in the first of which Mary praises God for His benefits to her;† in the second she praises Him for His judgments over the world ;‡ in the third she praises Him for His mercy towards Israel.§ Commentators justly observe that the expressions of the **Magnificat** being almost entirely borrowed from the Old Testament poetry, Mary could easily give vent to her feelings of gratitude in the poetical form under which they have come down to us.

3. **The Marriage of Our Blessed Lady.** ‖ The marriage customs of the East have ever differed considerably from those in vogue among the Western nations.

After the selection of the bride, the *espousals* or *betrothal* took place, and were formal proceedings undertaken by a friend or legal representative on the part of the bridegroom, and by the parents on the part of the bride. The *wedding* itself was simply the removal of the bride from her father's house to that of the bridegroom. But between the betrothal and the wedding an interval might elapse varying from a few days to a full year for virgins. During this period the communications between the bride and bridegroom were conveyed by " the friend of the bridegroom," and the bride was considered as a wife, so that any unfaithfulness on her part was punishable with death, the husband having, however, the option of putting her away.

It is in the light of these Eastern customs that we should understand the marriage of our blessed Lady, as recorded by St. Matthew.

* LUKE i. 40–46 *a*. † LUKE i. 46–49. ‡ LUKE i. 50–53. § LUKE i. 54, 55.
‖ LUKE i. 56 ; MATT. i. 18–25.

After an abode of about three months Mary left the *house of Zachary** to "RETURN TO HER OWN HOUSE."[†] This last expression seems to indicate that Mary, "betrothed" to St. Joseph,[‡] had not yet been taken to him, as we learn in a more explicit manner from the following words of the first gospel : "When His mother Mary was espoused to Joseph, **before they came together,** she was found with child."[§]

After Mary's return to her own house her pregnancy was now so advanced that it was very soon noticed either by her parents or by the friend of the bridegroom : "*She was found with child,*" *i. e.,* she was recognized as such, and the fact, being ascertained, was made known to Joseph.

Great was the anxiety of Joseph, her husband, at this news, for he was considered as such after the betrothal, and as a "just man," *i. e.,* a faithful observer of the Law, he felt bound to repudiate Mary. This he might do in two ways. He could either summon her before the law-courts to be judicially condemned and punished,—this course would have "PUBLICLY EXPOSED HER,"—or he could choose a milder course : he could put her away by a bill of divorce written before witnesses, but without assigning the cause of the divorce ; and to this latter course he inclined : "*being not willing publicly to expose her, was minded to put her away privately.*"[‖] While thinking on those things, viz., how to put her away, the angel of the Lord appeared to him and, manifesting the innocence of Mary, directed him to take her unto himself, *i. e.,* to bring her into his house.[¶]

Joseph, obedient to the divine command, took Mary, his

---

* LUKE i. 40.   † LUKE i. 56.   ‡ LUKE i. 27 ; MATT. i. 18.
§ MATT. i. 18; cfr. also DEUTER. xx. 7.   ‖ MATT. i. 19.
¶ MATT. i. 20, 21. All these details could be fully realized by the Jewish converts for whom the first gospel was written, and to whom they must have appeared a striking fulfilment of the prophecy of ISAIAS (vii. 14) quoted by St. MATTHEW (i. 22, 23).

wife, unto himself, "and he knew her not till she brought forth her first-born Son." *

§ 2. *The Nativity.*

1. Christ Not Born in Nazareth. It might naturally have been expected that Mary's child would have been born in Nazareth, but an enrolment prescribed by Augustus made a distant village the birthplace of Jesus.†
This enrolment was most likely a registration of persons and property, a census which would serve as basis for future taxation ; and, as St. Luke tells us, it extended throughout the whole Roman empire.

Strong objection has been taken to the statement of the Evangelist that a universal census was carried into effect in Judæa before the death of Herod. In point of fact no *explicit* statement can be found in any contemporary writer concerning the taking of a universal census at this time. But many things make it probable that it was actually taken : (1) from his accession to the empire Augustus was anxious to have a uniform system of taxation applied to the provinces ; (2) under him a census was certainly effected in provinces such as Gaul and Spain ; (3) it is well established that he commenced, if he did not carry out, a complete geometrical survey of the empire ; (4) several Latin writers ‡ refer to Augustus's Breviarium Imperii, *i. e.,* to a little book written out in the hand of the emperor himself, and treating of the number of his soldiers, of the taxes, imposts, etc., of the empire. Under Herod, Judæa was not yet, it is true, a Roman province, but its reduction to that condition sooner or later was already determined, and it is beyond question that if Augustus ever wished to have a census taken in Palestine during the lifetime of

* MATT. i. 24, 25. † LUKE ii. 1 sq.
‡ TACITUS, i. 11 ; SUETONIUS, Aug. chaps. xxviii., ci.

Herod, the obsequious king would not attempt to resist.*

A still greater difficulty has been found in the statement of St. Luke that this enrolment took place when Cyrinus was governor of Syria, because it seems to conflict with the following data gathered from other sources : Cyrinus filled the governorship of that province some ten years later than this, and then took a census of Judæa. The actual governor of Syria at the time of the death of Herod—an event which is usually placed not long after Our Lord's birth—was not Cyrinus, but Quintilius Varus.† Nay, more, Tertullian, in his treatise against Marcion,‡ affirms as a positive fact "that the census which could give official information regarding the family and descent of Christ had been taken in Judæa by Sentius Saturninus "—that is, by the immediate predecessor of Varus in the governorship of Syria.

It would be a long and tedious work even to enumerate all the theories which have been advanced to show how St. Luke's statement harmonizes with the data which have just been mentioned, and the accuracy of which cannot well be denied.   Suffice it to say (1) that recent investigations have proved that Cyrinus was twice governor of Syria, and (2) that it may be supposed that the census was begun by S. Saturninus, so that Tertullian could speak of it as taken by this officer, and that it was completed by Cyrinus during his first governorship : in this way St. Luke could no less accurately ascribe it to the latter. §

In carrying out the imperial edict Herod was careful

---

* Cf. FOUARD, i., p. 41 sq.; ANDREWS, pp. 71-82 ; SCHÜRER, division I., vol. ii., pp. 105-143 ; PLUMMER, St. Luke in Internat. Critical Commentary, pp. 48, 49.

† JOSEPHUS, Antiq. of the Jews, book XVII., chap. xiii., § 5; book XVIII., chap. i., § 1.

‡ Book IV., chap. xix.

§ For an able discussion of this question, besides FOUARD, ANDREWS, and SCHÜRER, above referred to, see VIGOUROUX, Nouveau Testament et Découvertes Archéologiques, p. 102 sq.; GLOAG, Introduction to the Synoptic Gospels, p. 269 sq.; WIESELER, Synopsis of the Four Gospels, section i., chap. ii.

not to override the national customs of the Jews, according to which they should be enrolled at the place with which they were connected by the ties of tribe or family. This brought Joseph into Judæa, to the city of David, for, as we learn in detail from the two genealogies of Our Lord,* Joseph was of the house and family of David.†

Both genealogies manifestly profess to give the human pedigree of Our Lord, and yet they present several important differences. St. Matthew, writing for Jewish Christians, begins with Abraham ; St. Luke, writing for Gentile Christians, goes back to Adam, the father of all men. In St. Matthew the genealogies are introduced by the word "*begot*"; in St. Luke, by the genitive with the ellipsis of the word "*son.*" St. Luke gives twenty-one names between David and Zorobabel, whilst St. Matthew gives only fifteen, and all the names, except that of Salathiel, are different. Again, St. Luke gives seventeen generations between Zorobabel and Joseph, whilst St. Matthew gives only nine, and all the names are different. Finally, while St. Matthew calls Joseph the son of Jacob, St. Luke calls him the son of Heli.

Two principal theories deserve notice in connection with Our Lord's genealogies. The first maintains that St. Luke gives the genealogy of our blessed Lady, while St. Matthew gives that of St. Joseph. This solution would indeed do away with all the differences mentioned above ; unfortunately it finds no basis in tradition, and seems opposed to the natural meaning of St. Luke (iii. 23). The second theory considers both genealogies as the genealogies of St. Joseph ; but while St. Matthew shows that Our Lord is the son of David by *legal* succession, St. Luke shows that He is such by *natural* succession. In this latter view both genealogies should also be considered as genealogies of Mary, inasmuch as, Mary being either the niece or the first

---

* MATT. i. 1-16; LUKE iii. 23-38.   † LUKE ii. 3-5.

cousin of Joseph, the ancestors of Joseph—both legal and natural—are also her ancestors.

Whatever may be thought of these opinions the Davidic descent of Christ had been predicted as one of the essential marks of His Messiahship, and its realization in Our Lord's person is put beyond question by the testimony of the New Testament writers and of tradition.*

It is at the end of the journey of Joseph to the seat of his ancestors that Mary—who had accompanied him, because doubtless at this particular time she was unwilling to be left alone at Nazareth—gave birth to Jesus, "her first-born Son."† This leads us to speak of the exact date of Our Lord's birth.

The precise YEAR in which Christ was born is still a matter of discussion among scholars. They agree generally that, when in the 6th century our received chronology was framed, an error—which has hitherto remained uncorrected—was made in the calculation of the year of Our Lord's birth : but they are at variance in their estimate of the extent of this error.‡ The most common view among them is that the date of Our Lord's birth was five years earlier than is represented in our common chronology (749 instead of 753 U.C.) ; and we may remark that this view harmonizes well with our data regarding both the *latest*

---

* For further information see FOUARD, vol. i., appendix iii.; ANDREWS, pp. 58-65, etc.

† It should be borne in mind that the title of "first-born," given to Jesus by St. Matthew (i. 25) and St. Luke (ii. 7), was a technical expression applied to all who had a right to the privileges of primogeniture, without regard to the fact that they were or were not the only children of their parents.

‡ The dates admitted by ancient and modern critics and chronologists are as follows :

7 B.C. = 747 U.C. Sanclemente, Ideler, Patrizi, Wallon, Bacuez, Mémain, Rault, Zumpt, Keim.
6   = 748   Kepler, Cornely, Lewin.
5   = 749   Tillemont, Petavius, Lesêtre, Lecanu, Schegg, Fouard, Fillion, Bruneau, Gloag, Godet, Andrews, Edersheim, etc.
4 " = 750   Lamy, Bengel, Ellicott, Pressensé, Wieseler.
3 " = 751   Tertullian, St. Jerome, Baronius.
2 " = 752   Clement of Alexandria, St. Epiphanius, Caspari.

and the *earliest* year at which the birth of Christ can be put.

The *latest* year to which Our Lord's birth can be assigned would seem to be the year 750 U.C.; for on the one hand, St. Matthew tells us that Jesus was born during the lifetime of Herod the Great,[*] and not long before his death ; [†] and on the other hand, Josephus [‡] relates facts which point to the conclusion that the death of the Jewish king took place between the 13th of March and the 4th of April, 750.[§]

The *earliest* year at which Our Lord's birth can be put would seem to be 749 U.C.; for (1) at His baptism a few months before the Pasch of 780 U.C., Jesus was "about" thirty years of age, and the word " about," under St. Luke's pen, hardly allows us to admit that Christ was then one full year more or less than thirty ; (2) the universal enrolment which was carried out in Judæa, and occasioned Our Lord's birth in Bethlehem, must be put as near as possible to the beginning of the administration of Cyrinus, and Cyrinus was governor from the autumn of 750 to 753 U.C.

Thus, then, the choice remains possible between the latter part of 749 and the beginning of 750 U.C.; the probabilities are in favor of 749 U.C., or five years before the Christian vulgar era.

The **month** in which Our Lord was born may be determined in the following manner : From St. Luke [‖] we gather that the conception of John the Baptist took place in either the month of April or of October, and counting onwards fifteen months—for six months intervened between the annunciation to Zachary and that to Mary, and nine months between this latter event and the birth of Jesus— we reach *June* and *December*, in one or other of which Christ's birth is to be placed. Now when we bear in mind

* MATT. ii. 1–6. † *Ibid.*, 19.
‡ Antiq. of the Jews, book XVII., chap. viii., § 1, and chap. vi., § 4.
§ See art. Chronology, in HASTINGS, Dictionary of the Bible, pp. 403, 404.
‖ LUKE i. 5, 24.

that in the night Our Lord was born the shepherds tended their flocks,* we feel that the month of June cannot be thought of, because in this month the fields are absolutely parched around Bethlehem ; in the month of December, on the contrary, the earth is clothed with rich verdure, so that this is most likely the month in which Jesus was born.   In fact, an early tradition of the Church designates this month as the time of Our Lord's birth.

The **day** itself on which Christ was born is believed to have been the 25th of December, through an immemorial tradition of the Western Church.†

2. Birth of Christ in Bethlehem.‡   It was, then, on this memorable day (25th of December, 749 U.C.), that the Incarnate Word of God was born in Bethlehem, the little city of David, according to the prophecy of Micheas (v. 2).

The town, as it now stands, is situated about 5 miles south of Jerusalem, on a narrow ridge running pretty nearly east to west.   The slopes of the ridge are in many parts covered by terraced gardens, shaded by rows of olives, with figs and vines.   On the top of the hill lies the village in a kind of irregular triangle, at about 150 yards from the apex of which is the noble basilica of Justinian, now surrounded by three convents: Greek, Latin, and Armenian.   The houses have flat roofs, and the streets are narrow and crooked ; the population is about 8000 souls.

Joseph and Mary reached Bethlehem by the northwest, and on their arrival they failed to find accommodation in the inn, crowded by earlier comers.   Then, as now, an Eastern inn was simply an enclosed space surrounded by open recesses, of which the paved floor is raised above the ground. In the centre there is the courtyard and water for the

---

* LUKE ii. 8.
† ANDREWS, pp. 1-21. A Catholic Dictionary, art. Christmas. FOUARD, i., p. 48, etc.
‡ LUKE ii. 4-7.

cattle ; behind is found the stable, which in that region
consists sometimes of a cave of limestone ; and when no
place can be had *in* the inn, travellers must be satisfied
with a corner in the courtyard or else in the stable. So
was it with Joseph and Mary when they reached the inn
of Bethlehem, for the manger spoken of by St. Luke [*]
suggests that they either withdrew to the stable of the inn
itself, or to some neighboring cave used at the time for the
purpose of a stable. The *cave*, now shown as the Grotto of
the Nativity, is southeast from the town and covered by the
Latin convent. It has been modified through ages, and
is now 38 feet long by 11 wide, and 9 feet high. A
silver star in a marble slab at the eastern end marks the
precise spot where Our Lord was born. Here is the inscription : *Hic de virgine Maria, Jesus Christus natus est.* Fine
silver lamps are always burning around. The manger was
taken to Rome in 1486 by Pope Sixtus V., but a marble
one has taken its place.[†]

The tradition, however ancient, which speaks of an *ass*
and an *ox* as standing over the crib, is probably without
sufficient grounds.[‡]

3. **The Adoration of the Shepherds.**[§] The first to
worship the new-born Saviour were humble shepherds who,
on the night of Our Lord's birth, tended their flocks in the
fields, or on the eastern hills near Bethlehem. A brilliant
light suddenly dazzled their eyes, and an angelic voice broke
upon their ears. Bidding them not to fear, it announced
the birth of the Lord Christ, and gave them a sign whereby
they would find Him in the city of David. Instantly a
heavenly choir chanted the praises of God, saying :

> Glory to God in the highest,
> On earth peace,
> Good will towards men !

[*] Luke ii. 7.
[†] ANDREWS, pp. 83–87 ; VIGOUROUX, Dictionnaire de la Bible, art. Bethlehem.
[‡] Cfr. FOUARD, vol. i., p. 47, footnote 3. [§] Luke ii. 8–20.

Obedient to the heavenly message, the shepherds hastened
to make proof of the mysterious sign and found the Babe in
the manger.

Having offered their homage to the divine Infant, they
withdrew praising the God of Israel and proclaiming all
that they had seen and heard.

SYNOPSIS OF CHAPTER IV.

THE EARLY INFANCY

I. THE EIGHTH DAY AFTER THE NATIVITY:

1. Circumcision and Naming of Our Lord.

II. THE FORTIETH DAY AFTER THE NATIVITY:

1. The Two Ceremonies: Purification of Mary / Presentation of Jesus — Described.

2. The Two Meetings: Simeon: The personage. / Canticle and words to Mary.

Anna the prophetess.

Historical Conclusion of St. Luke ii. 39.

III. THE EPIPHANY:

1. Adoration of the Magi:
   1. Time of arrival of the Magi.
   2. Country they came from: Arabia? / Chaldæa? / Persia?
   3. Their quality, number, and names.
   4. The star (conjectures—how a sign to the Magi?).

2. Massacre of the Holy Innocents: An historical fact. / Number of children murdered.

3. Flight into Egypt: The road followed; the distance. / Place and length of sojourn.

47

CHAPTER IV.

THE EARLY INFANCY.

§ 1. *The Eighth Day after the Nativity.**

1. Circumcision and Naming of Our Lord. Born under the Law,† our divine Lord willed to comply faithfully with its various prescriptions. Among the many rites it enjoined ‡ was the religious ceremony of the circumcision which every male child in Israel had to undergo as a sign of its incorporation into the chosen people of God. The rite was to be performed exactly on the eighth day after the birth of the child, even though it were a Sabbath day.§ On the eighth day, then, after His birth, Our Lord received in His sacred flesh the bloody incision, the spiritual import of which was death to sin.‖

From the brief notice which St. Luke gives to Our Lord's circumcision it may be inferred that everything took place according to the ceremonial with which it had gradually come to be surrounded ; in presence of ten witnesses, the father, or some other member of the family, made the bloody incision and then pronounced the accustomed blessings.

The **place** where the ceremony was carried out is not mentioned in the Gospel, but it was most likely either the inn of Bethlehem, or the house where the Magi found Our Lord later on, ¶ and in which St. Joseph had provided accommodation as soon as possible for Jesus and Mary.

---

* LUKE ii. 21.   † GALAT. iv. 4.   ‡ LEVIT. xii. 3.   § JOHN vii. 22, 23.
‖ DEUTER. x. 16 ; xxx. 6 ; ROM. ii. 28, etc.   ¶ Cfr. MATT. ii. 11.

Together with the circumcision, Our Lord publicly received the name which had been destined for Him by God, the sacred name **Jesus**. This name corresponds to the **Josue** of the Old Testament, and means " JEHOVAH'S SALVATION " : it was given to Our Lord to indicate " that He should save His people from their sins." * The name of **Jesus** is the personal name of Our Lord, and that of **Christ** is added to it to identify Him with the expected Messias. It must be noticed that others besides Our Lord have borne the name of Jesus.†

§ 2. *The Fortieth Day after the Nativity.*‡

1. The Two Ceremonies of that Day Described. In connection with the birth of a male child, the Jewish Law required that the mother should remain forty days separated from holy things,§ and that at the end of this period she should appear at the Temple with the sacrifice of a yearling lamb for a burnt-offering, and a turtle dove or a young pigeon for a sin-offering. Those who could not afford to bring a lamb were allowed to offer a turtle dove or a pigeon as a substitute ; and it is an evidence of the humble station of Mary that she brought two turtle doves—the offering which was permitted to the poor.

To comply with these requirements of the Law, Mary started for the Temple early on the fortieth day. She had to appear in the **Court of the Women** as soon as the morning incense had been offered. There her two turtle doves, bought either from the Temple officer, or from the merchants who had changed the **Outer Court** into a noisy bazaar, would be taken from her by the Levites into the **Court of the Priests** to be burned on the altar. After a

* MATT. i. 21.
† Cfr. for example, in the Old Testament, the Prologue to ECCLESIASTICUS, and in the New Testament, COLOSS. iv. 11.
‡ LUKE ii. 22–38.　　§ LEVIT. xii. 4 sq.

time, a priest would come with some of the blood, and hav·
ing sprinkled her with it, would pronounce her clean.

The second ceremony to be gone through on the fortieth
day, was prescribed by the Jewish Law in connection with
the birth of a *first-born son.* In order to keep alive the remembrance that God had delivered the Hebrews from
Egypt by the death of the Egyptian first-born, the Law required that every first-born male should be sacred to Jehovah, * and after subsequent modifications † it finally prescribed that all the first-born should be presented before the
Lord, as a symbolical act of surrender for His service, but
they could be redeemed for five shekels (about $2.85), from
the service of the tabernacle.

On the prescribed day, Joseph and Mary were in the Temple to present Jesus to God and redeem Him from the service of the altar. Joseph declared formally to the priest
that Jesus was his first-born Son, whom he offered to him as
to God's representative. Upon being asked which he preferred, either to give up his first-born or to redeem Him, he
answered that he wished to redeem Him, and handed the
money to the priest with a prayer. The priest then proclaimed the redemption of the child, and concluded the
ceremony with a prayer.‡

2. **The Two Meetings on the Fortieth Day.**
While Joseph and Mary were still before the gate of the
Court of the Israelites, a man named **Simeon** entered this
same Court by the **Nicanor** gate. Traditions represent
him as an aged man, and this is naturally suggested by his

---

* EXOD. xiii. 2.   † NUMB. iii. 12; xviii. 15, 16.

‡ The details connected with the ceremonies of the fortieth day—as indeed most of
those referring to old Jewish customs throughout the present work—are not found in the
Gospel narrative, but in authoritative Jewish traditions which are recorded chiefly in
the *Talmud* or uncanonical written law of the Jews. Many of these traditions reach
up to the earliest times of Christianity, and have been used with great success by
eminent scholars (such as Lightfoot, Schöttgen, Zunz, Jost, Grätz, Sepp, writers in Bible
cyclopædias and dictionaries, etc.), to illustrate the biblical narrative. While freely
availing ourselves of the results of their labors, we will refrain from mentioning our
sources of information, in order not to overburden our pages with references.

words, as recorded in St. Luke (ii. 29 sq.). Some attempts have been made to identify him with Rabban Simeon, the son of the great Hillel, and father of Gamaliel, who was afterwards president of the Sanhedrim.*

The Gospel narrative describes him as a just and devout man in close union with God, whose mind was filled with an earnest longing for the Messias, as the " *Consolation of Israel.*" He had been favored with a divine assurance that he should not die until his desire had been fulfilled. Under the guidance of the Holy Spirit, he came into the Temple and recognized in the holy Child the object of his ardent desires. Taking Him in his arms, he blesses God, and bursts forth into the canticle known in the evening office of the Church, as the " *Nunc Dimittis.*" Simeon desires no longer to live, for he has seen the Saviour promised by Jehovah to all nations—to the Gentiles as a light, and to the Jews as their glory. While Joseph and Mary were wondering at these words, Simeon blessed them in his transports of joy and love, and with prophetic insight spoke of the future of the Child and His mother.

At that instant, we are told, an aged woman (she was eighty-four years old) of the tribe of Aser, coming in, approached the gate. She had lost her husband after seven years of marriage, and had ever since persevered in her widowhood. Her long life had been spent in deeds of piety, either actually dwelling in the Temple or scarcely leaving it for necessary purposes. She also gave praise to Jehovah, and spoke of the Child to " all that looked for the redemption of Israel."

St. Luke concludes this section of his Gospel by this statement, that when Joseph and Mary " had performed all things according to the law of the Lord, they returned into Galilee, to their city of Nazareth." † This seems to conflict with what is said in the narrative of St. Matthew,‡

*ACTS v. 34.   † LUKE ii. 39.   ‡ MATT. ii. 1-12.

who places the flight into Egypt *from* Bethlehem and *before* the departure for Galilee. Several solutions of this difficulty have been proposed. By some it has been supposed that Joseph and Mary went at once to Nazareth to settle their affairs and came back to Bethlehem, their return being followed by the adoration of the Magi and the flight into Egypt. Others hold that they went to Galilee only after their return from Egypt, and that St. Luke fails here, as on other occasions,[*] to mark accurately the sequence of events, either because he was not concerned about it or because he followed simply his sources of information, in which the order of events was not taken into account.

§ 3. *The Epiphany.*

1. **The Adoration of the Magi.**[†] The holy Child was sought and recognized not only by Jews (the shepherds, Simeon, and Anna), but also by representatives from the Gentile world. These were the Magi, who were seen in Jerusalem inquiring for the birthplace of the King of the Jews. The particular time at which this occurred has ever been a matter of discussion, although an early tradition places the visit of the Magi on the thirteenth day after Our Lord's birth (January 6th), and this date seems to be in harmony with St. Matthew who apparently connects the adoration of the Magi directly with the birth of Jesus in Bethlehem.

It seems, however, impossible to place this event **before** the Purification in Jerusalem on the fortieth day, for Joseph, who left Bethlehem immediately after the departure of the Magi, remained in Egypt "till after the death of Herod," that is, several months, and then withdrew to Galilee without coming to the Holy City.[‡]

---

* Cfr. Luke iv. 14.   † Matt. ii. 1-12.   ‡ Cfr. Matt. ii. 13, 14, 19-22.

The time at which the Wise Men arrived at Bethlehem may therefore be determined with considerable accuracy: they came after, and most likely only a few days after, the Purification. But the country from which they came cannot be indicated with the same amount of probability.

The Gospel tells us that the Magi came "FROM THE EAST," a general expression which includes all the nations east of Jerusalem, even Arabia and Persia. Three countries in particular have been suggested by commentators : (1) Arabia, because the gifts offered by the Magi are native to this country, and also because of the prediction in Psalm lxxi. 10, 15, "The kings of the Arabians and of Saba shall bring gifts. To him shall be given of the gold of Arabia." But the gifts offered were common throughout the East, and Arabia is perhaps too far south ; (2) Chaldæa, because more east than Arabia, and a great seat of astrology ; (3) and with greater probability, Persia, because of the historical association of the word "Magi" with a priestly Persian caste, and also because early pictures in the catacombs represent the Magi wearing the Persian dress.

The name of Magi originally belonged to a high sacerdotal caste among the Persians and Medes. They formed the king's privy council, and cultivated astrology, medicine, and occult natural sciences. During the time of the Chaldæan dynasty there also existed an order of Magi at the court of Babylon,* of whom Daniel was made the president.† Subsequently the name was applied to Eastern astrologers, interpreters of dreams, and even to those sorcerers who made pretension to supernatural knowledge.‡ The whole story of the visit of the Magi leads us to admit that the Wise Men who came to worship Our Lord were not of this last description That they were astrologers or students of the heavens may be inferred from St. Matthew

* JER. xxxix. 3.　　† DAN. ii. 48.　　‡ ACTS xiii. 8.

(ii. 2), "*we have seen His star in the East.*" If they came from
Persia, their name of Magi—which in Persian means *priest*
—would naturally suggest that they belonged to the priestly
caste of that country.   They are often spoken of as *kings :*
it is more probable, however, that this quality was ascribed
to them on account of Psalm lxxi. 10, and this only in the
sixth century.

Early pictures in the catacombs represent **three** Magi
worshipping the infant Jesus.   The names of **Melchior,
Balthasar,** and **Caspar** were given them only at a much
later period.

Many conjectures have been made about the star which
guided the Magi from Jerusalem to Bethlehem.   Some take
it to have been an extraordinary meteor or comet, or a passing star such as has been seen in later times to blaze suddenly forth and rapidly disappear.   The great astronomer
Kepler calculated that some time before Our Lord's birth
(747 U.C.) there was a remarkable conjunction of *Saturn*
and *Jupiter* in the sign of *Pisces*, to which in the spring following *Mars* was added : this conjunction many take as the
star of the Magi.   Others finally—and with greater probability—consider this star as a purely miraculous sign having the very peculiar motion indicated by St. Matthew (ii. 9),
shedding down its rays in some remarkable way so as to
indicate a peculiar spot, and bearing in the Gospel narrative the generic name of "*star.*"*

But whatever the star was, the Wise Men took it as a sign
of the birth of the great King of Judæa, the land ruled by
that section of the heavens in which it was seen.   They may
have been helped to this conclusion by the prophecy of
Balaam,† by the prophecies of Daniel, and by the general
expectation which at the time seems to have pervaded the
East, that a king should arise in Judæa to rule the world ;

---

* See FOUARD, i., p. 382 ; ANDREWS, pp. 6-10.

† NUMB. xxiv. 17

moreover, great multitudes of the Jews were spread through the East, and their Messianic hopes were most likely known to the Magi. However all this may be, the sight of the star and the inner workings of divine grace determined them to undertake a journey to the far-distant land of the Jews.

After a journey of about four months, if they started from Persia, and of about seventy days, if they came from Chaldæa, the Magi arrived at the Jewish capital expecting to obtain there full information about the particular place where the new King of the Jews was born. Their question much more than their dress excited the curiosity of the Holy City.

Scarcely was Herod informed of their question, " Where is He that is born King of the Jews ? " when he trembled for his crown and formed an artful plan to get rid of the royal descendant of David, whom all expected at that time as the Messias. He therefore consulted the chief priests and scribes as to the *place* where this great monarch should be born, and the Magi regarding the *time* when the star had appeared. Then he sent the latter away to Bethlehem, the city of David, bidding them return and report the finding of the Babe to him, on the pretext that he, too, wished to worship Him.*

As they went, the star reappeared, and guided them to "the house" where Jesus was. Entering, they fell down before the Babe and presented their gifts : gold, frankincense, and myrrh ; after which, in compliance with a divine warning, they left for their own country without coming back to Jerusalem.

2. **The Massacre of the Holy Innocents.†** The departure of the Magi from Bethlehem was soon reported to Herod, for this village is but a few miles distant from the Holy City. In a frenzy of passion the aged tyrant gave orders for the massacre of all the male children in Bethle-

* MATT. ii. 3-8. † MATT. ii. 13-18.

hem and its neighborhood " from two years old and under."
This fact is not recorded by Josephus, it is true ; but his
silence may be accounted for in various ways. Neither is
it mentioned by heathen writers; but they knew little about
Jewish internal history. At any rate, the order to slaughter
the Holy Innocents is in full accordance with the historical
character of Herod as we described it in Chapter II.

Herod's edict extended to " Bethlehem and its neighborhood " ; its victims were to be children "of two years old
and under." This latter expression indicates that on the
one hand two years was the extreme limit beyond which the
tyrant did not think it necessary to go, and that on the
other hand he did not know what exact relation the time of
the appearance of the star had to the birth of Jesus.

The number of children cannot have been large : perhaps
fifty were slain; some writers even conjecture that the number did not exceed ten or fifteen.*

3. **The Flight into Egypt.** † Upon the departure of
the Magi, St. Joseph, warned from heaven, fled into Egypt
with the mother and the divine Infant, so that the cruelty
of Herod missed its mark.

The *route* followed by the Holy Family was, according to
tradition, by way of Hebron, Gaza, and the desert ; and as
this is the most direct way, it is very likely the true one. A
few hours sufficed to place them out of danger; and after
about three days' journey they reached the Egyptian boundary.

Egypt was, at the time, a convenient place of refuge,
because easily reached from Judæa, outside of Herod's
power, and full of Jewish residents. The *particular place*
where St. Joseph settled in this foreign land is probably
Metaryîeh, near Heliopolis, and about two hours distant
from Cairo. There he waited until he received a new message from heaven, i.e., "until the death of Herod." ‡

* ANDREWS, pp. 100-102.   † MATT. ii. 13-15.   ‡ MATT. ii. 15.

SYNOPSIS OF CHAPTER V.

LIFE OF CHRIST IN NAZARETH.

I. FIRST YEARS OF THE LIFE OF JESUS:

1. The Return from Egypt: { At what time? By what road?

2. Developments of His Human Life:
   - Physical: developments both real and normal.
   - Mental:
     - Apparent words of St. Luke.
     - Real: { Protestant views. Catholic teaching.

3. Apparition among the Doctors: { At the age of twelve. Appeal of Mary. Response of Jesus.

II. YOUTH AND EARLY MANHOOD OF CHRIST:

1. His Surroundings:
   - The Place: { The province of Galilee described. The town of Nazareth.
   - The People: { A mixed population. The Jewish element.
   - Family and Relatives:
     - Parents: St. Joseph disappears.
     - " Brothers and Sisters ": { Not full brothers and sisters. Either half brothers and sisters, Or only cousins.

2. His Occupations: { The trade of St. Joseph. No special training under any great Rabbi. The rest: A matter of conjecture.

CHAPTER V.

LIFE OF CHRIST IN NAZARETH.

§ 1. *First Years of the Life of Jesus.*

1. **Our Lord's Return from Egypt.*** The date of Our Lord's return from Egypt is intimately connected with the date of Herod's death. For on the one hand, the Gospel tells us that St. Joseph remained in Egypt till he received word from God,[†] and on the other hand, there are good grounds to admit that St. Joseph received the divine message very soon after the death of Herod, and that he then did not delay, but rather hastened his return.

Considering how numerous were the Jews in Egypt, how constant their communications with Palestine, how great their hatred of Herod, it is certain that the news of Herod's death would have soon reached St. Joseph in the ordinary way ; but it was first made known to him by the angel of the Lord,[‡] so that a very short interval must be admitted between the death of the monarch and the angelic message. That St. Joseph hastened his return upon this divine message is implied in the fact that he did not know that Archelaus was Herod's successor till he reached the Holy Land.[§] Now, as is very probable, Herod died in April, 750 U. C., so that Our Lord's return is most likely to be placed in this same year, after about two months of sojourn in Egypt.[||]

* MATT. ii. 19-23. † MATT. ii. 13, 19, 20. ‡ MATT. ii. 19.
§ MATT. ii. 22 || Cfr. ANDREWS, p. 1 sq.

The intention of Joseph was to settle down in Bethlehem as the proper place in which to rear the Son of David, near Jerusalem, from which the Messias was expected to extend His rule over the world. He therefore started by the great caravan road which connects Egypt with Damascus. This road passes by Gaza and Ramleh ; and it is probably in this last-named town—which is connected by a branch road with Jerusalem—that Joseph, in obedience to a new divine message, gave up his purpose to reside in Bethlehem, and withdrew into Galilee. To reach this province, now under the rule of Herod Antipas, he had only to pursue his way on the caravan road, first northward through the plain of Saron, and next eastward across the mountains, into the plain of Esdrælon. A little north of the plain of Esdrælon lies the upland town of Nazareth, in which Joseph took up his abode again, and in which "THE CHILD GREW AND WAXED STRONG." *

2. Developments of Our Lord's Human Life. The words of St. Luke, just quoted, point to what all grant to have been the real condition of Our Lord's *physical* life, viz., a condition of natural development. After its miraculous conception in the virginal womb of Mary, † Our Lord's body was subject to the ordinary laws of growth : from helpless infancy ‡ it passed through the stage of childhood,§ and the natural increase in strength and age,‖ into the full vigor of man's estate.¶ The physical developments of Christ's human life were then both real and normal.

As to the developments of His *mental* life, they are the object of considerable difficulty. When St. Luke writes (ii. 52) "AND JESUS INCREASED IN WISDOM AND AGE," it is plain that the Evangelist refers to such an intellectual growth of Our Lord as *appeared* to His contemporaries no less real than His actual increase in years and bodily strength. The

* LUKE ii. 40.   † MATT. i. 20; LUKE i. 42.   ‡ LUKE ii. 7, 12.
§ LUKE ii. 40.   ‖ LUKE ii. 40, 52.   ¶ LUKE iii. 23 ; JOHN viii. 57.

difficulty is to know whether such growth was *real* after the manner in which the mind of a child gradually expands into all manner of knowledge.

Here, recent Protestant writers depart considerably from the teachings of past ages. They admit that the growth undergone by Our Lord's mind was a strictly human growth, with all its weaknesses and imperfections and its gradual acquisition of positive knowledge. According to them, Jesus did not know from the beginning that He was the true Son of God; and it was only after long years of prayer and reflection that He became absolutely sure of His Messianic calling. Such a conception of Our Lord's mental life is hardly reconcilable with His divine character, and contradicts not only the constant teachings of ecclesiastical tradition, but also the impression which the Gospel narrative produces upon the mind of an impartial reader, concerning Our Lord's knowledge during His mortal life. *

The common teaching of Catholic theologians is entirely different. They admit that Our Lord's mind was endowed with a twofold knowledge which was not susceptible of increase, viz.: the *beatific vision* and an *infused* knowledge, in virtue of which He was *ever* "full of wisdom and of truth." † But besides, they hold that His mind acquired an *experimental* knowledge, the actual development of which depended upon the natural and gradual exercise of His mental powers acting on the data of His senses, and in virtue of which He was truly *advancing in wisdom as He increased in age.*‡ Such a co-existence of growth in knowledge, with a possession of all its ultimate results, is not without parallel in ordinary human life ; the telescope, for instance, may verify a result of which we have been previously informed by a mathematical calculation ; and we are all con-

---

* Cfr. LUKE ii. 40 ; JOHN i. 14 ; ii. 24, 25.
† JOHN i. 14 ; LUKE ii. 40.
‡ LUKE ii. 52.

stantly learning by direct observation, things already known to us.*

3. Our Lord's Apparition among the Doctors. †

At the age of twelve, a Jewish boy began to be instructed in the Law and to be subject to its regulations. Among these stood prominent the obligation to appear before the Lord three times a year, and as Joseph and Mary had no longer to fear the cruelty of Archelaus, who had been banished the year before by Augustus, they took up with them to the Holy City, and for the first time, the Child Jesus.

This was on the occasion of the Paschal feast of the year 761 U.C. [8 A.D.]. It was the greatest of all the Jewish solemnities, lasted seven days, and was attended by countless Jews who came to Jerusalem from every part of the world. When the seven days were over and the various caravans formed of kinsmen and fellow countrymen proceeded on their homeward journey, relatives could easily be separated without feeling any anxiety. Thus it was that Joseph and Mary did not feel any anxiety when they first noticed the absence of Jesus ; they simply thought that " He was in the company," ‡ and that they would easily find Him at the end of their first day's journey home, most likely at Beeroth, about 10 miles north of Jerusalem. Not finding Him, however, "AMONG THEIR KINSFOLK AND ACQUAINTANCE," they spent the next day in returning to the Holy City and seeking Him there. But it was only on the following day—the third after the separation—that they found Him within the sacred precincts of the Temple.

The precise part of the Temple where Our Lord was sitting with the Jewish doctors cannot be identified with certainty. It was most likely, however, the **Hall of Gazith,**

---

* Cfr. A Catholic Dictionary, art. Christ, p. 153 sq.; DEHAUT, Evangile médité, etc.. i., p. 397 sq.; LIDDON, The Divinity of Our Lord, p. 457.

† LUKE ii. 41-50.   ‡ LUKE 43-44a.

where the Sanhedrim, together with the scribes, ordinarily assembled.   During the Paschal festivities in particular, the eminent Jewish doctors of the time sat surrounded by great throngs eager to be instructed by them.   Jesus was among their auditors, and He soon astonished all by His questions and answers.

At the sight of Jesus, Mary could not help addressing to Him a maternal reproach, which was at the same time an appeal to His filial love for Joseph and for her. " Son, why hast Thou done so to us?   Behold Thy father and I have sought Thee sorrowing."   To this tender appeal of His mother Jesus made an answer full of mysterious meaning : " How is it that you sought Me?   Did you not know that I must be about the things that are My Father's?"   Even Joseph and Mary did not realize the full sense of these words, for we are expressly told that " they understood not the word that He spoke unto them."

§ 2. *Youth and Early Manhood of Christ.*

1. **His Surroundings.** The return of Jesus to Nazareth was followed by a long period of silent subjection and obscurity, of which the Gospel narrative says nothing, beyond this brief statement " He (Jesus) went down with them (Joseph and Mary), and came to Nazareth, and was subject to them." *   But, with our present knowledge of the circumstances of the time and place, it is possible, and may prove interesting, to obtain a distinct idea of Our Lord's surroundings during the long years of obscurity which preceded, and in some measure extended to, His public ministry.

The **province** in which Jesus spent no less than thirty years of His mortal life is Galilee, the northernmost of the three parts of Palestine, west of the Jordan.   It lay almost

* LUKE ii. 51.

wholly inland, and was divided into **Upper** and **Lower**
Galilee. *Upper* Galilee comprised the mountain range, a
prolongation of Anti-Lebanon, which lay between Phenicia
and the upper Jordan. As the town of Capharnaum was
in *Upper* Galilee, this district must have touched to the
east the lake of Genesareth, while to the west it reached
to the coast of Tyre and Sidon.* *Upper* Galilee was more
especially the "Galilee of the Gentiles." † *Lower* Galilee
included the great triangular plain of Esdrælon, with its
offshoots which run down to the Jordan and the lake of
Genesareth, and the whole of the hill country adjoining it
on the north, to the foot of the mountain range.

From the writings of Josephus ‡ it may be gathered that
the Galilee of Our Lord's time had a rich and well-culti-
vated soil, that it abounded in fruit and forest trees, and
that numerous large towns and populous villages—amounting to no less than 240—thickly studded the face of the
country. And there is no doubt that *Lower* Galilee, in
particular, was ever one of the richest and most beautiful
sections of the Holy Land.

The **town** of Nazareth—called Our Lord's "own country" in the Gospels, § lies on the western side of a small
valley of *Lower* Galilee, a little north of the plain of Esdrælon, about 14 miles from the Sea of Galilee and 66
miles north of Jerusalem, in a straight line. It is reached
from the plain of Esdrælon by rocky and precipitous
paths, and its population in Our Lord's day is variously
estimated from 5000 to 15,000 inhabitants. Its flat-roofed
houses are to-day, in general, built of stone, and have a
neat and comfortable appearance, but its streets or lanes
are narrow and crooked, and after rain are so full of mud
and mire as to be almost impassable. Nazareth enjoys a
mild atmosphere and climate, and all the fruits of the

* MARK vii. 31. † MATT. iv. 15.
‡ Wars of the Jews, book III., chap. iii., § 2; Life, § 45. § MATT. xiii. 54, etc

country—as pomegranates, oranges, figs, olives —ripen early and attain a rare perfection. Its present population is about 7500 souls. At the northeast of the town is the *Fountain of the Virgin*, whither, it is supposed, Jesus often accompanied Mary when she went to draw water, as the women of Nazareth do in the present day.

The village is surrounded by some fifteen heights, several of which rise to an altitude of 400 or 500 feet. They have rounded tops and present a pleasing aspect, diversified as they are with the foliage of fig trees, wild shrubs, occasional fields of grain, and countless gay flowers. From the top of the hill northwest of Nazareth there is a most remarkable view often described by travellers, and preferred by Porter even to that which is enjoyed from the top of Mount Thabor. Finally, a prevalent tradition indicates as the *Mount* from the summit of which the inhabitants of Nazareth wished to throw Our Lord,* a hill about 2 miles southeast of the town.

If from the country and town we pass to the **people** in the midst of which Jesus spent His youth and early manhood, we easily notice that it was a mixed population, the various foreign elements of which—Assyrians, Phenicians, Greeks, Romans, Arabs—had been brought thither by trade, exercise of power, or the natural intermingling of the neighboring populations, as Galilee was the great thoroughfare between Syria and Egypt. The Galilean Jews were fervent worshippers of Jehovah, and crowded to the Holy City at the feasts and to the local synagogues on Sabbath days. Far from admitting new doctrines, they remained extremely faithful to the Law, most likely because of the influence of the Pharisees and doctors of the Jews, who seem to have been settled in every town. Contact with strangers did nor affect their morals, and their courage could not be questioned ; and yet they were despised by the

---

* LUKE iv. 29.

Jews of the south, who boasted to live near the Temple, amid a less mixed population, on a holier soil, to possess a greater culture and to speak a purer dialect.

That Nazareth had a worse name among them than any other Galilean town is not proved.[*]

In the home itself at Nazareth we find two persons most dear to Jesus and whom the gospels call His *parents;* 1. Mary, His true mother, of the race of David, married young to Joseph, and who survived both Joseph and Jesus. 2. Joseph, a descendant of David, working at his trade for his daily bread, the foster-father of Jesus, and who died before Him—a tradition says when Jesus was eighteen years old.

Besides His parents Our Lord had relatives, who lived also in Nazareth, and perhaps under the same roof with Him. They are indeed called in the gospels " HIS BROTHERS " and " HIS SISTERS," [†] never His cousins or kinsmen ; but all grant that this does not necessarily define the degree of relationship which they bore Him, and in fact scholars are still divided respecting this difficult question. [‡]

Many Protestant writers think that these relatives were the *full* brothers and sisters of Jesus, or children both of Joseph and Mary, the mother of the Lord. This view would have the advantage that it takes the words " brothers " and " sisters " in their strictest natural sense ; and after

---

[*] Cfr. JOHN i. 46.

[†] Cfr MATT. xii. 46–50 ; xiii. 55, 56 ; MARK iii. 31 ; vi. 3 ; LUKE viii. 19, 20 ; JOHN ii. 12; vii. 3, 5 ; cfr. also ACTS i. 14 ; 1 COR. ix. 5.

[‡] Catholic writers on this question : FILLION, Commentaire sur St Matthieu, p. 183 sq.; VIGOUROUX, Manuel Biblique, iii., N. 181 ; Livres Saints et Critiques Rationalistes, tome iv.; REITHMAYR, Introduct. au Nouveau Testament, ii., p. 346, sq.; FOUARD, l. p. 383 sq.

Non-Catholic writers : LANGE-SCHAFF, Commentary on St. Matthew, p. 255 sq.; ANDREWS, pp. 111–123 ; MILL, Observations, ii., p. 221 sq.; ELLICOTT, On Galatians, ch. i., 419 ; SALMON, Introduction to the New Testament, p. 474 sq.; LIGHTFOOT, Dissertations on the Apostolic Age, pp. 1–45.

Bible Dictionaries, cfr. SMITH, art. James, Brother, etc.; A Catholic Dictionary, art. Mary, p. 155 sq.; HASTINGS, art. Brethren of the Lord.

having been admitted by ancient heretics,[*] written down by St. Jerome, it has been revived in Germany by Herder, Strauss, etc.; in England by Alford, Edersheim, etc.; and in America by Schaff, Lyman Abbott, Easton, Gould, etc. But it is irreconcilable with the ancient and constant tradition of the Church, which has made the perpetual virginity of Mary an article of Catholic belief. It is also repugnant to the common instinct of Christians, who have ever felt " that the selection of a woman to be the mother of the Lord carries with it as a necessary implication that no other could sustain the same relation to her, and that the selection of a virgin still more necessarily implied that she was to continue to be so." [†] Even from a lower standpoint this view is hardly compatible with the fact that our dying Saviour intrusted His mother to St. John, if she had other children to take care of her.[‡] Finally, while the words " brother," "sister," may certainly be understood otherwise than in their strict natural sense, it is significant that nowhere in the gospels are those relatives of Jesus called the *children of Mary*, the mother of the Lord. It is plain, therefore, that the "brothers " and "sisters " of Jesus were not His *full* brothers and sisters.

When this erroneous view has been set aside two opinions remain, each with its respective amount of probability. The first maintains that these relatives of Our Lord were only His half-brothers and half-sisters, or children of Joseph by a former marriage. This view goes back to the earliest ages of Christianity ; it has been admitted by many of the Fathers, both Greek and Latin, and is in the present day the current notion of the *Greek* Church. It does not present any unsurmountable difficulty, and has the advantage that it takes the words " *brothers,*" " *sisters,*" in a natural sense.

The second opinion takes the words " *brothers,*" " *sis-*

---

[*] HELVIDIUS, JOVINIAN.   [†] ALEXANDER, quoted by ANDREWS, p. 122.
[‡] JOHN xix. 26, 27.

ters," in a broad sense as equivalent to "_cousin_." This view was strongly advocated, and, indeed, to all appearance, started, by St. Jerome. Under the influence of this great Doctor it has become the current opinion of the Latin Church. There is no doubt that the words "_brother_," "_sister_," may be understood as equivalent to "_cousin_." Again, if Our Lord had no brother in the natural sense of the term we understand easily why He gave John to Mary as her son. It has also been noticed that Jesus is designated at Nazareth by an appellation usual to the _only son_ of a _widow_.* For these and other such reasons this third opinion remains very probable, although its partisans seem, at times, to rely too much on conjectures to strengthen their position.

2. **Our Lord's Occupations.** The life of Jesus in Nazareth was indeed a life of obscurity. Subject to His parents,† as all good children are, He was simply known as the " carpenter's son "‡ and as the " carpenter."§ This last expression implies that He had learned and that He actually toiled at the humble trade of His foster-father. We can gather also that He received none of the curious learning of the time, and was subjected to no special training under any great rabbi, such as St. Paul had under Gamaliel for we are told that "the Jews wondered, saying : How doth this man know letters, having never learned ?" ‖

This is all we know for certain about Our Lord's occupations during His youth and early manhood. Several attempts have been made to fill up the gaps of the sacred narrative and to present a fuller picture of the life of Jesus in Nazareth.

The first of these attempts goes back to the early times of Christianity, when it gave birth to legendary accounts, samples of which have come down to us in the gospel of Thomas and the Arabic gospel of the infancy. No one

---

* MARK vi. 3. † LUKE ii. 51. ‡ MATT. xiii. 55. § MARK vi. 3. ‖ JOHN vii. 15.

can peruse these apocryphal gospels without feeling of how little use they must ever remain to complete the picture drawn from the sacred text. They hardly ever record a fact of real importance not already supplied by our canonical gospels, while they abound in wonders which they ascribe to Jesus, and of a character always unlikely, sometimes even childish.

This is also the case, to a large extent, with the descriptions of Our Lord's life in Nazareth which were drawn during the Middle Ages. They breathe the childlike piety of the time, but also bespeak its great lack of acquaintance with Oriental customs and manners. Only in our century have really scientific efforts been made to retrace in descriptions that would be true to life the youth and early manhood of Christ. Contemporary scholars have availed themselves of all the sources of information at their disposal to describe accurately the manner of life of a young and poor artisan of Galilee in the time of Christ, and they bid us contemplate in the picture thus drawn a faithful image of Our Lord's life in Nazareth. Like the other young men of His time and country, we are told, Jesus frequented the school of Nazareth and received the ordinary instruction imparted there ; attended divine service in the synagogue of that city on the Sabbath and festival days ; went up with the Galilean caravans to Jerusalem for the yearly celebration of the Pasch, etc. Of course, as the divine character of Jesus remained absolutely concealed during this period of His life, it is only natural to picture Him to ourselves as conforming to the ordinary ways of the young men of His time and condition. It remains true, however, that we have no positive information about the extent it pleased the Son of God to conform to, or dispense with, the natural conditions of the time, so that many features of His life in Nazareth as described by recent scholars must ever appear an object of more or less plausible conjecture.

SYNOPSIS OF CHAPTER VI.

THE SOCIAL AND RELIGIOUS CONDITION OF THE JEWS DURING THE LIFETIME OF JESUS.

SOCIAL CONDITION:

1. The Sons of Herod the Great: { Herod Philip II. Herod Antipas Archelaus } { Men; titles; territories. }

2. Immediate Roman Domination over Judæa: { When imposed? How exercised? { Under Augustus. Under Tiberius. } }

3. The internal Divisions: { Pharisees Sadducees Essenes Samaritans } { Origin; tenets; influence. }

II. RELIGIOUS CONDITION:

1. The Temple of Jerusalem: { Situation and general aspect. Description of enclosures and of Temple proper. }

2. The Aaronitical Priesthood: { The simple priests. The high priest (social and religious influence). }

3. The Synagogues: { Origin and development. Organization and authority. }

4. The Scribes: { Who they were and how divided? On what did they rest their traditions? }

5. The Sanhedrim: { Origin, constitution and authority. }

CHAPTER VI.

THE SOCIAL AND RELIGIOUS CONDITION OF THE JEWS DURING THE LIFETIME OF JESUS.

§ 1. *Social Condition.*

1. The Sons of Herod the Great. The last will of Herod the Great having, after a time, been confirmed by Augustus, Palestine was divided between three of his sons

(1) **Herod Philip II.**, a son of Herod and Cleopatra of Jerusalem, became tetrarch of Gaulanitis, Trachonitis, Batanea, and the district of Panæas.* He was a just and moderate ruler, entirely devoted to the duties of his office. He rebuilt Panæas, near the sources of the Jordan, and called it **Cæsarea**, in honor of the emperor. As he left no children, at his death his dominions were annexed to the Roman province of Syria. He ruled thirty-seven years, from B.C. 4 to A.D. 34.

(2) **Herod Antipas**, a son of Herod the Great and Malthace, a Samaritan, was appointed tetrarch of Galilee and Peræa.† In character he was unscrupulous, tyrannical‡ and weak, § cruel and cunning, ‖ though not remorseless. ¶ He was a truly Eastern despot, capricious and sensual. In defiance of the Jewish law he had married the wife of Herod Philip—his brother, who was then living as a private citizen in Rome—and this led him to the murder of John the Baptist. It was before this prince that Our Lord appeared at the time of His passion.

* Luke iii. 1.   † Luke iii. 1.   ‡ Luke iii. 19-21.
§ Matt. xiv. 9.   ‖ Luke xiii. 32.   ¶ Mark vi. 14.

His greatest architectural work was the erection of a city which he called **Tiberias,** in honor of the emperor. After his banishment to Lyons, in Gaul, his territories were given to Herod Agrippa I., his nephew. He was tetrarch forty-one years, from B.C. 4 to A.D. 38.

(3) **Archelaus,** like Herod Antipas, was a son of Herod and Malthace. He did not enter upon his possessions without opposition and bloodshed, but Augustus confirmed the will of Herod in its essential provisions. Archelaus received the title of *ethnarch,* with the promise of that of *king* if he should rule to the satisfaction of Augustus. His territories included Idumæa, Judæa, and Samaria. By his tyranny and cruelty he roused his subjects to appeal to Rome for redress. He appeared before the emperor, and after his cause was heard he was banished to Vienna, in Gaul. After a rule of ten years (B.C. 4 to A.D. 6) his territories were annexed to the Roman province of Syria, and thus **Judæa** was placed under the *immediate* Roman domination.*

2. **The Immediate Roman Domination over Judæa.** The Jews had asked for this *direct* government of Rome at the death of Herod the Great, in the hope that the Romans would allow them to manage their national affairs after their own customs, under their high priests. This hope was revived by the banishment of Archelaus, but it did not last long. Judæa and Samaria were united to Syria, of which Publius Cyrinus was made president or pro-prætor, while the immediate direction of affairs was given to a *procurator,* residing at Cæsarea. The powers of this inferior officer cannot be exactly defined. In general, he was subject to the president of the province; yet, in districts lying far from the main province, he seems to have had a large discretionary power, a considerable number of troops

---

* Cfr. SCHÜRER, division I., vol. ii., p. 10 sq.; SEIDEL, In the Time of Jesus, pp. 79-86.

at his disposal, and, in certain cases, the power of life and death.

The immediate Roman domination was exercised over the various provinces of the empire in an irritating, vexatious, and oppressive manner, but it was particularly so in Judæa, on account of the peculiar character of the Jews, which contrasted so much with that of the Romans.*

It must be said, however, that under Augustus the rule of Rome over the Jews was fairly tolerable; but the exercise of the Roman power required chiefly two taxes: a *poll* and a *land* tax, the latter tax amounting to one-tenth of all grain and two-tenths of fruit and wine. To establish these taxes a *second census* was necessary. The fiercer spirits in Judæa rebelled at the idea that the *fruits* of a land consecrated to Jehovah should be given to pagan strangers, and that *tithes* to be paid to God alone should henceforth be paid to a heathen lord. Judas, the Galilean, led the insurrection against the census: he perished, and his followers dispersed.†

Towards the close of the reign of Augustus the procurators of Judæa succeeded one another rapidly; but his successor, Tiberius, pursued a different policy. During his long reign Judæa had only two procurators: Valerius Gratus (A.D. 15–26) and Pontius Pilate (A.D. 26–36).

Under Gratus things went from bad to worse. He changed the high priests five times in eleven years, and the load of public taxes became so unendurable that the Jews appealed to Rome for relief; but in all probability their entreaties did not bring them any alleviation of misery. The successor of Gratus was Pontius Pilate, the very type of the rich and corrupt Roman of his age. He was a worldly-minded statesman, conscious of no higher wants than those of the present life, yet by no means unmoved by feelings

* See GEIKIE, Life of Christ, chap. xviii.
† Cfr. JOSEPHUS, Antiq. of the Jews, book XVIII., chap. i., § 1.

of justice and mercy. But all his better feelings were over-powered by a selfish regard for his own security.

As specimens of his administration we may notice the four following facts:

(1) He transferred the winter quarters of the army from Cæsarea to Jerusalem; hence the soldiers introduced into the Holy City the Roman standards, on which were the image of the emperor and the imperial eagle. No previous governor had ventured on such an outrage and Pontius Pilate had sent his men in by night. The Jews poured down in crowds to Cæsarea to obtain from him the removal of the odious symbols. Pilate yielded after five days of re-sistance, and the standards were withdrawn.

(2) On another occasion he hung up in his palace, at Jerusalem, some gilt shields which were simply inscribed with the names of the donor and of the deity to which they were consecrated. This the Jews so resented that they ap-pealed to Tiberius, and they obtained the removal of the shields objected to.

(3) On the appropriation by Pilate of the revenue arising from the redemption of vows to the construction of an aqueduct a riot ensued. It was suppressed by means of soldiers sent among the crowds, armed with concealed dag-gers, and who slew not only rioters, but also casual spectators. The aqueduct was completed without further hindrance.

(4) Later on he slaughtered certain Galileans at some great festival at Jerusalem. This apparently took place in the Outer Court of the Temple, since the blood of the wor-shippers was mingled with their sacrifices.*

The conduct of Pilate was equally tyrannical towards the Samaritans; and on their complaint to Vitellius, then presi-dent of Syria, he was ordered to go to Rome, whence it seems Caligula banished him to Vienna, in Gaul.†

---

* LUKE xiii. 1.

† Cfr. JOSEPHUS, Antiq. of the Jews, book XVIII., chaps. iii.. iv.; SCHÜRER, division I., vol. ii., pp. 83–87.

3. The Internal Divisions. The **Pharisees** formed the most prominent party or guild among the Jews during the lifetime of Our Lord. As their name indicates, they originally arose as champions of the *separateness* of the Jewish people from other nations.* They consequently held fast by the distinctive beliefs of the Jewish race, as, for instance, the hope of a great national deliverer in the person of a Messias, the doctrine of the immortality of the soul, of a divine Providence, of an *oral* tradition equal in authority with the *written* law. Nor were they less zealous in carrying out the external observances of their ancestors, such as fasts, prayers, tithes, ablutions, sacrifices, etc. They were ardent patriots, ever willing to lay down their lives for the national independence, and hating the foreign yoke with a bitterness mingled with scorn. The multitudes, although not actually enrolled among the Pharisees, were under their sway, and zealously adhered to a party so intensely national in politics and orthodox in religion. To the Pharisaic party belonged also most of the scribes. Finally, although there were found noble characters among the leaders of the party, self-conceit, arrogance, and hypocrisy had become the general characteristics of the sect.

The origin of the **Sadducees** is probably to be traced to a natural tendency opposed to that which gave birth to the Pharisaic party, viz., the desire to tide closely with the ruling power. Their opposition to the Pharisees extended both to religious tenets and to social customs. They notably denied the immortality of the soul, the existence of a divinely revealed oral tradition, etc. They ridiculed Pharisaic exclusiveness, affected Greek culture, enjoyed foreign amusements, and thought it useless to fight for the freedom of their country. They belonged chiefly to the upper and wealthy classes, and formed a kind of priestly aristocratic

---

* For details see Outlines of Jewish History, p. 351 sq.

party in close alliance with the ruling power ; an extreme section of them were the **Herodians**.

The origin of the **Essenes** is very obscure.   In the time of Josephus, the Essenes lived in small colonies or villages at long distances from the towns, principally in the neighborhood of the Dead Sea.   The differences between them and the Pharisees lay mainly in rigor of practice and not in articles of belief.   Those who wished to join them had to pass through two periods of probation.   They employed themselves chiefly in agriculture and were devoted to silence and contemplation.   Some of them lived in ordinary society, as, for instance, Menahem, a friend of Herod ; but they generally formed an exclusive and isolated community.   Their organization resembled closely that of our monastic orders.

For centuries the **Samaritans** had been despised by the Jews, as a mixed race descending from the Assyrian colonists who had settled in the land of Israel when the northern kingdom was destroyed in the eighth century before Christ. At the time of Our Lord, the hatred between the Jews and the Samaritans had reached its climax ;[*] and this is explained by several contemporary events : notably, by the connivance of the Samaritans with Herod the Great before his accession to the Jewish throne, by the favor which that prince ever showed to them, by their willing submission to the *census* and their ready adoption of Roman usages, and finally, by their daring violation of the Temple of Jerusalem during a Paschal festival.[†]

§ 2. *Religious Condition.*

1. **The Temple of Jerusalem.**   The great centre of the religious life of the Jews during the lifetime of Our Lord was the *Temple* of Jerusalem.   Herod had rebuilt it

---

[*] JOHN iv. 9.   [†] Cfr. SCHÜRER, division II. vol. ii. pp. 4-46.

on its original site, Mount Moria, east of the **Holy City.**
He had, however, considerably enlarged its enclosure to the
south ; and it is very probable that the present enclosure of
the so-called **Mosque of Omar** represents that of the
Temple as enlarged by Herod the Great.

When we think of the Jewish Temple, our impulse is to
picture to ourselves some building like a classical temple or
a great cathedral.   But the first effort of our imagination
should be to picture to ourselves a system of structures, one
quadrangle within another, the second standing upon higher
ground than the outermost. and the *Temple proper* upon a
position highest of all.   We should imagine the appearance
of a wide open space spoken of by the prophets as " THE
COURT OF JEHOVAH'S HOUSE," while " THE HOUSE " itself,
or Temple proper, was erected on the highest of a series of
successive terraces, which rose in an isolated mass from the
centre of the Court, or rather nearer to its northwestern
corner.*

The *Outer Court*—the first to be entered when approaching the Sacred Mount—was called " the Court of the Gentiles," not because it was set apart for them, but because
Gentiles rigorously excluded from every other portion of the
Temple enclosures were permitted, with all others, to enter
there.   In form it was a quadrangle, surrounded by a strong
and lofty wall, with but one gate to the east, one to the
north, four to the west, and two to the south.   On the *inner
sides* of this wall extended porticoes or cloisters of white
marble Corinthian columns : the ceiling was flat and finished
with cedar.   On three sides there were two rows of columns,
but on the southern side, the cloister (*the Royal Porch*)
deepened into a fourfold colonnade, and its axis was in a
straight line with the axis of the colossal bridge which
spanned the Tyropœon valley.   These porticoes or porches
around the Court of the Gentiles were most convenient

* CONYBEARE and HOWSON, St. Paul, chap. xxi.

places for friendly or religious intercourse, for meetings or discussions.* The open court was paved with stones of various colors, and in it the buyers and sellers congregated.†

From near the middle of the Court of the Gentiles arose the series of enclosed terraces, on the summit of which was the Lord's house. This more sacred ground was fenced off by low balustrades of stone, along which, at regular intervals, stood pillars with inscriptions in Greek and Latin, warning Gentiles not to proceed farther, on pain of death. Besides this barrier, a separation was formed by a flight of fourteen steps leading up to a platform or narrow terrace, beyond which arose the wall of the *Inner Court* with its four gates to the north and to the south, and one to the east.

The eastern portion of this second quadrangle or *Inner Court* was called the *Court of the Women*, not because it was set apart exclusively for their use, but because they were not allowed to advance beyond it. This court covered a space of more than 200 feet square, and its eastern gate—which formed the principal entrance into the Temple—was the *Beautiful Gate*.‡ All round the court ran a simple colonnade, and within it was the Treasury ; § finally, in each of its four corners were chambers, one of which was for the performance of the vows of the Nazarites.‖

From the western side of the Court of the Women fifteen semicircular steps led through the *Gate of Nicanor* into the narrow *Court of Israel*, reserved for the men who had accomplished certain acts of purification. Two steps led up from the Court of Israel to the *Court of the Priests*, with which it practically formed but *one* court, divided into two by a low balustrade one and one-half feet high. A colonnade ran around three sides of the Court of the Priests; and among its many chambers we may notice the hall *Gazith*, the meeting-place of the Sanhedrim. The Court of

* Cfr. JOHN x. 23 sq.; ACTS iii. 11.   † MATT. xxi. 12, 13; JOHN ii. 13-17.
‡ ACTS iii. 2.   § LUKE xxi. 1, 2.
‖ Cfr. EDERSHEIM, The Temple, its Ministry and Services, pp. 25-27.

the Priests surrounded the Temple proper, and contained the great *Altar of Burnt-offerings*, together with the apparatus required for its service.

The House, or Temple proper, remains to be described. Its form was that of an inverted T (⊥), and it was divided into three parts: the *Vestibule*, the *Holy Place*, and the *Holy of holies*.

The Vestibule was reached by a flight of twelve steps, and was wider than the rest of the House by 30 feet on each side. Its entrance was covered by a splendid veil, and within it a number of dedicated gifts were kept. Folding doors, plated with gold and covered by a rich veil, formed the entrance to the Holy Place, and above it hung a gigantic vine of pure gold, a beautiful symbol of Israel. In the Holy Place were, to the south, the golden candlestick, to the north the table of "the loaves of proposition," and beyond them the altar of incense, near to the entrance to the Holy of holies, or Most Holy Place. The latter was now entirely empty, a large stone, on which the high priest sprinkled the blood on the Day of Atonement, occupying the place where the Ark had stood. A wooden partition separated the Most Holy from the Holy Place, and over the door hung the "SECOND VEIL." * The Holy Place was but 60 feet long from east to west, and 30 feet wide; and the Holy of holies was 30 feet long and as many wide. On three sides of the Temple proper there were side buildings three stories high, and so arranged that the Temple proper rose above them like a clear-story rising above aisles, and bearing aloft a gabled cedar roof with golden spikes on it, and surrounded by an elegant balustrade.†

At the northwestern corner of the Temple enclosure stood the fortress **Antonia**, ever reminding the Jewish worshippers of the hated Roman yoke.

---

* HEB. ix. 3; MATT. xxvii. 51.   † EDERSHEIM, The Temple, pp. 34-37.

2. The Aaronitical Priesthood. The persons who had charge of the Temple, and a large number of whom were always in residence, were the priests, whose duty it was to mediate between Jehovah and His people.   They formed a sacred order, to which no one could be admitted who did not belong to it by birth; for according to the legislation of the Pentateuch, " THE SONS OF AARON " were alone entitled to the rights and privileges of the Jewish priesthood.   Physical defects, however,—amounting to 142 at the time of Our Lord,—disqualified a descendant of Aaron, not indeed for the priestly *order*, but for the *exercise* of its functions.   So that, before being selected for the discharge of the sacred duties of the priesthood, a man had to prove (1) that he was a legitimate descendant of Aaron, and (2) that he was exempt from all disqualifying bodily blemishes.

If a young man had duly established this to the satisfaction of the Sanhedrim, he was set apart for the priestly ministry by a special consecration, which originally lasted seven days, and consisted in sacrifices, purifications, the putting on of the holy garments, the sprinkling of blood, and anointing with oil.   It is probable, however, that the anointing with oil was no longer in use in Our Lord's time.

For the service of the Temple, the numerous descendants of Aaron had been divided by David into twenty-four courses, which would officiate in regular succession, changing every Sabbath, so that each course would be in attendance at the sanctuary at least twice a year.   It is true that only four of these courses came back from the Exile, but they were divided afresh into twenty-four courses, each of which formed a distinct body, with presidents and elders at its head.   After the return, the number of priests rapidly increased in the Holy Land: and yet, however numerous, they must have been comfortably provided for.   They had a considerable share in the victims which the Jews of all nations offered in sacrifice in the Holy City; and even independently of these sacrifices, dues of various kinds were paid to them, such as first fruits, tithes of the products of the ground, the redemption money for the first-born of man and beast, etc.

Although in some cases the priests exercised judicial functions, and were in charge to preserve and expound the Law, their duties were mainly sacrificial. They had to prepare and offer the daily, weekly, and monthly sacrifices, and such as were brought by individuals at the great festivals or on special occasions, and in general they conducted the public service of the sanctuary.

At the head of the whole Jewish priesthood was the *high priest.* He was to be a person especially sacred, hence any bodily imperfection or blemish excluded him from the office. There were, besides, other disqualifications, such as illegitimacy, idolatry, etc. Under the Romans this office was too often entrusted to persons who had neither age nor learning nor rank to recommend them.

The services of the consecration, which originally lasted seven days, consisted in sacrifices, anointing with oil, and putting on of the sacred garments. But in Our Lord's time the anointing had long ceased to be in use, and a simple investiture was gone through, together with the offering of the sacrifices. We have already noticed that under the Roman domination the high priests had become mere puppets in the hands of the Roman procurators, and that Gratus and Pontius Pilate were famous for the rapid deposition and substitution of high priests which they effected.

And yet the position of the high priest combined in one and the same person both a *civil* and a *sacred* dignity. To him alone belonged the right to officiate on the great day of Atonement. He alone could enter the Most Holy Place; he was also the supreme administrator of sacred things and the final arbiter of all religious controversies.

At the same time he presided over the Sanhedrim; and in all political matters he was the supreme representative of the Jews in their relations with the Romans.*

3. **The Synagogues.** During the captivity of Babylon the sacrificial services of the Temple were, of course, discontinued; hence, it is most likely to this period that we must ascribe the origin of a religious institution which at the return of the Jews was transplanted into Palestine, and which in Our Lord's time was spread everywhere, viz., the institution of the synagogues. No sacrifices could be offered in these meeting-places; but public prayers were put up, and Holy Writ was read and practically expounded. The synagogues often consisted of two apartments: one for prayer, preaching, and public worship; the other for the meetings of learned men, for discussions concerning questions of religion and discipline, and for purposes of education.

In the audience chamber of a synagogue we might notice the *first chairs;*† a *desk* for the reader; a *chest* in which the rolls of the Sacred Book were preserved; and perhaps some lamps for use at the evening worship. Over every synagogue there was a *ruler* ‡ whose duty it was to attend to the external affairs of the synagogue, and to maintain order in the meetings. *Elders* § were associated with him in the management; while the inferior duties connected with the synagogue were discharged by servants or *ministers.*‖

The rulers of the synagogue had the power to inflict excommunication or exclusion from the synagogue, a most important act of religious discipline, whereby those under excommunication were looked upon as no better than the heathen.¶

4. **The Scribes.** The chief interpreters of Holy Writ in the synagogues were the *Scribes*, who, far more than the

---

* See SCHÜRER, division II., vol. i., pp. 195–299.   † MATT. xxiii. 6.

‡ MARK v. 35.   § LUKE vii. 3 ; MARK v. 22.

‖ LUKE iv. 20.   ¶ JOHN ix 22; xii. 42; LUKE vi. 2; MATT. xviii. 17.

priests, guided and shaped the religious life of the people at large. They belonged to different tribes and families, and also to different sects, although most of them, while being Scribes by office, were Pharisees by religious and political profession. In the time of Our Lord they were spread everywhere, and because of their special skill in the Law and in the other Sacred Writings, they were reputed as men of great learning. They loved the title of *Rabbi*,* and required the greatest honors not only from their pupils, but also from the public at large.

By their theoretical and practical interpretation of Holy Writ they had gradually laid a most heavy burden upon the people, for it was their aim to apply the Law to all imaginable circumstances of daily life, and their work in that direction was characterized by slavery to the letter, and by subtle casuistry. Moreover, through their great attachment for the "traditions of the elders," they had gone so far as to "make void the commandment of God," † and to teach the people to neglect some of the most fundamental principles of the moral law.‡

The origin of the divine authority they ascribed to these traditions is to be referred to their theory that Moses himself had delivered to Israel an *oral* Law together with the *written* Law. This oral Law was as old as the Pentateuch, and had come down in an authentic form, through the prophets to Esdras, the first and greatest of the Scribes. Hence they inferred that the *whole* Law, written and oral, was of equal practical authority. Through this conception of a traditional law the Scribes were led into many a departure from the spirit of the written Word, § and indeed were betrayed into looking upon all their traditional customs and interpretations—however recent—as no less authoritative than the revealed precepts of the Law.

* MATT. xxiii. 6, 7.   † MARK vii. 2-23.
‡ MATT. xii. 1-6; xv. 1-20; xxiii.   § MARK vii. 12.

5. The Sanhedrim. It was in one of the halls of the Temple that, up to about A.D. 30, the *Sanhedrim*, or highest council of the Jews, made up of chief priests, elders, and Scribes, met under the presidency of the high priests. Its origin is unknown ; anu the view of the Jewish rabbis which identifies the Sanhedrim with the council of seventy elders on whom the Holy Spirit was poured to assist Moses in the administration of justice, is without serious grounds. This supreme tribunal of the Jews counted seventy-one members of pure Israelite descent and was governed by a president and two vice-presidents ; besides, there were secretaries and other officers.

During Our Lord's lifetime the power of the Sanhedrim extended to matters of the greatest importance. Among others, we may notice that it superintended the ritual of public worship, regulated the Jewish calendar, enforced the exact fulfilment of the Law, punished false prophets, and even exercised judicial control over the high priests. However, its privilege of carrying into effect a sentence of death it had pronounced had been taken from the Sanhedrim and reserved to the Roman procurator. The supreme authority of the decrees of the Sanhedrim was acknowledged by all the Jews dispersed throughout the world.

SYNOPSIS OF CHAPTER VII.

THE PUBLIC WORK OF CHRIST.

I. ITS DIFFICULTIES:
1. National Susceptibilities (Romans, Samaritans, Jews).
2. Narrowness or Fears of Jewish Bodies and Authorities.
3. Popular Mistaken Notions concerning the Messias.

II. ITS MEANS:

1. Prudence of Action:
   - Never a collision with Roman power.
   - Action in perfect harmony with the distinction between the authority and the personal life of the Jewish authorities.
   - Gradual
     - Removal of popular prejudices.
     - Disclosure of what He is and purposes.

2. Power of Words (Chief Characteristics of His Public Discourses).

3. Miracles (Perfect Mastery over all Nature, invoked as a Proof of His Statements).

III. ITS LENGTH:

Various Theories held successively through Ages: Opinion now Prevalent.

Data of the Gospels:
- The Synoptists mention only one Pasch—but imply a second one.
- St. John speaks certainly of three Paschs—probably of a fourth.

Conclusions certain or simply probable concerning that question.

84

SECOND PERIOD:

OUR LORD'S PUBLIC MINISTRY.

CHAPTER VII.

THE PUBLIC WORK OF CHRIST.

1. The Difficulties of Our Lord's Work. The social and religious condition of the Jews in Our Lord's day— which we have briefly described in the foregoing chapter— naturally created many difficulties against the acceptance of His teachings.

One of these difficulties arose from the national antipathies and susceptibilities of Our Lord's contemporaries. The Romans despised, it is true, the Jewish nation and thought they could easily quell any revolt against their domination ; yet they were naturally jealous of their authority, and would certainly resent Christ's open assumption of the title of the Messias and His preaching of a new kingdom, for both could easily lead the Jewish multitudes to new uprisings against the hated power of Rome. Again, the Samaritans and the Jews were no less at variance between themselves than the Romans and the Jews ; hence, any special favor shown by Jesus to the members of either community would certainly tell against the influence of His words and miracles upon the minds and hearts of the other.

A second and greater difficulty to Our Lord's work was to

be found in the narrowness or the fears of the Jewish leaders.
To be welcome as a teacher to the Scribes and the Pharisees
of His time, Jesus should have belonged to the learned class
of the " Masters in Israel," * and like them He should have
pledged Himself to uphold all the " traditions of the elders " ;
but more particularly, He should have felt bound to comply
with the rules of the Scribes and the Pharisees, since " all the
Jews " †—even the Sadducees—carried them out faithfully;
and the Gospel records prove that to be faithful to His mission, Our Lord had to set all these traditions aside and to
unmask fearlessly the pride and hypocrisy of this the most
influential of the Jewish sects. The Sadducees were no less
opposed to the work of Our Lord than the Pharisees. His
doctrine was in direct contradiction in several points to that
of the Sadducees, and His public mission appeared to them
most objectionable. On the one hand, these cautious poli-
ticians saw that the multitudes were more and more won to
His cause, and feared lest they would ultimately crown Him
King and rebel against Rome ; and on the other hand, they
were fully persuaded that Jesus had not at His disposal the
forces necessary to cope successfully with the Roman
legions. These various elements of opposition to Our
Lord's work were all represented in the Sanhedrim, and
their ultimate combination against His work and His life
led to His trial and to His execution.

It must be said, however, that the greatest difficulty our
divine Lord had to contend with in the discharge of His
public mission arose from the mistaken notions concerning
the Messias, which were so prevalent in the minds of His
contemporaries. As we have seen in Chapter II., the Jewish expectations respecting the person and work of the
Messias, the nature and conditions of the Messianic kingdom, ran directly counter to what the Redeemer of the
world had to be and to establish upon earth.

---

* JOHN iii. 10.   † MARK vii. 3.

2. The Means used by Our Lord in His Public Work. One of the most remarkable features of the conduct of Our Lord during His public ministry is His prudence of action. During His entire public work we find no trace of the least collision with the Roman power. He usually moves in Galilee, far from immediate contact with the Roman officials, avoids assuming the Messianic title, never shows the least desire for the royal dignity, and when pressed by His enemies to declare whether it is lawful to pay the tribute to Cæsar or not, He answers in a manner which had to be distorted in order that it might be brought against Him at the time of His passion.

Our Lord did not act with less prudence in His relations with the Jewish authorities. Here, however, the avoidance of a collision was an impossibility. His mission of Saviour of souls required that He should unmask His opponents to the people and contend openly with them, and this He did repeatedly, with a severity proportionate to the ardor of His zeal. But outside these cases He acted towards them with the utmost kindness. Indeed, it may be said that His conduct was ever in perfect harmony with this most wise distinction between the authority and the person of the Jewish leaders : " All whatsoever they shall say to you, observe and do ; but according to their works do ye not." *

It is in the same prudent way that Jesus did not go at once against the mistaken Messianic notions of the people, or even of His chosen disciples. He knew that inveterate prejudices must not be handled roughly, and that a gradual light is not only more welcome, but also more effective. Hence He suggested in various ways, but especially through striking parables, the truths regarding the nature of the kingdom of God, its growth, conditions of entrance, etc., which He could not have disclosed openly without hurting uselessly the most cherished hopes of His contemporaries.

* MATT. xxiii. 3

And it is only towards the close of His work that He fully disclosed His equality with the Father and His true relations to the Jews and to the world.

A second means which Our Lord employed for the fulfilment of His mission is the wonderful power of His words. His discourses are a spirit, an impulse, a direction, not a series of abstract, dry enactments, so that every one of His hearers could at once feel their importance and their beauty. They are also characterized by great originality, for even when He took up the religious truths of the Old Testament revelation, He divested them of their grosser interpretations and gave them a spiritual meaning hitherto unsuspected. In opposition to the method of the Scribes, the teachers of the time, "He spoke with authority," never repeating the opinions of interpreters before Him, never sustaining a statement by the authority of some master. Seldom He discussed with His hearers, but when controversy was engaged, either with the Pharisees or the Sadducees, He ever and easily remained victorious. So great, indeed, was the power of His words, that the multitudes, in their eagerness to hear Him, pressed upon Him in great numbers, and followed Him everywhere, forgetful of the very necessaries of life.

The miracles which our divine Lord performed were, however, the very powerful means by which He won the admiration, gratitude, and authority necessary to cope successfully with the opposition of the Jewish leaders. He multiplied these wonders at each step, and they were such as no man had wrought before Him. All the elements of nature, all the diseases of the body, life and death, and even invisible spirits felt the effects of His divine power. A simple touch, a single word was sufficient to exercise this power over the most inveterate diseases, and even His presence was not necessary for the performance of such wonders. The most hidden thoughts of His hearers, as well as the most remote events, were equally known to Him. Not only did He perform miracles Himself, but on different occasions He imparted a similar power to His messengers. It was, therefore, plain to His contemporaries that He was endowed with a perfect mastery over all creatures. The multitudes instinctively felt that the coming Messias could not be expected to perform greater miracles, and were led to consider Him as being Himself the Messias who, as they thought, by His miraculous power was to drive the foreigners from the Holy Land, submit the Gentiles to the Jews, and start a new era of material and religious prosperity. Only blind leaders, who wilfully blasphemed against the Holy Spirit, could ascribe such beneficent works to the agency of the Evil One. Finally, Our Lord Himself repeatedly appeals to His works as clear proofs of His divine mission and superhuman power.

3. **Length of Our Lord's Public Work.** The ministry of Our Lord includes, indeed, the period between His baptism and His ascension ; but how long this period was, is a question which has ever been debated in the Church.

During the first three centuries the prevalent opinion was that the ministry of Christ lasted not more than a year and a few months, and included only two Paschal celebrations, viz., that which followed soon on His baptism, and that which immediately preceded His crucifixion. Some writers, however, during the third and following centuries, regarded Our Lord's ministry as including three Paschal festivals. Eusebius, who wrote in the first part of the fourth century, was the first who represented the ministry of Christ as including four Passovers ; his opinion did not prevail at once, for during the latter part of the fourth century several Church writers, among whom was St. Augustine still, retained the ancient opinion, viz., that it included two Passovers only. Subsequently, however, and up to the middle of the eighteenth century, the view of Eusebius was received without misgiving, and at the present day it is by far the most prevalent among biblical scholars ; it maintains that the public ministry of Our Lord lasted three years and a few months, and that it included four Paschal celebrations.*

If we consult the Gospel records we shall find that none of the Evangelists states explicitly either the exact duration of Our Lord's ministry or the number of Passovers included within the period between His baptism and His ascension. Again, we may notice that the *Synoptists* mention only one Pasch, namely, the last one He celebrated in Jerusalem before His death, while they incidentally refer to facts which clearly imply another Paschal festival as having occurred during Our Lord's public ministry.† Finally, we find that St. John speaks certainly of three Passovers,‡ and probably of a fourth one in Chapter v. 1. In the last passage just referred to, the fourth Evangelist tells us that " there was a festival of the Jews and Jesus went up to Jerusalem." Now it can be shown with great probability that this " festival of the Jews " was first of all, distinct from either of the Passovers spoken of in Chapter ii. 13, and in Chapter vi. 4, and next, from either the feast of Pentecost or that of Tabernacles.§

We therefore conclude that while it is beyond doubt that Our Lord's ministry included at least three Paschal celebrations, it is very probable that it included a fourth Passover, and that consequently the entire duration of the public work of Jesus extended to three years and a few months.

* Cfr. CARPENTER, Harmony of the Gospels, dissertation I. pp. xiii.-xx.

† Cfr. MATT. xii. 1; LUKE vi. 1; MARK ii. 23, compared with MARK vi. 39; vi, 56–52. See also HASTINGS, Bible Dictionary, art. Chronology of the New Testament, 406.

‡ JOHN ii. 13; vi. 4 ; xi. 55; xiii. 1.

§ VIGOUROUX et BACUEZ, Manuel Biblique, vol. iii., n. 142. SMITH, Bible Dictionary, art. Jesus Christ, p. 1359. ANDREWS, Life of Our Lord, pp. 189-198.

SYNOPSIS OF CHAPTER VIII.

THE EARLY DAYS OF CHRIST'S PUBLIC MINISTRY.

I. IMMEDIATE PREPARATION FOR PUBLIC MINISTRY:

1. The Preaching of St. John:
   - Time and place.
   - Nature (essentially a preparation for the coming of the Messias).
   - Influence (extent and reasons).

2. The Baptism of Our Lord:
   - The baptism administered by John (where and why received by Jesus?)
   - How was Jesus manifested to John?
   - Date of the baptism: Jesus "about the age of thirty years."

3. The Temptation:
   - Where and why undergone by our divine Lord?
   - Duration and nature.

II. BEGINNING OF PUBLIC MINISTRY:

1. The First Five Disciples:
   - Their names, places of birth, and station in life.
   - When and how brought to Jesus?
   - First relations with Our Lord.
   - The Titles Given to Jesus:
     - The Lamb of God.
     - The Son of God, the King of Israel.
     - The Son of Man.

2. The First Miracle:
   - The Occasion: A wedding at Cana of Galilee.
   - The Miracle:
     - The request of Mary: Its motives.
     - The answer of Jesus.
     - The change of water into wine.

91

CHAPTER VIII.

THE EARLY DAYS OF CHRIST'S PUBLIC MINISTRY.

§ 1. *The Immediate Preparation for Public Ministry.*

1. **The Preaching of St. John.** Our Lord was soon to commence His public life, when John, the son of Zachary, was directed by heaven to begin his mission of precursor. St. Luke tells us that this happened " in the fifteenth year of Tiberius Cæsar." * This " fifteenth year " is most likely to be reckoned from the time when this prince was associated with Augustus in the government of the empire, and consequently, it corresponds to the year 779 U.C. (A.D. 26). That it was a *Sabbatical* year is regarded as probable by some authors, who explain in this manner how the people could flock to John in great numbers and from all parts of the land.†

Long years before this moment " of his manifestation in Israel," the son of Zachary had lived in the Wilderness, or eastern portion of Judæa proper.‡ In this desolate region, some 9 or 10 miles in width, by about 35 in length, he had taken his abode, most likely in some cave in the depth of a gorge to shelter himself from the glare of an Eastern sun. His food had consisted of locusts which leaped and flew on the bare hills, and of wild honey which the bees deposited in the clefts of the rocks. Thus, far from

---

* LUKE iii. 1, 2.
† MATT. iii. 5. See FOUARD, i., p. 96; ANDREWS, pp. 23-29; 145, 146; WIESELER Chronological Synopsis, p. 184 sq.
‡ LUKE i. 80.

a corrupt world, in silence and prayer, he had slowly prepared himself for his difficult mission, and he now stood
before all, a living example of sincerity and disinterestedness.

The holy precursor began his instructions in the wilderness of Judæa, * and then he moved northward, apparently
following the course of the Jordan.† He announced the
near coming of the Messias and of His kingdom, and bade
his hearers prepare for this most important event by genuine
sorrow for sin and a true change of life.   His words went
directly against one of the most mischievous errors of his
contemporaries, who felt sure of a place in the kingdom of
the Messias simply because of their descendance from
Abraham and of their scrupulous, though soulless, discharge
of outward practices of penance and religion.   His language
assumed a particularly severe tone when addressed to the
Pharisees and the Sadducees, whom he called " offspring of
vipers " because of their hypocrisy, which turned religion
itself into a vice and hid a deadly malice under the appearance of zeal.   As a body, these Jewish leaders rejected His
exhortations to repentance and moral reform, and were far
from desiring the baptism which John administered to the
humble and truly repentant multitudes.‡

The fame of the new prophet spread rapidly, and as St.
Matthew informs us, " Jerusalem and all Judæa and all the
country about Jordan went out to him."§   Even the most
unspiritual elements of society, such as the publicans and
the soldiers, felt deeply the influence of his preaching and
were willing to follow his counsels.‖   Very soon the ministry
of the precursor caused so general an excitement and so lively
an expectation that " all were thinking in their hearts of
John, that perhaps he might be the Christ."¶

---

* MATT. iii. 1.   † LUKE iii. 3.
‡ MATT. iii. 2, 5-12 ; MARK i. 4-8 ; LUKE iii. 3. 7-9 ; MATT. xxi. 28-32.
§ MATT. iii. 5.   ‖ LUKE iii. 10-14.   ¶ LUKE iii. 15.

When we inquire into the causes of an influence so wide-spread and so considerable, we find that they were chiefly three : (1) the personal appearance of John, which was in striking contrast with that of the teachers of the time and forcibly reminded the multitudes of the ancient prophet Elias ;* (2) the character of his preaching, so earnest in its tone, so striking in its images, so disinterested in its motives, so practical in its bearing, so perfectly in harmony with his own life ; (3) the expectation of the Messias, which was more than ever prevalent among, and dear to, the multitudes, and which the very preaching of John had rendered more lively and more certain.

2. The Baptism of Our Lord.† From the summary accounts which the Gospels give us of the preaching of St. John, we easily gather that the burden of his teachings was the necessity, even for the Jews, to prepare for the Messianic kingdom by a hearty renunciation of sin and a real amendment of life. And it is this necessity which he symbolized by administering to the multitudes a baptism hitherto required only from proselytes to Judaism. He had been sent to baptize with water,‡ and his baptism shared in the preparatory character of his entire mission, inasmuch as it taught the Jews the true frame of mind in which they should receive "the baptism with the Holy Ghost," which was reserved to Him whom John announced.

St. John had been baptizing for some time when Jesus, leaving Nazareth, "went to the Jordan " to be baptized by the holy precursor. The precise place of Our Lord's baptism is not indicated in the Gospel narrative, and remains doubtful down to the present day, St. John having baptized the multitudes at different points of the river. The most common opinion, however, is that Jesus was baptized on the lower Jordan, near Jericho, at a place named Bethany.§

* 4 KINGS i. 7, 8.   † MATT. iii. 13-17; MARK i. 9-11 ; LUKE iii. 21-23.
‡ JOHN i. 33.   § Cfr. JOHN i. 28 ; x. 40.

Ecclesiastical writers have suggested various motives why Jesus submitted to a rite expressive of inward repentance and intended reform. The motive the most probable, because suggested by Our Lord's words to St. John,[*] is that He wished thereby to comply with a general disposition of divine Providence, that He should not be exempt during His mortal life from the rites enjoined by God upon the Jews of the time.[†]

It has been affirmed that the words of St. John by which he stayed Jesus, saying, " I ought to be baptized by Thee, and comest Thou to me ? " implied a previous and personal acquaintance of the precursor with Our Lord. But such an acquaintance with the person and character of Jesus is by no means certain. The homes of John and Jesus were far removed, and the sojourn of the precursor in the wilderness extended to the very moment " of his manifestation in Israel." We must, therefore, consider it much more probable that John had never seen Jesus before,[‡] and that he was able to discern His exalted character only through an inward inspiration. Such supernatural discernment of character was sometimes given to the prophets of old, and it should be remembered that this same precursor, when yet in his mother's womb, had leaped for joy at the salutation of the mother of the Lord. Yet it was not till St. John had seen the appointed sign, the descent of the Holy Ghost, that he could bear official witness to the Messianic dignity of Jesus.[§] There is no reason to suppose that the apparition of the Holy Spirit, in a bodily shape " as a dove," was seen by the multitude. Jesus saw it,[‖] and John also, whose mission it was to bear witness to others that Jesus " is the Son of God " [¶] and apparently no one else.

St. Luke (iii. 23) informs us that Our Lord at His baptism was " about the age of thirty years," an expression the

* MATT. iii. 15.   † Cfr. KNABENBAUER, in S. Matthæum, i. pp. 137, 138.
‡ JOHN i. 31-34.   ‖ MATT. iii. 16.   ¶ JOHN i., 31, 32, 34.

natural meaning of which is, that Jesus was some months
or parts of a year more or less than thirty. He was not just
thirty, nor twenty-nine, nor thirty-one years of age. Whence
it follows that Jesus, born in December, 749 U.C., was baptized towards the end of 779, or the beginning of 780 U.C.
The probabilities are in favor of 780 (A.D. 27).

Now the first Pasch which followed Our Lord's baptism
fell upon the 11th of April; so that in the interval between
this Pasch and His baptism we must place various events—
the forty days' temptation, the return of Jesus to Galilee,
where He attended the wedding at Cana, and Our Lord's
few days' sojourn in Capharnaum immediately before going
up to Jerusalem—which occupied upwards of two months.
This naturally leads us to look for the traditional month of
January as the month in which Jesus was baptized in the
Jordan, and the climatic peculiarities of Palestine offer no
valid objections to this month.*

3. The Temptation.† Immediately after His baptism,
Jesus was led by the Spirit into the wilderness of Judæa, to
be tempted by the Devil. The wild aspect of this place has
already been referred to, and its descriptions by travellers
enable us to realize the perfect accuracy of St. Mark's
statement, that in the wilderness the Son of God "WAS
WITH BEASTS." ‡ Tradition points to a high mountain
a little west of Jericho as the "very high mountain " from
which the Tempter showed Our Lord all the kingdoms of
the world. This mountain, a limestone peak, exceedingly
sharp and abrupt, and overlooking the plain of the Jordan
and beyond, has been called the **quarantania**, in allusion
to the fast of forty days.

That the true Son of God should have been tempted by
the Evil One will ever remain a most mysterious, though
most certain, event in the history of mankind. Nothing, of

---

* ANDREWS, pp. 21-35.   † MATT. iv. 1-11; MARK i. 12, 13; LUKE iv. 1-13.
‡ MARK i. 13.

course, could allure to sin a divine person, and it is difficult to understand how victory over temptation could secure merit for a soul which could not sin. Various reasons, however, have been set forth to explain why our divine Lord was tually tempted. Thus, in the Epistle to the Hebrews* we are told that in Jesus "we have not a high priest, who cannot have compassion on our infirmities; but one tempted in all things such as we are [yet] without sin."† Again, it has been said that the second Adam suffered this humiliation, that all Adam's sons might share in His victory; and there is no doubt that Christians under temptation have ever found in the pattern of their tempted Saviour both an instructive example and a great source of power to overcome their ghostly enemy.

If we had only the narratives of St. Matthew and St. Mark, we would naturally suppose that Our Lord's temptation consisted simply in the three assaults which St. Matthew records in detail, and consequently that it lasted but a short time. But St. Luke's narrative is decisive, to the effect that Jesus was actually tempted during all the forty days He remained in the wilderness, and that it was at the end of this long period that He underwent these three great assaults.

It is not necessary to detail and refute here the various theories invented by Protestants and Rationalists, against what ecclesiastical tradition has ever believed to have been the true nature of the Tempter, and of his three final assaults against Our Lord. An impartial study of the Gospel records proves beyond all doubt that the Evangelists intended to describe a real external occurrence, in which a personal Tempter appeared to Jesus in a bodily form, spoke audible words, went visibly from place to place, and finally departed. It is clear, furthermore, that Our Lord, having no inordinate inclination towards any thing, could not be

---

* HEB. iv. 15.   † Cfr. also HEB. ii. 17.

tempted to deviate from His appointed path of duty by the inward solicitations of appetite, of ambition and of worldliness, but only by the outward suggestions of the Evil One. These suggestions appealed to the threefold concupiscence of our fallen nature, and Satan hoped that they would prove the more easily successful against Jesus, because he presented them when Our Lord's physical frame had been greatly weakened by a rigorous and prolonged fast, and also because in using them he simply proposed to Jesus to act as the worldly Messias whom the Jews expected. But Satan's hope was doomed to disappointment. For whether approached by the Tempter in the wilderness, or led by him to the top of one of the platforms of the Temple's enclosure, or to the summit of a high mountain, Jesus never swerved in the least from what He knew to be the divine will in His regard. He met promptly, firmly, all the suggestions of Satan by direct appeals to Holy Writ—which St. Paul in his inspired language will call later "the sword of the Spirit "*—and finally put this enemy to flight.

The direct, and as it were personal, conflict between Jesus and Satan was over till the time of Our Lord's ignominious passion and death ;† and heavenly spirits came and ministered to Jesus. ‡

§ 2. *The Beginning of Public Ministry.*

1. **The First Five Disciples.**§ The opening events of Our Lord's public life are recorded only by the beloved disciple, who had been a witness of them all. He pictures to us Jesus attaching to Himself His first five disciples : Andrew, and another left unnamed in the Gospel narrative, but who was no other than John, the modest writer of the

---

*Ephes. vi. 17.   † Luke iv. 13 ; xxii. 53.
‡ Matt. iv. 11, cfr. Fouard, i., p. 121 sq. ; Dehaut, l'Evangile Expliqué, etc., voL i., p. 485 sq. (Paris, 1873) ; Fillion ; Godet, and other commentators.
§ John i. 35-51.

Fourth Gospel ; Simon and Philip ; and finally Nathanael, who is most likely identical with the apostle Bartholomew. They were all Galileans by birth ; and Andrew, together with Simon and Philip,* and probably John, † were of Bethsaida, on the western shore of the lake of Genesareth, while Nathanael was of Cana in Galilee.‡ Tradition represents the latter as of nobler birth than the other four, who were poor fishermen, although the father of St. John seems to have been a fisherman of some means. §

The exact time at which these five men became the disciples of Jesus cannot be determined. It was, however, not long after Our Lord's return from the scene of the Temptation, and when His holy precursor was still baptizing at Bethany, and had just given a public testimony to Christ's Messianic character.‖ St. John the Baptist was, in fact, the direct means of bringing Andrew and John to Jesus, by pointing to Him as "the Lamb of God."¶ Both were soon convinced that they had indeed "found the Messias," ** and they immediately went in quest each of his own brother, to impart to them the good news. Andrew was the first to find Simon, his brother, and he led him to Jesus. The next day occurred the first direct call from Jesus Himself. When about to go forth into Galilee He found Philip, and at once made him His disciple by these simple words : " Follow me." No sooner had Philip recognized Jesus as the Messias than he sought a friend of his to impart to him the same belief. This friend was Nathanael, who was at first reluctant to admit that anything good could come from Nazareth, but who soon became a fervent disciple of Jesus.††

The Gospel narrative does not describe in detail the first relations of these five disciples with their new Master. It briefly tells us of Jesus inviting Andrew and John to His

---

* JOHN i. 45.　　† Cfr. JOHN i. 44, and LUKE v. 10.　　‡ JOHN xxi. 2.
§ MARK i. 20; JOHN xix. 27. Cfr. FOUARD, i., p. 135, footnote 3.　‖ JOHN i. 19-24.
¶ JOHN i. 35-40.　　** JOHN i. 41.　　†† JOHN i. 45-50.

temporary abode and spending long hours with them, *
changing the name of Simon into that of Peter, † bidding
Philip simply to follow Him, ‡ and finally manifesting to
Nathanael a knowledge more than human. §   But this nar-
rative, however brief, clearly proves two things : (1) that
Our Lord had from the very beginning of His public life a
most distinct knowledge of His entire mission ; (2) that
His first five disciples derived from their first relations with
Him a real conviction that he was the long-expected
Messias.

This same narrative is also remarkable for the three titles
we find therein given to Jesus.   The first is that of " *the
Lamb of God,*" applied to Our Lord by St. John the Baptist. ‖
Jesus was thereby pointed out as the " Servant of Jehovah,"
spoken of by Isaias (liii.), who would make atonement for the
sins of the people by His vicarious sufferings.   The second
title was that of " *the Son of God, the King of Israel,*"¶ addressed to Jesus by Nathanael.   In this twofold designation
we should not see anything else than an emphatic recognition of Our Lord's Messianic dignity, which, in the eyes of
His new disciple, exalted Him far above all those—whether
men or angels—who could be styled "the sons of God,"
and made Him " the Great King " of the Jews.   The last
title was that of " *the Son of Man,*" which Our Lord applied to Himself in His conversation with Nathanael.** This
was another Messianic designation in the phraseology of
the time, and it was preferred by Jesus to any other in connection with His Messianic dignity, chiefly because it re-
called less sensibly to the minds of His hearers their false
notions of material prosperity and glory during the Messianic era. ††

2. **The First Miracle.** ‡‡ The faith of the first five disciples of Christ, however real, needed to be strengthened by

---

* John i. 38, 39.   † John i. 42.   ‡ John i. 43.   § John i. 47, 48.
‖ John i. 36.   ¶ John i. 49.   ** John i. 51.
†† Fouard, i., p. 137 ; Fillion, St. Matt., p. 322 ; St. Jean, p. 21. ‡‡ John ii. 1-11.

the sight of those miracles which the Messias was expected
to perform in Israel, and this sight was first granted to them
on the occasion of a wedding at Cana of Galilee.

Two towns have been pointed out as the place of Our
Lord's first miracle : (1) **Kana el-Jelîl**, about 9 miles
north of Nazareth; (2) **Kefer Kenna**, only 4½ miles northeast of Nazareth. Even granting that the modern name
Kana el-Jelîl is nearer to the ancient name "Cana of
Galilee," yet it must be maintained that the traditional
Kefer Kenna is more probably the place of the wedding,
because of its proximity to Nazareth, and because of its
situation on the direct road between Nazareth and the lake
of Genesareth.*

Upon his return from the Jordan, Jesus had not gone
directly to Cana, but to Nazareth, where, however, He and
His disciples did not find Mary, for " on the third day "—
apparently the third day after His departure for Galilee—
" there was a marriage in Cana of Galilee ; and the mother
of Jesus was there." † Thither He directed His steps, either
previously invited, or called with His disciples as soon as
His coming was known.

Wedding festivities usually continued for a week, and a
bridegroom in humble circumstances—such as the one
spoken of in the Gospel narrative—could ill afford to make
provision for an entertainment of so long duration. It has
also been supposed that the unlooked-for arrival of Our
Lord's five disciples contributed to make more apparent, if
indeed it did not cause, the insufficiency of the supply of
wine. However this may be, Mary, who was the first to
notice that the provision of wine was running short, was
anxious that no one else should perceive this evidence of
poverty, and betaking herself to Jesus, she said, " They
have no wine."

* FOUARD, i., p. 140; ANDREWS, p. 162 sq.; and also, article Cana, in VIGOUROUX,
Dictionnaire de la Bible, p. 111 sq.
† JOHN ii. 1.

In these simple words of Mary, it is easy to see a modest request, prompted by her thoughtful charity and by her implicit trust in the hitherto hidden power of Our Lord to perform miracles. It was a secret, a brief appeal of His mother to One who had ever been ready to comply with her least desire, and it was made at the time which she thought the most opportune to spare a public disgrace to the family which had invited Him and His disciples. It is true that Mary was asking for a miracle, but in so doing she cannot have been guilty of fault, since she asked, or rather suggested, the very thing which Jesus did.

In answer to the request of His mother, Our Lord said : " Woman, what is to Me and to thee ? My hour is not yet come." These words sound harsh to our ears, but on the lips of Our Saviour they had not the same meaning as in our modern languages. First of all, the word " woman " was compatible with the utmost respect, for Jesus will use it later on, when about to die on the cross He will give to Mary one of the most tender proofs of His affection,* and passages from the classics might be quoted, where the same word is used without implying the least tinge of disrespect or blame.† The title "woman," here given to Mary, seems simply to indicate that a relation different from that of mother to son is referred to. The next words, "what is to Me and to thee ?" have not necessarily a reprehensive sense in Semitic languages.‡ They denote usually, however, some divergence between the thoughts and ways of persons so brought together. Perhaps Jesus used them here to express the following opposition. His mother seemed to imply that He was ever to be in the same dependence on her maternal wishes and suggestions, whereas, now that He was entering on His public career, Our Lord intended to work independently of them. The last words of Our Saviour to Mary,

* JOHN xix. 26.
† See FOUARD, vol. i., p. 145, footnote 2.
‡ Cfr. JUD. xi. 12; 2 KINGS xvi. 10.

"My hour is not yet come," have been understood in various ways, and it may be that the best one—because in greater harmony with other expressions of Jesus—is that the time appointed for Him to work miracles had not yet fully come.   But our blessed Lady, fully confident that her divine Son had not completely rejected her request, or rather that He would grant it, said to the waiters, " Whatsoever He shall say to you, do ye."

The details which follow in the sacred narrative, about the change of the water into wine, bespeak the report of an eye-witness.   St. John speaks not only of water-pots used for the frequent ablutions of the Jews—in which consequently no wine could be supposed to remain—but of their number, of their material, and of their approximative size ("they contained two or three measures apiece," that is, between about eighteen and twenty-seven gallons).   He remembers the astonishment of the chief steward of the feast, who, not knowing the miraculous origin of the wine he had just tasted, hastened to address complimentary words to the bridegroom, whom he thought had kept till then his best wine.   Finally, he had apparently ascertained the reality of the miracle from the mouth of the waiters who had drawn the water and had carried it to the chief steward, and his faith and that of his fellow disciples was strengthened by this first manifestation of the miraculous power of Jesus.*

* See MALDONATUS, in Joannem; DIDON, Jesus Christ; Revue Biblique, 1897, pp. 405-422.

SYNOPSIS OF CHAPTER IX.

FIRST YEAR'S MINISTRY.

(April A.D. 27—March A.D. 28.)

I.

LEADING FEATURES OF THE GOSPEL NARRATIVE:

1. Its Contrast with Ordinary History or Biography.

2. Difficulty in Harmonizing Details.

II.

EVENTS IN JUDÆA (April–December A.D. 27):

1. The First Pasch in Jerusalem: The cleansing of the Temple. Conversation with Nicodemus.

2. Ministry through Judæa (its character and duration).

III.

JESUS IN SAMARIA:

1. The Province of Samaria and its Inhabitants in the Time of Our Lord.

2. Jesus and the Samaritans (John iv. 1–44).

IV.

MINISTRY IN GALILEE:

1. The City of Capharnaum and its Importance in the Public Life of Christ.

2. Principal Features of Our Lord's Work in Galilee.

CHAPTER IX.

(April A.D. 27—March A.D. 28.)

§ 1. *Leading Features of the Gospel Narrative.*

1. Its Contrast with Ordinary History or Biography. It is particularly in their narrative of Christ's public ministry that our canonical Gospels approach the form of ordinary history or biography. Here the Evangelists record in detail a large number of His words and deeds, and picture Him in the most varied circumstances of His public and private life. With their assistance we can follow Him in His journeys through Galilee or on His way to Jerusalem ; we can hear Him reasoning with His enemies, teaching the multitudes, or imparting special instructions to His disciples ; we can observe Him performing ordinary actions or working great miracles, passing " the whole night in the prayer of God," or giving vent to His inmost feelings in public prayer to His heavenly Father. As we peruse the sacred pages we naturally admire the transparent simplicity of the narrative, together with its skilful selection and arrangement of events which gradually enable us to grasp the very spirit of Christ and to realize the principal features of His life and character. In a word, we feel instinctively that in their narrative of Our Lord's public ministry the Gospels exhibit, more than anywhere else, the general characteristics of a faithful though brief history of the public life of Christ.

Even here, however, the leading feature of the Gospel records is much less that of resemblance to, than that of contrast with, ordinary history or biography, ancient or modern.

While in ordinary history or biography the circumstances of place and time rule the narration, in the Gospels it is the spiritual import or some other aim which predominates. In none of them is the strict chronological sequence the standard of the arrangement of facts, and hardly any of them supplies distinct connections of detailed events. Indeed, as Westcott * justly observes, "the style of St. Matthew produces the greatest appearance of continuity, though probably he offers the most numerous divergences from chronological order."

No less striking than this absence of chronological order is the fact that the Gospel narrative does not aim at completeness. Events of such importance as the raising of Lazarus, or the solemn promise of the Holy Eucharist, are recorded by one Evangelist alone, although they must needs have been known to the other three writers. Further, time and again, general formulas † sum up entire categories of facts and discourses, and prove that each narrator simply purposed to give to his contemporaries, after a special design of his own, an extract of the deeds and teachings of the Son of God.

Thus the unchronological and fragmentary character of the Gospels, even in their narrative of Our Lord's public life, clearly proves that they are **memoirs** rather than histories or biographies generally so called.

2. **Difficulty in Harmonizing the Details of the Gospel Narrative.** The contrast just pointed out between the Gospel narrative and ordinary history or biography accounts to a large extent for the difficulty which has

---

* Introd. to the Study of the Gospels, chap. vii.
† Cfr. JOHN ii. 23 ; xx. 30 ; LUKE iv. 14 ; MARK i. 39, etc.

ever been felt in harmonizing its details. Incompleteness in the description of the same event by several Evangelists gives rise naturally to many variations in detail, while it oftentimes deprives us of the data necessary for showing the perfect harmony of the several accounts. True, in such cases, commentators or harmonizers are seldom at a loss to suggest plausible ways of reconciling opposite statements ; but in the absence of positive information their suggestions hardly ever appear more than probable solutions of a difficulty. To secure for their theories something like certainty, it would be necessary for them to throw upon the events about which the discrepancy has been noticed the full light of the circumstances of time and place in the midst of which these events occurred, as this light would in some measure make up for the lack of details afforded by the Gospel narrative. But in most cases the exact circumstances of time and place can be so imperfectly determined that the same fact which is assigned by one writer to the very beginning of Christ's public life is considered by another as belonging to a much later period, or is even placed towards the very end of Our Lord's mortal career, while a third declines to assign it to any specific period, or even endeavors to prove its identity with another fact from which most writers distinguish it.

In view of these, and other such obscurities which surround the details of the Gospel narrative, we shall not make in the following pages elaborate attempts to show that these details can be forced into the semblance of a complete and connected narrative. We shall, rather, confine ourselves to a summary view of the principal events of Christ's public ministry, and mention only incidentally the differences in detail noticeable in the sacred records.

§ 2. *Events in Judæa* (*April–December*, A.D. 27).

1. **The First Pasch in Jerusalem** (April 11–18).
After the wedding festivities at Cana were over, Jesus, together with His mother, His brethren, and His disciples,
went down to Capharnaum,[*] a town some 20 miles distant
from Cana and situated on the northwestern shore of the
Sea of Galilee. The Pasch of the Jews was near at hand,
and Capharnaum would be a convenient place to join the
annual pilgrimage to Jerusalem.

Leaving Capharnaum after only a few days' sojourn, Our
Lord probably took the road usually followed at that time
by the caravans which left the western shore of the Sea of
Galilee. This road passed through Scythopolis, Archelais,
Phasaelis, and Jericho, crossed in a westerly direction the
wilderness of Judæa, and traversing Bethany and Bethphage, led to the Mount of Olives and the Holy City.

After a journey of about 90 miles Jesus reached
Jerusalem, probably a few days before the Paschal celebration, which this year fell on the 11th of April, and which
marks the beginning of Our Lord's public ministry in
Judæa. St. John, who alone records the events connected
with this sojourn of Our Lord in Jerusalem, mentions first
a cleansing of the Temple by the Son of God,[†] and this
cleansing is plainly distinct from the later one recorded by
Matthew xxi. 12–16 ; Mark xi. 15–19 ; Luke xix. 45–48.[‡]
On the occasion of this the greatest Jewish solemnity, the
Outer Court of the Temple had gradually been transformed
into a market-place particularly for the convenience of the
Jews who, coming from distant countries, were obliged to
purchase in this court the victims for their offerings, and to
exchange their foreign money, stamped with idolatrous images, into the sacred shekel with which alone the Temple

---

[*] JOHN ii. 12.   [†] JOHN ii. 14–22.

[‡] FILLION, St. Jean, p. 40; MEYER, on St. John, American Edition, p. 111.

dues could be paid. From the strong language of Our Lord in driving out of the place the traders in sheep, cattle, and pigeons, and in overthrowing the tables of the money-changers, it seems probable that not only a fair and honest, but even an extortionate, traffic was carried on within the *Court of the Gentiles.* Be this as it may, it is plain that the close neighborhood of a noisy market must have greatly interfered with the religious stillness requisite within the *Inner Courts* for either the silent prayer of the solitary worshipper or the deep recollection of the multitude when attending the more important ceremonies. All this was, indeed, a great desecration of God's house, but the Jewish priests derived a large profit from the whole traffic, and hence they had sanctioned what they should have considered as an intolerable profanation of the Temple.

It was, then, the honor of His Father's house that Jesus came forward to vindicate when driving out the buyers and sellers. With an irresistible majesty, as St. Jerome says, He exclaimed, " Make not the house of My Father a house of traffic." Any Jew might rise up in a holy zeal against public abuses,* but the most ardent zealots generally justified their proceedings by unquestionable signs of the divine approval.† By His conduct Jesus had rebuked not only the people at large, but also the Jewish leaders. The Temple officials came, therefore, to Him and requested a sign whereby He would prove His authority "to do these things." ‡

" Destroy this temple," replied Jesus, " and in three days I will raise it up." These words seemed to refer to the Temple in which He and His questioners were standing; but they referred to a much holier sanctuary of the divinity. " He spoke of the temple of His body." § The great proof which Our Lord was to give to all was indeed His resurrection; but this connection between His answer

* NUMB. XXV. 7.   † 3 KINGS xviii. 23, 24.   ‡ JOHN ii. 18.   § JOHN ii. 21.

and their question was not realized even by His disciples until a much later day, when they remembered His prophetic words and derived from their fulfilment an increase of their faith. *   The words of Jesus were therefore understood as referring to the magnificent edifice, the rebuilding of which, begun long years before by Herod, was still in progress; and they were maliciously construed by His enemies into a blasphemous boast against the house of Jehovah.†

In addition to the cleansing of the Temple, St. John records that during the Paschal festivities Our Lord performed in Jerusalem several miracles which he does not report in detail. They made such an impression that "many believed in His name," that is, believed Him to be the Messias.‡   But Jesus, knowing that these believers were far from possessing deep convictions, showed towards them the greatest reserve.§

It was different, however, with Nicodemus, a personage whom St. John introduces as a Pharisee, and a member of the Sanhedrim.‖   This man feared, indeed, the hostility of most of his colleagues, who were already opposed to Jesus; yet, having seen the miracles which Our Lord had performed, and being convinced that Jesus was a teacher truly sent by God, he desired to inquire from Him the nature of the kingdom of heaven and the manner in which men were to enter into it.   He therefore came to Jesus during the night, and learned, to his great astonishment, that, far from belonging to the new kingdom by natural right, the Jews had "to be born again of water and the Holy Ghost," that is, to be spiritually regenerated in the vivifying waters of Christian baptism, in order that they might be admitted into the kingdom of God.¶   The action of the Spirit which gives to the waters of baptism their vivifying power is, in-

---

* JOHN ii. 22.   † JOHN ii. 19; MATT. xxvi. 61.   ‡ JOHN ii. 23.
§ JOHN ii. 24, 25.   ‖ JOHN iii. 1; vii. 50.   ¶ JOHN iii. 3-5.

deed, hidden, but because of its hiddenness its action should not be denied, any more than that of the wind, the presence of which is ascertained only by its effects.*

After his summary of Our Lord's dialogue with Nicodemus, the beloved apostle reports the substance of a beautiful discourse delivered by Jesus, apparently in connection with His interview with Nicodemus.†

2. Ministry through Judæa.‡ When the companies of pilgrims started from Jerusalem for their homes, Our Saviour went with His disciples "into the land of Judæa," that is, into the province of that name, as distinguished from its chief city. It is impossible to determine the extent of Judæan territory through which Our Lord went at this time. From St. John (iii. 22 *b*, and iv. 3, 4), it may, however, be inferred that He visited several parts of Judæa, and from Acts x. 37 it seems probable that He went through most, if not all, the rural districts of that province.

The same uncertainty prevails about the character of Our Lord's teaching during this same period. It may be conjectured, however, that His preaching was of the same preparatory kind as we find described a little later in St. Matthew (iv. 17), where we read: " FROM THAT TIME JESUS BEGAN TO PREACH AND TO SAY: DO PENANCE, FOR THE KINGDOM OF HEAVEN IS AT HAND," and that consequently it was substantially the same as the preaching of His holy precursor. Those who listened to His words received from the hands of His disciples § a baptism which was most likely identical with the rite administered by St. John the Baptist.‖

Meanwhile the forerunner of Jesus was still baptizing in a place called " ENNON, NEAR SALIM," which it is impossible to identify at the present day. It was more probably

---

* JOHN iii. 7, 8. † JOHN iii. 11-21. ‡ JOHN iii. 22-36.
§ JOHN iii. 22 *c*; iv. 2. ‖ See FILLION, St. Jean, p. 58.

on the west side of the Jordan,* in Judæa, and apparently not far distant from the place where Our Lord's disciples baptized the repentant multitudes.†

This circumstance of Jesus and John teaching and baptizing at the same time in the vicinity of each other naturally excited some speculation among the people. Some of John's disciples fell into an argument "concerning PURIFICATION"—that is, concerning *baptism*—with a Jew, and they referred the question to John himself for his decision. These disciples were jealous of their master's honor and could not bear that Jesus, whom they thought greatly indebted to John, should baptize and attract more followers than did the holy precursor.‡ But John, far from sharing this feeling of jealousy, earnestly endeavored to remove it from the heart of his disciples. He reminded them that he had always asserted that he was not himself the Christ, but greatly inferior to Him ; and in the most emphatic manner he reasserted his own secondary station. He was but the humble attendant on the bridegroom ; Christ was the bridegroom Himself ; his own doctrine was that of earth, that of Christ was of heaven ; it was only right that the Son of God and the author of eternal life "should increase," and his precursor "decrease."§

Our Lord's ministry in Judæa extended until the month of December, A.D. 27, as we may infer from His words to His disciples when passing by Sychar : "there are yet FOUR MONTHS, and THEN THE HARVEST COMETH,"‖ for these words can be understood only of the first crops which, in Palestine, are gathered during the month of April. His departure was a hasty one,¶ most likely because of an imminent danger due to the very great offence which His success, far greater than that of John, gave to the Pharisees who, at the time, wielded so much power in the province of

---

* Cfr. JOHN iii. 26.   † See ANDREWS, pp. 173-175.   ‡ JOHN iii. 25, 26.
§ JOHN iii. 27-36.   ‖ JOHN iv. 5, 35.   ¶ JOHN iv. 4.

Judæa.* We learn, moreover, from the Synoptists† that the imprisonment of John the Baptist, which probably occurred at this time, contributed to Our Lord's return into Galilee.‡

§ 3. *Jesus in Samaria.*

1. The Province of Samaria and its Inhabitants in the Time of Our Lord. Between Judæa and the northern province of Galilee lay the district of Samaria. Since the accession of Herod to the throne it had been a province of the Jewish kingdom, and after the deposition of Archelaus, had passed, together with Judæa, under a Roman procurator. According to Josephus§ the Samaritan territory "begins at a village in the great plain (the plain of Esdrælon) called Ginæa and ends at the district, or *toparchy*, of Akrabim, and is entirely of the same nature as Judæa. Both countries are made up of hills and valleys, the soil is suitable for agriculture, and is very fertile. . They are not watered by many rivers, but derive their chief moisture from the rains. The river water is exceedingly sweet, and the cattle fed upon the excellent grasses yield more milk than those of other places. Both countries are very populous."

As already remarked in a preceding chapter (Chapter VI.) the inveterate enmity between Jews and Samaritans reached its climax in the time of Christ. They both utterly despised each other,‖ and the Jews, in their pilgrimages to Jerusalem, usually avoided passing through Samaria in order to escape words of abuse or deeds of violence. Josephus loses no occasion to tell us of Samaritan tricks and outrages, and there is no reason to question his statements; and if we had a Samaritan historian we would undoubtedly hear quite as much that was no less true on the other side.

---

* Cfr. JOHN vii. 1-3, 25, 32.   † MATT. iv. 12; MARK i. 14; LUKE iv. 14, 15.
‡ See ANDREWS, pp. 178-182.   § Wars of the Jews, book III., chap. iii., § 4.
‖ Cfr. JOHN viii. 48; iv. 9.

"This people were, nevertheless, of the same faith as Israel. They adored the one God of the patriarchs of old, and avoided carefully all practices of heathenism in their worship of Jehovah. The only sacred books in their possession were the Mosaic writings, and so far as their exclusion from the sanctuary in Jerusalem permitted, they kept strictly to the statutes of the Pentateuch. The popular Jewish expectation of the Messias was indeed foreign to them, for the politico-national element in it could not but find them unsympathetic, since they were excluded from the "Kingdom." They, too, hoped for the Messias ; but on the ground of a passage from the Law,* they thought of Him more as an ethical reformer than a mighty converter or restorer." †

2. **Jesus and the Samaritans.‡** Such were, briefly, the country and the people which Jesus had to visit as He wished to reach quickly the friendly province of Galilee. A rapid and fatiguing journey brought Him to the neighborhood of Sychar, a small Samaritan town most likely to be identified with a village known as 'Askar, on the southern base of Mount Hebal, some 40 miles north of Jerusalem. At the foot of Mount Garizim, on the other side of the valley of Sichem, was the well which the patriarch Jacob had dug when he bought the ground "of the children of Hemor, the father of Sichem."§ This well still exists, although it seems there is water in it only during the rainy season. It has a diameter of 9 feet and its present depth is about 75 feet. It is on the low wall of masonry built around the brim of Jacob's well that Our Lord sat to rest Himself while His disciples entered the town to purchase provisions. It was about the sixth hour, or midday, according to the Jewish manner of reckoning from sunrise to sunset; the usual hour, indeed, for

* DEUTER. xviii. 15.   † WEISS, Life of Christ, vol. ii., p. 33, Eng. TransL
‡ JOHN iv. 1-44.   § GEN. xxxiii. 19; JOHN iv. 12.

the principal meal of the Jews,[*] but not the usual one for women to come to fetch water. While, however, Jesus sat waiting at the well a woman came from the town with her waterpot on her shoulder to draw water from this famous spring.

Then occurred between Our Lord and the Samaritan woman a conversation too well known to be repeated here. Its summary in our fourth Gospel reveals the zeal of Jesus for the conversion of souls, makes known to us the Messianic hopes of the Samaritans, and proves that from the beginning of His public mission the Saviour of the world had a perfect knowledge both of His Messianic dignity and of the manner of divine worship He was to introduce into the world.

The conversation was interrupted by the return of the disciples with the provisions they had bought. They wondered that Jesus talked with one of the hateful race, but they did not dare to question Him about it. Meanwhile the woman had quickly returned to the town and made known to the inhabitants what had occurred between her and One who might be the Messias. Accordingly, the Samaritans went forth to see Our Saviour, and invited Him to tarry with them. Complying with their request, He remained two days in Sychar ; and to the number of those who had believed in Jesus on the woman's report of His supernatural knowledge, many more were added who, having heard His sacred words, were convinced that He was "indeed the Saviour of the world."

§ 4. *Ministry in Galilee.*

1. The City of Capharnaum and its Importance in the Public Life of Christ. Proceeding from Sychar, Our Lord soon entered Galilee and directed His

---

* JOSEPHUS, Life, 54; ANDREWS, pp. 184, 185.

steps towards Cana. As He went along He preached repentance and the near coming of the kingdom of God.* In the various villages He traversed people welcomed Him, for they had witnessed His miracles at the Pasch, which they also had celebrated in Jerusalem.† Not long after His arrival at Cana the rumor of His return reached Capharnaum, only about 20 miles distant. Thereupon "a certain ruler, whose son was sick in Capharnaum," and who is thought by many to have been Chusa, the steward of Herod Antipas, came to Jesus beseeching Him to come down to that city and heal his son, but Jesus wrought the miracle requested of Him without departing from Cana.‡

Soon after this great miracle§ Christ was Himself on His way to Capharnaum, which was at the time one of the most important towns of Galilee. Situated on the north-western shore of the Sea of Galilee—whether at **Khan Minyeh,** at the northeastern end of the plain of Genesareth, or at **Tell Hum,** about 2½ miles northeast of Khan Minyeh, does not appear,‖—Capharnaum stood on one of the great caravan roads between the East and Egypt. It

---

* MATT. iv. 17; MARK i. 15.

† JOHN iv. 45.

‡ JOHN iv. 46-54.

§ The question whether Jesus went to Nazareth before repairing to Capharnaum is still a matter of discussion among scholars. Those who think that He did not visit Nazareth at this time identify the visit spoken of in LUKE iv. 16-30 with the one recorded in MATT. xiii. 53-58, and MARK vi. 1-6. (See BRUNEAU, Harmony, p. 46.)

‖ Cfr. VIGOUROUX, Dict. de la Bible; ANDREWS, Life of Christ, pp. 224-238; HASTINGS, Dict. of the Bible.—The Sea of Galilee, called also the lake of Genesareth, is about 60 miles northeast from Jerusalem and 27 east from the Mediterranean Sea, and in size and shape it is somewhat similar to Lake Lucerne, in Switzerland. It is an irregular oval, the broad end of which is towards the north, and it is 13 miles in length by 4 to 7 miles in width, and 165 feet in depth in its deepest part. Its shores are surrounded by hills, which on the west side are broken by broad valleys with streams descending to the lake, and between the hills and the water edge there is a narrow level belt which in the springtime is covered with verdure (MATT. xiv. 19, etc.). On the western shore the principal towns were formerly *Bethsaida, Capharnaum, Corozain, Magdala,* and *Tiberias*; but they have all long disappeared, except the town of Tiberias and the wretched village of El Mejdel (ancient Magdala). In Our Lord's time, as at the present day, the waters of the lake abounded in fish, and were subject to sudden and violent storms.

was a customs-station,* and had a Roman garrison† under the command of a centurion, who thought it worth while to ingratiate himself with the Jewish population by building them a synagogue.‡

After His rejection by Nazareth,§ Jesus selected this flourishing city as His own home,‖ and as the centre of His work. Capharnaum had much to recommend it to Our Saviour for this twofold purpose. He could feel more at home in a place far removed from the Judæan authorities, amid a mixed and consequently less fanatic population, and near the residence of the grateful courtier of Herod, whose son He had quite lately healed. Again, in this fishing-town His disciples could easily pursue their avocation of fishermen and He himself could at any time be carried to the eastern shore of the Sea of Galilee, where He could find greater quiet and security. Finally, from Capharnaum, as from a centre of operation, He could easily start on His missionary journeys through Galilee on the west, Trachonitis on the north, Decapolis and Peræa on the east and south.

2. Principal Features of Our Lord's Work in Galilee. It was not long after settling in Capharnaum, that Jesus, not satisfied with preaching and performing miracles in that city,¶ resolved to pay a visit to other places in Galilee.**

Accordingly, He started with His disciples—to whom He had but lately extended a second call on the occasion of the miraculous draught of fishes ††—on His first circuit or missionary journey through that province. "We have no sufficient data to determine the local order of these visitations ; but it is only natural to suppose that He would first visit the places near Capharnaum and then those more remote."‡‡

---

* MATT. ix. 9. † MATT. viii. 5. ‡ LUKE vii. 5. § LUKE iv. 16–30.
‖ MATT. ix. 1. ¶ Cfr. MARK i. 21–34; LUKE iv. 31–41; MATT. viii. 14–17.
** MARK i. 35 sq.; LUKE iv. 42 sq. †† MARK i. 16–20. ‡‡ MARK i. 38.

In going "through all Galilee* His common mode of
action was apparently this: on entering a city where there
was a synagogue, He availed Himself of the privilege which
His reputation as a rabbi and prophet gave Him, to teach
the people from the Scriptures. This He did upon the
Sabbaths and synagogue days.   At other times He
preached in the streets or fields, or sitting in a boat upon
the sea; in every convenient place where the people were
willing to hear Him.   His fame as a healer of the sick
caused many to be brought to Him, and He appears in general to have healed all.†   His sojourn in any single village
was necessarily brief, and therefore those who had been
really impressed by His works or words, and desired to see
or hear Him more, followed Him to the adjoining towns or
sought Him at Capharnaum.   The disciples do not appear
to have taken any public part as teachers.   The expenses
of these journeys were probably borne by the contributions
of the disciples, and by the voluntary offerings of those who
had been healed, and of their friends.   .   It should
also be noted as a characteristic of the beginning of His
ministry, that we do not find any open avowal of His Messianic claims."‡

The Gospel narrative affords us no particulars of Our
Lord's first missionary journey. Only one miracle, the healing of a leper, is recorded in detail, and this because the
cure of a leper was in every instance and by all traced to
the direct agency of God. This helps us to understand why
Jesus, knowing perfectly the stupendous effect which the
news of such a miracle would produce on the people's
minds, strictly imposed silence on the healed man, lest erroneous Messianic hopes should be confirmed among the Jewish people.§

After Christ's return to Capharnaum two events occurred

* MARK i. 39.   † MARK vi. 56; MATT. ix. 35.
‡ ANDREWS. pp. 241, 242.   § MATT. viii. 1-14; MARK i. 40-44; LUKE v. 12-14.

which do not require more than a passing mention here. The first was the healing of a paralytic, which Jesus effected as a proof that "the Son of Man" had the power to remit sins, and which filled the Pharisees and Doctors of the Law who witnessed it with indignation towards one whom they considered as a blasphemer. The second is the call of Levi the tax-gatherer, who, while sitting at the receipt of custom —probably at the point where the great road from Damascus comes to Capharnaum—heard from Jesus these simple words, " Follow Me." And the publican Levi—called also Matthew—leaving all things, rose up and followed Christ.*

* MARK i. 45; ii. 14; LUKE v. 15-28; MATT. ix. 2-9.

SYNOPSIS OF CHAPTER X.

SECOND YEAR'S MINISTRY.

(March A.D. 28—April A.D. 29.)

I. SHORT SOJOURN IN JERUSALEM:	Occasion:	"A Festival Day of the Jews" (John v. 1). Probably a Second Pasch.
	Prominent Features (John v. 2–47).	

II. JESUS AND THE TWELVE:	1. The Twelve selected	Where? How? Why? Who they were?
	2. Their Temporary Mission:	Why sent forth? With what instructions and powers?

III. CHRIST'S PUBLIC TEACHING:	1. The Sermon on the Mount: Place, Audience, General Object.
	2. The Parables: Nature, Principal Teachings.
	3. The Discourse in the Synagogue of Capharnaum (John vi.).

IV. HIS GROWING INFLUENCE IN GALILEE:	1. Principal Causes.
	2. Climax towards the End of Second Year's Ministry.

CHAPTER X.

(March A.D. 28—April A.D. 29.)

§ 1. *Short Sojourn in Jerusalem* (*March–April*, A.D. 28).

1. Occasion of Our Lord's Sojourn in Jerusalem.
The second year of Our Lord's public ministry is marked, like the first, by a short sojourn in Jerusalem. St. John, who alone makes us acquainted with this event, states that it was occasioned by the desire of Jesus to celebrate in the Holy City " a festival day of the Jews," but as he does not say *which* Jewish festival this was, biblical scholars are divided between four important feasts which Our Saviour might have celebrated in Jerusalem after His return from Judæa in December of the preceding year.

These festivals are (1) that of **Purim**, falling in March, and instituted to commemorate the deliverance of the Jewish exiles from the cruel designs of Aman ;* (2) that of the **Passover**, in April ; (3) the feast of **Pentecost**, occurring this year on the 19th of May ; (4) the feast of **Tabernacles**, falling on the 23d of September. Strong arguments point to the **Paschal** festival as the one referred to by St. John, and indeed the Passover was pre-eminently the " festival day of the Jews." †

2. Prominent Features of Our Lord's Sojourn in Jerusalem. This visit of Jesus to the Holy City has a special importance in the public life of Our Lord, for on

---

* Cfr. ESTHER iii. 7; ix. 24.   † FOUARD, i., appendix vii.; ANDREWS, pp. 189–198.

the occasion of the miracle at the pool of Bethsaida, which He wrought at this time,* He manifested His Messianic and divine character more openly than before, and in consequence the official classes of Judæa showed themselves more hostile to Him.

The pool of Bethsaida was most likely situated on the northeast side of Jerusalem, a little northwest of the present church of St. Anne and not far from St. Stephen's gate. † It had five porches, and was much resorted to for the miraculous power of its waters. Among the crowd of sufferers who had gathered there Our Saviour took notice of one who had been disabled by disease for thirty-eight years; and as he had no friend to immerse him in the waters of the pool "when they were troubled," Jesus took pity on him, healed him by His word, and sent him away carrying his bed (a thin mattress or blanket) with him.‡

This happened on a Sabbath, and the carrying of any burden on such a day was looked upon as one of the most heinous offences against the Law, so that the sight of a man thus violating the statute in a public place naturally excited the greatest attention. The clamor of the official classes was raised at once against the man, and when they learned that Jesus was the author both of the cure and of the violation of the Sabbath, they resolved on putting Our Saviour to death, and summoned Him before the Sanhedrim.

Our Lord availed Himself of this trial to declare more openly than on His first visit to Jerusalem His equality with the Father, His Messianic character, His right to divine honor, and to prove to His judges that His claims, however astonishing they might appear to them, rested not on His own assertion alone, but also on the unquestionable tes-

---

* JOHN v.

† About the probable site of the pool of Bethsaida (in Greek *Bethesda*), cfr. VIGOUROUX, Dictionnaire de la Bible ; EASTON, Bible Dictionary ; FOUARD, vol. i., appendix viii. ; HASTINGS, Dict. of the Bible, art. Bethesda.

‡ Cfr. VIGOUROUX, Diction. de la Bible ; FOUARD, i., appendix viii.

timony of John the Baptist, of His own miraculous works, and even of the writings of Moses, their great law-giver.

These assertions appeared blasphemous in the eyes of " the Jews," and they determined to ᴾress more earnestly against Jesus the capital charge. The sacred narrative does not state whether any sentence was passed against Him on this occasion. Yet it may be gathered from other passages of the fourth Gospel * that a sentence was actually passed, that Jesus was publicly banished from Judæa, and that He would be seized and put to death if found in that province.

§ 2. *Jesus and the Twelve.*

1. **The Twelve Selected.** Banished from Judæa, Our Lord withdrew to the safer province of Galilee, but His actions were henceforth closely watched by His enemies, especially on Sabbath days. † The miracles of healing which He performed at this time secured to Him, however, such popularity that His enemies could not carry out their criminal designs against Him. ‡

Thus freed from open opposition, yet knowing that He should continue to labor but a short time, Our Lord made provision for carrying on His work in a more extensive manner during His mortal life, and for pursuing it after His departure by the selection of faithful assistants in His ministry. § With this object in view St. Luke tells us that " He went out into a mountain to pray, and that He passed the whole night in the prayer of God." When it was morning He called His disciples and out of them He chose twelve— a number which occurs with significant frequency in Holy Writ—and named them His apostles. Seven of them He had already especially called to be His followers, namely,

* Cfr. JOHN vii. 1, 25-32.
† Cfr. MATT. xii. 1-14 ; MARK ii. 23—iii. 6 ; LUKE vi. 1-11.
‡ Cfr. MARK iii. 7-12 ; LUKE vi. 17-19.
§ MARK iii. 13-19 ; LUKE vi. 12-16 ; cfr. also MATT. x. 2-4.

Andrew and Simon his brother ; James and John, the sons of Zebedee ; Philip and Nathanael or Bartholomew ; and Levi or Matthew the publican. To these He now added Thomas or Didymus (*a twin*) ; James and Jude, the sons of Alpheus ; Simon Chananeus (*zelotes*) ; and finally, the only apostle from Judæa proper, the traitor Judas Iscariot (*the man from Kerioth*). [*]

These are the men whom Jesus especially called to witness His miracles, to profit by His teachings, to help Him in His ministry, and to preserve and spread His religion. Apparently they had little to recommend them to His choice, for they were almost all uneducated, without wealth, social rank, and personal influence ; but in selecting them Jesus was laying the basis of one of the best arguments for the divine origin of Christianity, namely, that the world should have been converted by means of so few and so humble instruments. [†]

2. **Temporary Mission of the Twelve.** It was during one of His missionary journeys through Galilee that Our Lord sent His chosen twelve on a temporary mission. As He went about the towns and villages, He was moved with compassion at the forlorn condition of their inhabitants, who " were distressed and lying like sheep that have no shepherd." He therefore resolved to send to them in the person of His apostles, men entirely devoted to their temporal and spiritual welfare. A further reason for this sending forth of the twelve is to be found in Christ's desire to prepare for the ministry in a more practical manner than heretofore, those who were soon to be the continuators of His work. For more than a year the apostles had contemplated in the Saviour a model of zeal and disinterestedness which they were to reproduce in their own lives. They had seen Him work the most convincing miracles in proof of His divine mission, and it was now to be their privilege

---

[*] Cfr. FOUARD, vol. i., pp. 246-258.   [†] Cfr. 1 COR. i. 27 sq.

to wield the same miraculous powers for the conversion of their brethren. In a word, the sending forth of the twelve towards the end of Our Lord's second year's ministry was to be for the apostles a real initiation into their future ministry, and to prove beneficial both to themselves and to the sheep of the house of Israel to whom they were sent.

Great indeed must have been the joy of the twelve when Jesus gave them a mission practically identical with His own, sending them "to preach the kingdom of God"; when He imparted to them powers co-extensive with His own, "giving them power over unclean spirits, to cast them out, and to heal all manner of diseases and all manner of infirmities." True, in sending them forth He gave them directions* as to the places where they should go, the manner in which they should use their powers, etc., which under other circumstances might have appeared rather severe; but at that moment they were only too willing to accept them, and they set off, "going about through the towns, preaching the gospel and healing everywhere."†

§ 3. *Christ's Public Teaching.*

1. **The Sermon on the Mount.** The place pointed out by tradition as the scene of the selection of the twelve is a hill on the road from Tiberias to Nazareth, and called from its peculiar shape "the Horns of Hattin." After having chosen His apostles Our Saviour descended with them from the mountain peak to a more level spot,‡ and sitting down in the formal attitude of a teacher, He delivered His discourse so well known under the name of the **Sermon on the Mount.**§ His immediate audience was indeed made

---

* It is probable that the recommendations recorded by St. Matthew (chap. x. 16 sq.), in connection with this temporary mission of the twelve, were made by Our Lord only at a later period (cfr. Luke xii. 2 sq).

† Cfr. Matt. x; Mark vi. 7-13; Luke ix. 1-6.

‡ Luke vi. 17.

§ Matt. v-vii; Luke vi. 20-40.

up of His apostles and disciples, and of the great multitudes that had gathered around Him. But He also spoke for future generations, describing a kingdom and a blessedness very different from those which His contemporaries expected, and laying down the Christian form of life for all ages.

This discourse of Jesus, so exalted in its teachings and so authoritative in its tone, filled the multitude with admiration,[*] and will ever exercise the deepest influence upon the readers of the Gospel.

2. **Teaching in Parables.** Instead of this formal manner of teaching the people at large, Our Lord substituted soon afterwards another no less in harmony with the Oriental mind of His hearers, which has ever been fond of mystic and figurative language. Parables, to which He now resorted as a means of conveying His doctrine, were stories describing events of common occurrence in such a manner as to suggest to reflecting and well-disposed minds truths of the spiritual order. Jesus used them freely henceforward, because on the one hand the time had come when He should make known to the Jews the true nature and principal features of the kingdom of God, and on the other hand their national prejudices and Messianic misconceptions did not allow Him to speak too plainly.

There is hardly any doubt that in delivering His parables Christ intended to correct gradually the false notions of His hearers respecting the kingdom of God,[†] and that in each parable He suggested mainly one feature of this same kingdom. His principal teachings in this respect may be briefly summed up as follows :[‡]

The kingdom which the Jews should expect is the kingdom of God in its modest, secret, and as it were, insignifi-

---

* MATT. vii. 28, 29.
† Cfr., for instance, MARK xii. 12; LUKE xix. 11.
‡ Cfr. BRUCE, The Kingdom of God; BRIGGS, The Messiah of the Gospels.

cant origin. It is submitted to the laws of organic growth as all living things are, and hence its planting and early developments do not attract much attention ; but it is not so with its further extension, destined as it is to pervade and transform the whole world. *

The real worth of this kingdom is that of a hidden treasure and of a precious pearl,† which if even accidentally found must be preferred to all things else. This kingdom is indeed rejected by those who, like the men invited to the marriage feast,‡ or the two sons spoken of in the parable in St. Matthew (xxi. 28–32), had the first claim to its possession and apparently were best qualified for entering into it; but all those who earnestly avail themselves of the invitation of the Gospel will be admitted. As long as God's kingdom exists in this world it is necessarily composed of good and bad men, so that the certain separation between them must be postponed to the end of time.§

This is really a new kingdom of God with a new nation and a new set of rulers (as is taught in the parable of the wicked husbandmen),‖ although it is no less truly the continuation of the kingdom of God under the Old Covenant. Once this kingdom is organized upon earth, the King goes to a far country, relying upon His representatives to be more faithful than the rulers of the old kingdom, and expecting that all His servants shall bear fruits proportionate to their several trusts, else each and all will be visited, as were the unfaithful rulers and subjects of the old kingdom, with meet punishment.¶

At the return of this King this kingdom of grace will be transformed into a kingdom of glory, when all trials here

---

* Cfr. MATT. xiii. 1-23, and parallel passages; MARK iv. 26-29; MATT. xiii. 31-33 and parallel passages.

† MATT. xiii. 44-46.　　　‡ MATT. xxii. 1-14.

§ Parables of the Cockle and the Drag Net, MATT. xiii. 24-30, 47-50.

‖ MATT. xxi. 33-43.

¶ MATT. xxiv. 45-51, and LUKE xii. 41-46; MATT. xxv. 14-30; LUKE xix. 11-27, etc.

below will be at an end, but as the day and hour of this second coming of the Son of Man remains one of the divine secrets, the duty most pressing upon all is that of constant watchfulness.* Finally, the duration of this kingdom on earth will outlive the ruin of the Holy City and of its Temple. It will be coextensive with the preaching of the Gospel to all nations, and this, when accomplished, will be an unquestionable sign of its near approach.†

3. The Discourse in the Synagogue of Capharnaum.‡ Of course, it should not be supposed that Jesus never addressed His hearers otherwise than in parables. Although this formed His chief means of teaching the people during the second year—as well as during the last year—of His public ministry, yet He did at times deliver public addresses, one of which has been preserved to us in the sixth chapter of St. John's Gospel.

It was in the synagogue of Capharnaum and under peculiar circumstances that Jesus addressed this important discourse to the Galilean multitudes. For a full year their devotion to Him had been steadily growing, and they had recently wished "to take Him by force and make Him King." § Their hopes of a temporal kingdom had now reached their highest point, and when Our Lord entered the synagogue of Capharnaum on this memorable occasion, they were confident that He was at length to proclaim Himself the Messias and start at once His glorious rule. In the midst of such high-strung but mistaken hopes, Jesus saw that the time had come when He should make known in explicit terms the true nature of the kingdom He had come to found. He therefore declared openly that the object of His mission was not to confer temporal, but rather spiritual, benefits, and that to secure to themselves these invaluable blessings, His hearers should believe in Him and in His heavenly descent.

* MATT. xxv. 1-13.   † Cfr. MATT. xxiv. 3-36, and parallel passages.
‡ JOHN vi.   § JOHN vi. 15.

Great was the astonishment of the Jews at words so unexpected. Many among them even murmured, saying, "Is not this Jesus the son of Joseph, whose father and mother we know? How then saith He, I came down from heaven?" This, however, was but a prelude both to the announcement which Jesus proceeded to make, and to the scandal it occasioned. He declared repeatedly to His hearers the necessity under which they all were "to eat His flesh and drink His blood to have life in them," and this statement so greatly shocked several of those who had up to this time faithfully followed Him, that they exclaimed "This saying is hard, and who can hear it?" In vain did Jesus insist upon the necessity of faith in His words; His endeavors to banish from their minds the unbearable thought that He required of them the inhuman practice of cannibalism were likewise fruitless. "Many of His disciples went back and walked no more with Him." But the twelve remained faithful through all, and Peter undoubtedly gave expression to their unflinching loyalty to their Master when he exclaimed: "Lord, to whom shall we go? Thou hast the words of eternal life. And we have believed and have known that Thou art the Christ, the Son of God."

§ 4. *Christ's Growing Influence in Galilee.*

1. Principal Causes of Christ's Influence in Galilee. The second year of Our Lord's public ministry has justly been called the year of "public favor." Hardly had He returned to Galilee from the Passover when He performed miracles of healing which won for Him the admiration and gratitude of multitudes from all parts of the country,* and throughout the year wonders of the most stupendous kind kept the attention of the people fixed upon Him. For centuries no miraculous deeds had been wrought in Israel, and

---

* MATT. iv. 25.

the Galileans naturally felt proud that the wonder-worker was their fellow countryman. Further, in the eyes of many, both in and out of Galilee, miracles so numerous, so easily performed, denoted not only the prophetical, but even the Messianic, character of their author.

Besides this first—and indeed greatest—cause of the growing influence of Jesus in Galilee, several others may be mentioned here. There was, for instance, His power of speech, His words having ever a special grace and authority. There were also His well-known compassion for the weak, the poor, the sinners, and His constant readiness to relieve the misery and sufferings of all around Him ; He was meek and lowly of heart, and this attracted powerfully the affection of all those who had hitherto been looked upon with contempt by their teachers. Again, the slanderous reports, artfully started and studiously spread about by Christ's enemies, contributed in their manner to increase His favor with the people at large. The real character of many of these calumnious charges was at times so evident that no one was deceived, while at other times those who had been first misled soon recognized their error; with the final result in both cases that through a reaction against the malice of His enemies, the popular attachment to Jesus grew gradually stronger and deeper. Finally, it should be borne in mind that the Jews of Galilee were, much less than those of the south, under the direct and all-powerful sway of the Pharisees and other enemies of Christ, while many of the leading men and women, especially of Capharnaum were His declared friends.

2. Christ's Influence at its Climax towards the End of Second Year's Ministry. These and other such causes contributed powerfully towards securing to Jesus an ever-growing influence in the northern province of Galilee. This steady growth of His favor with the people during His second year's ministry is particularly noticeable in the

Gospel narrative in connection with the miracles recorded. At first His miracles of healing attracted to Our Lord large multitudes, not only from Galilee and Judæa, but also from Idumæa, Decapolis, and the region about Tyre and Sidon.* The raising, a little later, of the widow's son at Naim—a town on the northwestern slope of Little Hermon and about 25 miles southwest of Capharnaum—produced the deepest impression upon the spectators, who proclaimed and spread far and wide their belief that Jesus was "a great prophet" truly sent by God.† Other miracles, hardly less astonishing, gradually led the multitudes to wonder whether He was not "the Son of David,"‡ and next to proclaim Him as such, regardless of the well-known opposition of the Pharisees.§ A little later the twelve were sent on a temporary mission. Being endowed with miraculous powers similar to those of their Master, and going two by two through the different towns of Galilee, they spread His doctrine very rapidly in remote places, and secured for it such publicity that Our Lord's fame now reached Herod for the first time. Finally, at the approach of the Paschal festival, two great events carried to its climax the hitherto growing influence of Christ in Galilee. The first was His feeding of 5000 men with five loaves and two fishes; this miracle aroused the grateful enthusiasm of the multitudes to such an extent that they strove "to make Him king." The second, which became known to them the next morning, was His miraculous walking upon the sea. The news of this last miracle caused the people to be so fully persuaded of a very near establishment of a worldly kingdom by Jesus, that He deemed it necessary to deal a death-blow to all their earthly expectations by His public discourse in the synagogue of Capharnaum, a summary of which has been given above.

* MATT. iv. 25.   † LUKE vii. 11-18.   ‡ MATT. xii. 23.   § MATT. ix. 27 sq.

SYNOPSIS OF CHAPTER XI.

FIRST PART OF THIRD YEAR'S MINISTRY.

(April—October 29 A.D.)

Section I. Jesus and His Enemies.

**I.
OPPOSITION OF
OUR LORD'S
ENEMIES.**

1. This Opposition can be Accounted for in Various Ways.
2. They Resorted to all Kinds of Means to Undermine His Authority.
3. They are now Fiercer against Him because of
   - Christ's repeated public censures of their doctrine and practices.
   - News of His wonderful success and widespread fame.
   - Diminution at last of His popular favor.

**II.
HOW JESUS MET
THE OPPOSI-
TION OF HIS
ENEMIES.**

1. The Open Rupture:
   - The occasion.
   - The aggressive words of Jesus.
   - Fierce resentment of the Jews.
2. Travels through the Northern Regions:
   1. The Territory of Tyre and Sidon.
   2. The Decapolis.
   3. Magdala and Bethsaida.
   4. District of Cæsarea Philippi.

   Principal incidents recorded.

CHAPTER XI.

SECTION I. JESUS AND HIS ENEMIES.

§ 1. *The Opposition of Our Lord's Enemies.*

1. The Opposition can be Accounted for in Various Ways. The active ministry of Jesus in *Galilee* was practically brought to a close with His discourse in Capharnaum.* During two years "He had gone about doing good and healing all that were oppressed by the Devil," and had thereby given to all manifest proofs that "God was with Him."† Yet, far from recognizing the divine character of His mission, the Jewish leaders had constantly opposed Him, and in a short while they will "THROUGH IGNORANCE"‡ put to death the "LORD OF GLORY."§

Of course their opposition and ignorance were criminal, yet they may be accounted for in various ways. From infancy they had been taught to consider the Sabbath as a most sacred day, and in the schools they had learned to set the traditions of the elders on a par with the revealed Law of Moses. These views they had taught and enforced upon others, and all Jews, whatever their political and religious tenets, strictly acted upon them in their daily life. Jesus, on the contrary, had repeatedly dared to violate public statutes on the Sabbath and to take no account of traditions which the whole nation regarded as sacred, and of which the Jewish leaders were the watchful guardians. Again, the

* JOHN vi.   † ACTS x. 38; JOHN iii. 2.   ‡ ACTS iii. 17.   § 1 COR. ii. 8.

Jewish officials were considered by the people at large as models of holy living, because of their strict compliance with the least enactments of the Mosaic law and because of their long prayers, rigorous fasts, and liberal alms; and hence they received from all the highest marks of honor and respect in the market-places or in the synagogues. But far from paying them this tribute which flattered their vanity, Our Lord had solemnly condemned their religious practices as unwelcome to God because tainted with pride and hypocrisy, and quite lately He had called them a generation of vipers and pronounced them guilty of an irremissible blasphemy against the Holy Spirit. If only the people had let Jesus alone, and had not crowded in the synagogues to hear Him, and had not followed Him in the streets and in the fields anxious to listen to His exalted teachings and believing in His miraculous power, the leaders of the Jewish nation would not have taken the trouble to pursue Him with their opposition. But every increase of His popularity had been a decrease of their own ; indeed, in every conflict the multitude had sided with Him, and in every defeat of His adversaries they had rejoiced ; in short, His success was His greatest crime.

And after all, who was He thus to stand in successful opposition to them ? In their eyes He was but a Galilean peasant, a poor carpenter of Nazareth, an uneducated rabbi who surrounded Himself with poor fishermen, and won popular favor by welcoming the lowest elements of society, for He was " the friend of sinners and of publicans." Evidently such a one could not be, was not, the great and holy King they expected as the political restorer of their nation. The pretensions of Jesus were lofty indeed ; He claimed an authority superior to that of the elders, and apparently to that of Moses himself. He assumed a power over the Temple of God, made Himself equal to the Almighty, claimed to be the Lord of the Sabbath, and very recently He had assumed

the divine power of remitting sins.   But twice, at least, He
had denied to the lawful judges of His claims, the great
sign which the Messias was to give at His coming.   The
testimony of John the Baptist which He appealed to either
did not refer to Him, or John was mistaken, for according
to them no prophet could come from Nazareth.   In their
eyes, therefore, Jesus was but a bold deceiver of the people, whom He strove to withdraw from their lawful teachers
and leaders, and to whom He taught a lax morality, inasmuch as by His free intercourse with sinners and publicans
He obviously aimed at destroying all moral as well as all social distinctions.   He was but a false prophet, such as Moses
described long centuries before ; * for by teaching men not
to mind observances which the Jews thought necessary for
the faithful discharge of the divine commands, and by ar-
rogating to Himself the divine nature and powers, He manifestly tended to withdraw men from the pure worship of
Jehovah, from the primary belief of the Jewish religion,
namely, the belief in one only God.   His miraculous powers,
they concluded, were not credentials of a divine mission,
but rather proofs of a league with the Evil One, like that of
the magicians of Pharaoh, who performed wonders in their
opposition to Moses.†

**2. Means Used to Undermine Our Lord's Au-
thority.**   These are some of the grounds on which Our
Lord's enemies based their opposition, and in such frame
of mind they naturally thought it lawful to resort to every
means to undermine His authority.   They secretly plotted
against Him, striving to win over to their views their very
political opponents, the Herodians.   Then they waited
until some imprudence on His part, or the fickleness of the
people, should place Him in their power. During the full flush
of His popularity they had to be satisfied with recalling His
lowly birth at Nazareth, and with pushing His friends to

* DEUT. xviii.   † EXOD. vii. sq

treat Him publicly as one out of His senses. At the same time, they entertained an active correspondence with the Pharisees who were at Jerusalem, and when re-enforced by a deputation from the latter, they ventured to accuse Him of a league with Beelzebub. But in spite of all their efforts, His prudence had been such as not to leave them a single tangible ground for accusation, and His popularity had been steadily increasing, until, after the death of John the Baptist, His favor with the people reached its climax in Galilee, as we saw at the end of the preceding chapter.

3. **The Opposition Now Fiercer Against Jesus.** But the longer their opposition had been kept down and the greater His influence over the people had become, the more also the diminution of their own power with the multitudes and their wounded pride imperatively required that they should as soon as possible take a signal revenge upon His public and repeated censures of their teachings and practices.

When, therefore, they left Galilee for Jerusalem on the occasion of the third Pasch of Our Lord's ministry, they naturally reported to the ecclesiastical authorities of Judæa all that had taken place during the last month : how His ever-growing success had long reduced to naught all their efforts, and how His fame had finally reached Herod himself. But they also added how Jesus having refused the royal diadem offered Him by the enthusiastic people, they had finally betrayed Him into a public declaration equivalent in the eyes of all to a denial of the Messianic dignity. Many of His disciples had in consequence forsaken Him, and only a handful of followers still clung to Him. Now, then, was the time to turn against Him all the national expectations of the people. This the Jewish leaders understood, and the Paschal celebration * was hardly over when they sent a new deputation of Scribes into Galilee to watch

* JOHN vi. 4.

and oppose Him, and probably also to bring about a close alliance with the Herodians against Jesus.

The third year's ministry of Our Lord opened, therefore, with a fierce opposition on the part of the Jewish leaders, and we must now study how Jesus met their efforts against Him.

§ 2. *How Jesus met the Opposition of His Enemies.*

1. **The Open Rupture.** Arrived at Capharnaum, the Scribes who had been deputed by the authorities of Judæa, soon noticed that Our Lord's disciples did not practise the washing of hands after the traditionally prescribed manner before meals ; accordingly they remonstrated with Jesus for not training well His disciples. In the eyes of these emissaries this was a grave neglect of one of the most sacred " traditions of the elders," with which " all the Jews " complied and which had just been re-enacted in the form of an absolutely unchangeable decree.* Without stopping to vindicate His disciples, Jesus called the Scribes " hypocrites " whose only concern was about outward demonstrations of piety, without any concern about inward devotion to God. He went farther still, and charged them with setting aside the clearest and most important commandments of God by means of their human traditions. He next endeavored to teach the multitude one of those great truths so much lost sight of at the time : true defilement does not proceed from the outside, but from the evil desires and passions of the heart.

These words of Our Lord, which were a heavy but necessary blow against merely human and misleading traditions, gave so great offence to the Scribes, that the disciples of Jesus were afraid of the possible consequences of their resentment ; but the calm and significant words of Jesus quieted these fears of His disciples.†

* EDERSHEIM, vol. ii., p. 9 sq.; FOUARD, vol. ii., p. 6 sq.
† MATT. xv. 1-20; MARK vii. 1-23.

Several features of Our Lord's reply to the Scribes deserve especial attention.   On the one hand, He not only rebuked them for their hypocrisy, as He had repeatedly done in the past, but He pronounced a wholesale condemnation against their traditions, and taught the people a doctrine absolutely opposed to theirs on a point which they considered of the utmost importance.   On the other hand, His enemies resented openly His conduct, and, apparently for the first time in Galilee, threatened to use violence against Him and His disciples.   In a word, we are in presence of a direct attack on His enemies by Our Lord, and of an open rupture between Him and the Jewish leaders.

2. **Travels through the Northern Regions.**   Our Lord's time, however, to face His opponents resolutely and to the end, though not far away, had not yet fully come. Accordingly, we shall soon hear Him recommending silence, both to His disciples and to those whom He healed ; and as He had already avoided going to Jerusalem for the third Pasch of His ministry, so He now avoids moving through Galilee openly as before.

He therefore turns away from Central Galilee and begins His journeys through the northern regions.   He was accompanied by the twelve, whom it was His purpose henceforth to train in a special manner in view of His approaching death.   For this purpose also He sought the greater quiet and seclusion of the heathen territory of **Tyre.**   "But He could not be hid," says St. Mark ; and after healing the daughter of the Syrophenician woman in answer to her wonderful faith, He left that region.*   Passing through the territory of **Sidon,** Jesus probably proceeded along the Phenician frontier to the Jordan, and journeyed along the eastern bank of that river.†

Thus Our Lord reached the heathen territory of the **Decapolis**—a district taking its name from *ten cities* and

* MATT. xv. 21-28 ; MARK vii. 24-30.   † Cfr. ANDREWS, pp. 334, 335.

now under the immediate Roman rule—where He healed, among others, a "deaf and dumb man," enjoining strict silence upon him and upon his friends.   But His injunction of silence was not heeded, and the rumor of these wonderful deeds attracted to Him ever-growing multitudes.   They continued three days with Him, beholding His miracles and listening to His discourses, and at the end of that time, Jesus, moved with compassion upon the needs of the 4000 men before Him, fed them with seven loaves and a few fishes.*

After this *second* miraculous multiplication of loaves,† Our Saviour crossed the Sea of Galilee, and arrived at Magdala.‡   He was soon met by Pharisees and Sadducees, now combined for the first time against Him.   They had come to tempt Him and ask Him for a sign from heaven. He reproved their hypocrisy and affirmed that no sign would be given them except the sign of the prophet Jonas.   He therefore left them and went across the lake towards Bethsaida, probably situated at the point where the Jordan flows into the Sea of Galilee, warning His disciples during the voyage against the leaven of the Pharisees and the Sadducees. §   Outside the city of Bethsaida He restored the sight to a blind man who was offered to Him, and sent him home with the order not to spread the rumor of the miracle.‖

From Bethsaida Jesus probably directed His steps northward and reached the region of Cæsarea Philippi, where, on one important occasion,¶ He asked His apostles, "Whom do men say that I am?"   In their answer the disciples gave the opinions which were then most current among the Galileans, and which amounted to this: "Men generally look upon Thee as one of the forerunners of the Messias." But Jesus continued, "Whom do you say that I am?"

---

* MATT. xv. 29-38; MARK vii. 31; viii. 9.   † Cfr. MARK viii. 19.
‡ MATT. iv. 39.   § MATT. xvi. 1-12; MARK viii. 10-21.   ‖ MARK viii. 22-26.
¶ See MACLEAR, A Class-Book of New Testament History, p. 218.

Simon Peter answered in the name of all, "Thou art the Christ, the Son of the living God."

Ecclesiastical writers have ever seen in this confession of Peter a distinct acknowledgment of Our Lord's Messiahship and divine nature, and have ever considered as a return for it, the promise of Jesus to make him the foundation of His Church, to constitute him the supreme steward of this immortal edifice, with full powers of binding and loosing in His kingdom. At tne same time, our divine Saviour commanded His disciples that "they should tell this to no man." *

* MATT. xvi. 4-20; MARK viii. 27-30; LUKE ix. 18-21.

SYNOPSIS OF CHAPTER XII.

FIRST PART OF THIRD YEAR'S MINISTRY.

(April—October 29 A.D.)

Section II. Jesus and His Disciples.

I. CONDITION OF MIND OF OUR LORD'S DISCIPLES:

1. At the Bening: { All the Jewish Prejudices in possession of their minds. Without any Personal Ambition. }

2. Conclusions now Reached: { Firm Belief that Jesus, their Master, is the Messias: { "Christ, the Son of the Living God." } Hope of a Great Future as a Recompense for having left everything to follow Him. }

3. Remaining Misconceptions as to { The Nature of the Kingdom of the Messias. The Conditions required for { Its Establishment. Its Membership. } }

II. THE TRAINING OF THE TWELVE BY OUR LORD:

1. Before the Transfiguration: { In Public. In Private. }

2. The Transfiguration (Time, Place, Object).

3. After the Transfiguration: { Renewed Predictions of His Death. More direct Moral Lessons. }

141

CHAPTER XII.

SECTION II. JESUS AND HIS DISCIPLES.

§ 1. *Condition of Mind of Our Lord's Disciples.*

1. **Their Frame of Mind at the Beginning.** Up
to the time of their selection by Our Lord, the twelve naturally shared all the prejudices of their contemporaries concerning the person and work of the Messias. At home,
and more particularly in the schools where they had studied
the traditions and history of their nation, they had learned
to derive comfort in the present misfortunes of the Jewish
race, from the glorious prospect that a mighty Son of David
should soon appear to drive the foreigner from the land of
Jehovah and introduce a world-wide empire with Jerusalem
for its capital. As all the faithful Jews of the time, they were
under the constant influence of the Scribes and the Pharisees, whose Messianic dreams are well known, and who felt
in duty bound to keep alive among their fellow countrymen
the hope of a worldly restorer of the Jewish theocracy.
No wonder, then, that the frame of mind of the disciples
constituted from the very beginning the chief obstacle to
their proper training by Our Lord.

It does not seem, however, that for a long time after
their first call the Messianic misconceptions of the disciples
led them to aspire after high positions in a Jewish kingdom
soon to be set up. This may be accounted for, to a large

142

extent, by the consideration of their lowly station in life and by the consciousness of their own defective education. But the main reason is probably to be found in Our Lord's conduct during the first year of His public life. At first His preaching and His baptism seemed to be but a continuation of those of His holy precursor. His miracles soon multiplied and were indeed astonishing, but they apparently pointed Him out simply as a great prophet, who, not unlike Elias of old, had to take to flight in order to escape the fury of His enemies. Moreover, He had never laid any public claim to the Messianic dignity during that same period ; nay, more, he had enjoined strict silence upon the evil spirits whom he expelled, as if their repeated assertions that He was the Messias were untrue and misleading. Finally, He had remained a poor rabbi, hardly able to provide for His own sustenance and for that of His disciples. In point of fact, the personal ambition of Our Lord's disciples was so little developed during long months after their first call, that they did not hesitate to fall back upon their former avocation as fishermen in order to secure their own living, and that it is only long after their second call that we discover in the Gospel narrative traces of their hope of a glorious reward for having followed Jesus.

Of course, the Gospels do not afford a complete picture of the frame of mind of Our Lord's disciples during their early training. It may be safely stated, however, that had not many things contributed, if not to shake, at least to obscure, their belief in Our Lord's Messianic dignity, and thereby long prevented them from conceiving feelings of personal ambition, their aspirations after a high rank in the future kingdom of their Master would have revealed themselves earlier in the Gospel narrative.

2. Conclusions now Reached by the Disciples.
The second year of Our Lord's ministry was marked by some important changes in the condition of mind of the twelve.

In spite of the relentless opposition of the Jewish leaders, of the obscure teaching in parables resorted to by Jesus, of His twofold refusal to give the expected sign of His Messiahship, of His disregard of tradition held as sacred by the people at large, the disciples gradually came to the conclusion that their Master was indeed the expected Messias. This was henceforth a settled conviction in their minds, and when a general desertion followed on the disappointment caused by Our Lord's discourse in the synagogue of Capharnaum, St. Peter simply expressed their intimate thoughts during the past months in his ardent reply to Jesus : " Lord, to whom shall we go? Thou hast the words of eternal life. And *we have believed* and *we have known* that Thou art the Christ, the Son of God."

That these words of Peter were no mere expressions of a transient enthusiastic belief is proved by his later repetition of them in the district of Cæsarea Philippi. Meantime the Galilean multitudes had in large numbers come to think that Jesus was not the Messias, and under the pressure of the fierce opposition of His enemies, our divine Saviour had withdrawn from Galilee and begun almost as an exile a series of journeys through the northern regions, so that the first enthusiasm of the future prince of the apostles had ample time and opportunities to vanish. And yet, in answer to Our Lord's question, " Whom do *you* say that I am?" he repeated with the same earnest conviction, " Thou art Christ, the Son of the living God." *

The apostles had therefore, by this time, reached a firm

---

* MATT. xvi. 16. The reader will notice that in the parallel passages, St. Peter's confession is simply recorded, "THOU ART THE CHRIST " (MARK viii. 29), " THE CHRIST OF GOD" (LUKE ix. 20), and that even in MATT. xvi. 20, Our Lord's injunction is to the effect that the disciples "SHOULD TELL NO ONE THAT HE WAS JESUS THE CHRIST " (cfr. also LUKE ix. 21). So that, although as the Fathers tell us, St. Peter's confession expressed his own belief not only in the Messiahship but also in the divinity of his Master, yet a special emphasis is manifestly laid in the Gospel narrative on Our Lord's *Messianic dignity;* and this is why we represent it here as a very important conclusion reached by the disciples of Jesus in contrast with the Galilean multitudes which had recently rejected it

belief in the Messiahship of their Master, and although He forbade them to publish that " He was Jesus the Christ," * He took opportunity of this fresh manifestation of their faith in Him gradually to prepare their minds for His coming passion and death. † This was all the more necessary because the glorious promise which Jesus had just made to St. Peter, that He would give him all the privileges of the supreme visible head of the Christian Church, was the starting-point in the minds of Our Lord's disciples for the hope of a great future in return for having left everything to follow Him. This hope they first cherished in secret ; but they soon " disputed among themselves which of them should be the greatest " ‡ in the future kingdom of their Master, and at length Peter ventured to put to Our Lord this direct question, which expresses so well their common anticipation, " Behold, we have left all things, and have followed Thee : what, therefore, shall we have ? " §

3. **Remaining Misconceptions of the Disciples.** Henceforth the chosen twelve will ever look upon Jesus as the expected Messias, and in this respect, their views regarding Our Saviour were very different from those of the multitudes which will soon crowd around Him again. But with their contemporaries, the disciples continued to cherish the patriotic dream that the work of the Messias—consequently of Jesus whom they recognized as such—would consist in the restoration of the Jewish theocracy in an unprecedented political and religious splendor. Jewish history and traditions had taught them to unite inseparably in thought, church and state, the political rule and the religious organization, so that Our Lord's promise to found His Church implied necessarily, in their eyes, both the renewal of the Jewish religion and the restoration and extension of the kingdom of Israel under the rule of the Messias, the greatest of David's sons. This was of course a capital mistake, but

---

* MATT. xvi. 20.   † MATT. xvi. 21 sq.   ‡ MARK ix. 33.   § MATT. xix. 27.

it had taken such a hold of the mind of the twelve that, despite Our Lord's teachings to the contrary, the disciples of Jesus never doubted, throughout the last year of His public ministry, that He would soon set up an earthly kingdom. Indeed, the inspired narrative of the Acts of the Apostles pictures them on the very day of the Ascension clinging still to this cherished hope with a tenacity which astonishes us at the present day, and which, at that last moment of His visible intercourse with them, led Jesus not to undeceive them. *

This, then, was the first remaining misconception of Our Lord's disciples at the beginning of the last year of His public ministry. They expected a kingdom " of this world," and as a necessary consequence they continued to cherish the false notions current at the time concerning the conditions required for the establishment and membership of the Messianic kingdom. Like all their contemporaries, they had entirely lost sight of the dark picture drawn by those prophecies of the Old Testament, which foretold so plainly the sufferings and death of the future Redeemer of the world, and they had dwelt with delight on the glorious prospect afforded by those prophecies which described a Deliverer coming with great power and majesty, and forcibly subjecting all His enemies to serve Him as a footstool. Only such a misconception on their part regarding the manner in which the Messianic kingdom should be introduced can fully account (1) for Peter's audacity in rebuking Our Lord as soon as He openly announced His approaching passion and death ;† (2) for the obtuseness of mind which the twelve evinced whenever Jesus spoke in the plainest language of these same future events ; (3) for the kind of stupor into which they were thrown by the death and burial of our divine Saviour.

Finally, during the remainder of this last year of Our

* Acts i. 2–8.   † Matt. xvi. 21 sq.

Lord's public ministry, the apostles shared also the mistaken ideas of their contemporaries with regard to the conditions of membership of the Messianic kingdom. In fact, several things, such as Our Lord's public statement that He had come not to destroy the Law, but to fulfil it, and His words in connection with the Syrophenician woman, * etc., might easily he construed by the disciples, as implying that the Mosaic Law was certainly to be binding on all the future members of the Christian Church, and that in this same Church the privileged people of God would naturally be superior to the Gentile converts. However this may be, it is plain, especially from the statements found in the inspired Book of the Acts, that in this respect the prejudices of the twelve had persevered in their minds, not only throughout the last year of Our Lord's public ministry, but also after the descent of the Holy Ghost. †

§ 2. *The Training of the Twelve by Our Lord.* ‡

1. **The Training before the Transfiguration.** Next to the preaching of the kingdom of God to the Jews of His time, the greatest concern of Our Lord during His public life was the training of those whom He intended from the first should be the continuators of His missionary labors, and His effective instruments in gathering both Jews and Gentiles into one and the same fold. But the twelve little suspected these intentions of their Master, and were far from prepared to take in His teachings so contrary to their own Messianic expectations. It was therefore natural that Jesus should disclose to them only gradually the nature of the kingdom He had come to found, and the exact conditions of its membership.

* MARK vii. 27-29.
† Cfr., for instance, ACTS x., xi.; xv. 1-31.
‡ For this question, see BACUEZ et VIGOUROUX, Manuel Biblique, vol. iii, n. 153; PROF. BRUCE, The Training of the Twelve, Passim.

This gradual character of the training of the twelve by our divine Saviour is particularly noticeable during the period which extends from their selection to Our Lord's Transfiguration. They had been chosen to be in constant attendance upon Jesus ; and hence from the first they witnessed His wonderful miracles, such as the healing of the centurion's servant, the raising of the widow's son, etc.; they heard His no less wonderful discourses, His conversations and discussions with the Scribes and the Pharisees ; they beheld His holy examples of self-denial, of meekness, of humility, of love of prayer, etc.; they noticed also that His favor with the people at large grew steadily and reached such an extent that the multitudes, struck with His unlimited power over nature, diseases, death and the spirit-world, were soon led to consider Him as being very likely the expected Messias. All this was indeed calculated to train the minds and feelings of the disciples for their future ministry, yet all this, or almost all this, was common to them and to many others who, eager to see and listen to Jesus, followed Him from place to place. Gradually, however, to this public was added a private mode of training. This we first notice in connection with Our Lord's public use of parables, the meaning of which escaped the minds of the disciples, and which was explained to them in private by their Master. *   Next, it was their privilege to witness miracles withheld from the gaze of the multitudes, † and at the same time, their faith in Our Lord was strengthened more and more both by His rebukes of their little faith, ‡ and by His direct appeals to their real convictions respecting His Messianic mission. §

Long, indeed, Our Lord pursued His fatiguing missionary journeys through Galilee, without apparently entrusting to

* Cfr. MATT. xiii. 11, 18, 36, 51, etc.
† Cfr. MARK iv. 35-40 ; v. 37 ; MATT. xiv. 24-33.
‡ Cfr. MATT. viii. 26 ; xiv. 31 ; MARK viii. 17 sq.
§ JOHN vi. 68 ; MATT. xvi. 15.

the twelve a direct share in His labors; but the time came when He judged it advisable that He should send them on a mission like His own, and that they should be furnished with the same miraculous powers as Himself. This was an invaluable training for the disciples, who had thus an opportunity to exercise something of their future ministry under the eyes of their Master. As upon their return they told Jesus "both what they had done and what they had taught," this must have given Our Lord an opportunity to make them remarks for future use. However this may be, as He saw they greatly needed rest He invited them to retire into a quiet solitude, thus teaching them to withdraw even from ministerial labors when prudence seems to require it.

Finally, in connection with this training of the twelve by Our Lord before His Transfiguration, two things more are worth notice: (1) His care on at least two occasions not to hurt their national prejudices,* while however preparing their minds for the admission of the Gentiles in preference to the unbelieving Jews;† (2) His long delay to speak to the twelve of His approaching passion and death, seeing that "He began" to announce to them these events so important, yet so contrary to their notions concerning the Messianic kingdom, only after St. Peter's emphatic confession in the district of Cæsarea Philippi.

2. The Transfiguration. Great, indeed, must have been the gloom of the twelve when, after the glorious promise of Jesus to Peter that He would make him the foundation of His Church, they heard their Master calling this same Peter "Satan, savoring not the things that are of God, but the things that are of men." Greater still must have been their gloom when they heard Jesus saying openly, not only to His disciples, but to the multitude He had called for the purpose: "If any man will come after

---

* MATT. x. 5; MARK vii. 26–29. † MATT. viii. 10–12.

Me, let him deny himself and take up his cross and follow
Me." They had never dreamed that they should pledge
themselves to a suffering and despised Messias, that they
should fearlessly acknowledge Him before man, under
penalty of forfeiting their share in His glorious kingdom,
so that they greatly needed the encouraging words which
Our Lord was then pleased to add : " There are some of
them that stand here who shall not taste death till they
see the kingdom of God coming in power."*

Most ancient interpreters find in the glory of the Transfiguration, which occurred six days afterwards, the fulfilment
of this comforting promise of Jesus to His disciples.† The
period of the day at which this wonderful event took place
is not stated in the Gospel narrative, but as Jesus did not
come down from the mountain of the Transfiguration till
the day following, ‡ it is very probable that He ascended in
the evening the holy mount with the three disciples, Peter,
James and John, spent there the night in prayer as was
His wont, was transfigured at the early dawn, and soon
after descended.§

The sacred writers do not name the mountain upon
which Our Lord was transfigured, and for centuries the
tradition of both Greeks and Latins has pointed out as this
favored spot Mount Thabor, in Lower Galilee, a few miles
east of Nazareth. Recently, however, travellers and biblical writers generally reject this tradition, which goes back
at least to the beginning of the fifth century, because they
think that the testimonies of Polybius, v. 70, 6, and
Josephus, Antiq. xiv. 6, 3 ; Wars i. 8, 7, prove that in
Our Lord's time the summit of Thabor was occupied by a
fortified city, and hence was not the *secluded* spot spoken of
in the Gospels. Furthermore, a careful study of the geo-

---

* MATT. xvi. 23-28 ; MARK viii. 33-39 ; LUKE ix. 23-27.
† MATT. xvii. 1-13 ; MARK ix. 2-13 ; LUKE ix. 28-36.
‡ LUKE ix. 37.
§ ANDREWS, p. 358 ; FOUARD, vol. ii., p. 28, footnote 1.

graphical details afforded by the first three Gospels in this connection has convinced them that at the time of His Transfiguration Jesus was out of Galilee * and still in the district of Cæsarea Philippi.   Thence they have inferred that the high and secluded mount of the Transfiguration is most likely one of the peaks of Mount Hermon, which arises north of Palestine to the height of more than 9000 feet above the level of the Mediterranean.†

Three apostles only, Peter, James and John, had been selected by Jesus to witness His Transfiguration, and in descending the mountain they were bidden "tell this vision to no man, till the Son of man be arisen from the dead." The contemplation of this glorious scene was therefore a great privilege granted to the three apostles, and it was well calculated to strengthen them against the dark approaching hour of their Master's passion and death. They complied with His injunction of silence till, long years after His Resurrection, their testimony that they had seen His glory on the Holy Mount served to confirm the faith of the early Christians.‡

3. Training of the Twelve after the Transfiguration.   After the great event of the Transfiguration, the training of the twelve assumed a more direct and more constant character.   This was required on the one hand, by the nearness of Our Lord's death and departure from them, and on the other hand, by their slowness to take in His references to His coming sufferings and death, and to understand the spirit which should animate them as ministers in Christ's kingdom.   Accordingly we see Jesus soon renewing with a peculiar distinctness and emphasis the prediction of His death,§ actually giving up His active work

* Cfr. MARK ix. 29.
† Cfr. FILLION, St. Matt., p. 334 sq.   FOUARD, vol. ii., p. 27, footnote 2, still holds for Thabor as the mountain of the Transfiguration.
‡ 2 PET. i. 16; JOHN i. 14.
§ MARK ix. 30; LUKE ix. 44.

in Galilee to devote Himself more exclusively to the instruction of the twelve* and availing Himself of every opportunity
to complete their training. Thus after the healing of a
demoniac, He taught them the great power of prayer and
fasting to cast out evil spirits ;† after the miraculous paying
of a national and theocratic tax for Himself and for Peter
—a fact which implied the great prominence of this apostle
and gave occasion to the others to discuss " which of them
should be the greater in the kingdom of heaven ? "—He inculcated on them the necessity of a childlike humility.‡
Among the lessons taught them at this time by their Master
we may notice those of opportune toleration ;§ of the necessity of good example ‖ of apostolic severity ; ¶ of sincere
and practically unlimited forgiveness of injuries.**

* MARK ix. 29, 30.   † MATT. xvii. 14–20 ; MARK ix. 13–28.
‡ MATT. xvii. 23 ; xviii. 4 ; MARK ix. 32–34 ; LUKE ix. 46–48.   § MARK ix. 37 sq.
‖ MATT. xviii. 6 sq.   ¶ MATT. xviii. 16 sq.·   ** MATT. xviii. 21 sq.

SYNOPSIS OF CHAPTER XIII.

SECOND PART OF THIRD YEAR'S MINISTRY.

(October—December 29 A.D.)

I. THE FEAST OF TABERNACLES (11–18 Oct.):

1. Departure from Galilee: "After His brethren were gone up"—and 'As it were in secret."

2. During the Celebration at Jerusalem:
   - Before the arrival of Jesus: Frame of mind of the authorities and of the people towards Him.
   - After the arrival of Jesus:
     - In the midst of the feast.
     - Incidents of the last great day of the festival.

3. After the Celebration:
   - Short sojourn in Judæa:
     - The woman taken in adultery brought to Him.
     - The blind man healed adores Jesus.
   - Return to Galilee.

II. LAST DEPARTURE FROM GALILEE:

Features of this Departure (Luke ix. 51, 52 a).

Incidents on His Way through
- Samaria:
  - Rejection from a certain town.
  - Sending of the seventy-two disciples; object of their mission; their return.
- Peræa:
  - Jesus instructs His disciples.
  - He makes a deep impression upon the people.
  - He unmasks more and more the hypocrisy of the Pharisees.
  - He laments over the sin and coming ruin of Jerusalem.

153

CHAPTER XIII.

§ 1. *The Feast of Tabernacles* (11–18 *October*).

1. **Departure from Galilee.** The feast of Tabernacles spoken of by St. John (vii. 2) was the most joyous of the three yearly festivals prescribed by the Law. It had been instituted to commemorate the dwelling of the Israelites in booths in the wilderness, and at the same time, to return thanks to Jehovah for the completed ingathering of the fruits of the goodly land which He had given to His people, and which He ever claimed as peculiarly His own. It fell on the fifteenth day of the seventh month—September or beginning of October—and was celebrated five days after the great day of Atonement, in which all the sins of Israel were declared forgiven, a circumstance which added very much to the joyous character of the feast of Tabernacles. During the seven days it lasted, the people dwelt in booths constructed of branches of trees, and erected on the terrace-like roofs of the houses, in the courts of the Temple, in the streets, etc.

Two ceremonies peculiar to this celebration are especially to be noticed. Every morning while the sacrifice was being prepared, a priest left the Temple accompanied by a joyous procession, and went to the pool of Siloe to draw water, and after his return he poured it in the sight of all before the Lord, as a memorial of the water from the rock of Horeb. * The second ceremony occurred at the close of each day in the Court of the Women, where four golden candelabra were lighted amid the joyful acclamations of the people, in remembrance of the pillar of fire which had guided their ancestors. †

As the feast of Tabernacles "was at hand" the "brethren" of Jesus,‡ on their departure from Capharnaum—probably a week or ten days before the festival began—came to Our Lord. Not believing in His Messianic claims, they ironically advised Him to leave the remote province of Galilee, and to avail Himself of this period of national assemblage at Jerusalem to display His wonderful miracles before all those who would wish to be His disciples.§

Jesus replied to His advisers that, differently from them, He had to choose the opportune time to present Himself in Jerusalem, because of the hatred the world had for His character and His mission. He then added, "Go you up to this festival day, but I go not up to this festival day; because my time is not accomplished." From these words of Our Lord His brethren understood that if He intended to go to Jerusalem for the feast of Tabernacles He did not care to start with them; accordingly they left Him behind in Galilee. Some time after their departure He also started for the Holy City, but with all the secrecy naturally required by the murderous designs of the Jewish authorities.‖

2. During the Celebration at Jerusalem. Meantime, the festivities were going on in Jerusalem, and both the authorities and the people were on the lookout for Jesus. Murmurs secret or half-stifled "for fear of the Jews" ran among the multitudes, some exalting His virtues, others representing Him as a dangerous man.¶

* Exod. xvii. 1-7.
† Exod. xiii. 21, 22. See Edersheim, The Temple, its Ministry and Services, chap. xiv.
‡ The meaning of the word "brethren" in connection with Our Lord has been already discussed, chap. v., § 2.
§ John vii. 1-5.   ‖ John vii. 6-10.   ¶ John vii. 11-13.

"About the midst of the festival" Jesus appeared in the
Temple and took His station as a public teacher. Not
having graduated in the rabbinical schools of the time,
He was not supposed to have either the knowledge or the
mission required to be considered as an official teacher of the
people. Soon, however, His enemies noticed that He had
a wonderful knowledge of Holy Writ, and they learned from
His own lips that He had received both His doctrine and
His mission from a higher authority than theirs, namely,
from God. Having thus defended Himself against encroaching upon the rights and privileges of the Jewish
authorities, Our Lord directly charged His enemies with
violating one of the clearest precepts of the Mosaic Law.
His words referred to the unjust sentence of death pronounced against Him at His last sojourn in the Holy City,
because He had healed on the Sabbath the paralytic at the
pool of Bethsaida, and all those who were aware of this
sentence wondered at the fact that the Jewish rulers should
allow Jesus to speak freely after they had decreed He
should be arrested whenever found in Judæa. Some of His
hearers asked, therefore, "Have the rulers known for a
truth that this is the Christ?" Others rejected His Messiahship because unable to reconcile their knowledge about
Our Lord's origin with their notions respecting the origin of
the Messias, while more, on the contrary, believed in Him
on the strength of His miracles.

Amid this confused discussion, no one complied with
the standing order of the authorities to arrest Jesus ; nay
more, when the Pharisees finally sent officers to apprehend
Him, their messengers, overawed by the calm and solemnity
of His words, failed to carry out their mandate. †

On the seventh, "the last and great" day of the festival,
Jesus publicly alluded to the first ceremony above described,
the drawing of water from the pool of Siloe, and applying it

† JOHN vii. 14-36.

to Himself, He invited all to come to Him to quench their thirst by means of the waters at His command. * This started new discussions among the multitudes about Our Lord's Messiahship, and there were actual though unsuccessful attempts to secure His person. Meanwhile, the Sanhedrists found that they could not depend on their own officers to apprehend Jesus, and they censured them for surrendering themselves to the popular deception in favor of one condemned by all the rulers of the nation. Whereupon, one of these very rulers, the Sanhedrist Nicodemus (he that came to Him by night),† interfered in Our Lord's behalf, and pointed out to his colleagues the illegal character of a condemnation of any man without a hearing. His moderate words met with a violent accusation of favoring a self-condemned party, since it was a foregone conclusion in their eyes that "out of Galilee a prophet riseth not." Their meeting, however, was broken up without coming to any decision, perhaps because some members of the assembly agreed with Nicodemus. ‡

3. **After the Celebration.** Early the next day, which was also observed as a festival by the Jews, Our Lord, who had spent the night at the Mount of Olives, came into the Temple and began to teach the people. This the Jewish rulers had anticipated, and with a view to entrap Him they brought to Him a woman taken in adultery and requested His decision concerning her. With His divine prudence, Jesus escaped the many snares hidden in their request, skilfully turned against His enemies the feelings of the surrounding multitudes, and dismissed the adulteress with these simple words : " Go, and now sin no more." §

---

* Cfr. ISAI. xii. 3.　　　　　† JOHN iii. 1 sq.

‡ JOHN vii. 37-53 ; cfr. MILMAN, History of Christianity, book I., chap. vi.

§ JOHN viii. 1-11. The arguments *for* and *against* the genuineness of the episode of the woman taken in adultery are well set forth and examined in FILLION, St. Jean, pp. 163-166. Cfr. also FOUARD, vol. ii., pp. 57, 58 ; DIDON, vol. ii., Appendix O ; ALFORD, The Greek Testament, vol. i St. John, vii. 53.

On this same eventful Sabbath day, and apparently in the
Court of the Women, where stood the candelabra which
were lighted every night during the feast of Tabernacles,
Our Lord, alluding to this ceremony, uttered these memorable words : " I am the light of the world ; he that followeth
Me walketh not in darkness, but shall have the light of
life." * This high claim of Jesus was at once challenged
by His opponents, and this gave Him an opportunity to
multiply His allusions to His Messiahship and divine
descent. The careful reader of the sacred text cannot
help feeling that the animosity of the Jews was steadily
growing as Jesus unfolded His lofty claims, and as He reproached His enemies with their criminal unbelief and
murderous designs. At length their animosity reached its
height when He identified Himself with Jehovah in these
significant words : " Before Abraham was made, I am," and
they would have stoned Him to death had not Jesus hid
Himself and gone out of the Temple. †

Leaving the Temple, Our Lord saw a man blind from his
birth, and He miraculously cured him, to the great amazement of the people, who could hardly believe that the one
cured was the very man they were wont to see begging at the
gate of the Temple. As the cure had taken place when the
Sabbath was not yet over, information respecting it was conveyed to the Jewish authorities, who, being divided among
themselves regarding the character of one who did not keep
the Sabbath, resolved to investigate the case with the utmost
care. Accordingly, the man who was reported to have been
healed was subjected to a lengthened and searching examination. Next, his parents were summoned and closely questioned. Finally, the evidence in favor of the miracle proving unassailable, the Sanhedrists did their best to overawe
the healed man, and thereby prevent him from ascribing

* Cfr. ISAI. lxii. 1.   † JOHN viii. 12-59.

the miracle to Jesus, of whom they spoke as a sinner, as a man without clearly proved mission. But the one who had received his sight argued so powerfully in favor of Our Lord's holiness and divine mission, that, no longer able to bear with him, the Sanhedrists pronounced against him a sentence of excommunication.

The news of this excommunication soon reached Jesus, who, having sought out the healed man, imparted to him the knowledge that He was the "Son of God," and received from him a fervent homage of grateful adoration.[*]

It is highly probable that after these events Jesus did not remain long in the territory of Judæa, but rather hastened to return into Galilee; for the Jewish rulers, who were bent on His destruction even before the feast of Tabernacles,[†] must have been much exasperated by their discussions with Him and among themselves during its celebration.[‡]

§ 2. *Last Departure from Galilee.*

1. Features of this Departure.[§] After a brief sojourn in Galilee, Jesus left this province for the last time. This departure was an important step in the closing period of Our Lord's life, and this is why it is described by St. Luke in words peculiarly solemn and impressive: "And it came to pass, when the days of His assumption were accomplishing, that He steadfastly set His face to go to Jerusalem." From the beginning of this journey to the Holy City, Jesus contemplated the ignominious passion and death which awaited Him there, and He gave vent to feelings in harmony with this prospect. To those around Him He appeared like one who, conscious of great perils to be encountered, fears, yet unflinchingly faces them. ‖

St. Luke mentions another feature of this last departur

---

[*] John ix. 1-38.   [†] John vii. 1.   [‡] Cfr. also St. John ix. 39; x. 40
[§] Luke ix. 51, 52 *.   ‖ Cfr. Mark x. 32.

of Our Lord from Galilee, namely, its great publicity. **Far**
from going up to Jerusalem "in private," as He had done
quite lately, He now appears surrounded with numerous followers. Indeed, their number is so great, that to secure for
them sufficient food and lodging in the places they will
traverse, He feels it needful to send before Him many messengers. The mission of seventy-two other disciples very
soon afterwards added considerably to the public character
of this journey, at the end of which Jesus entered Jerusalem in triumph at the head of countless multitudes. *

2. **Incidents on His Way through Samaria.** Leaving Galilee, Jesus proceeded southward through the plain
of Esdrælon, and soon reached the border-land lying
between Galilee and Samaria. Meanwhile, His messengers
having arrived at a Samaritan village—very probably
Ginæa †—had announced His coming as that of the Messias on His way to Jerusalem. The inhabitants of this village shared manifestly the enmity of their race against the
Jews, and hence they declined to have anything to do with
Galileans who professed to be on their way to the Jewish
capital. James and John would have punished this refusal
of hospitality by calling down fire from heaven, and thus
would have crushed the first attempt at resistance against
Jesus, who they thought was about to assert His royal
claims in Jerusalem. But Jesus rebuked His apostles, saying : "You know not of what spirit you are," and they went
into another town, probably in Galilee. ‡

From this town Jesus passed eastward to the Jordan, and
soon afterwards entered Peræa.§ Before, however, penetrating into this province, He selected and sent before Him
seventy-two of His disciples. This large deputation was
naturally calculated to gather crowds around Jesus in the

* Cfr. JOHN xii. 19.
† See JOSEPHUS, Antiq. of the Jews, book XX., chap. vi. 1 ; ANDREWS, p. 386.
‡ LUKE ix. 52 b-56.   § Cfr. JOHN x. 40.

places He would traverse, the more so because Our Lord's messengers were to confirm their message by great miracles. The instructions which they received were about the same as those given to the apostles in their temporary mission through Galilee, and on the occasion of the menaces threatened against those who will not receive them, Jesus uttered awful woes against the unbelieving cities of Corozain, Bethsaida and Capharnaum, which about thirty years afterwards were but heaps of ruins. *

The seventy-two rejoined their Master at a fixed place, and evinced the greatest joy because even evil spirits had been subjected to them in Our Lord's name. Jesus rejoiced at their success, seeing in it the presage of the downfall of the empire of Satan, but at the same time He taught them that the moral worth of His ministers is proportionate, not to their wonderful powers even over demons, but to their persevering faithfulness to God's grace. Then Jesus praised the divine decree that while the proud minds would not understand the things of God, the humble would enjoy this inestimable privilege. †

3. **Incidents on the Way through Peræa.** While journeying through Peræa Our Lord availed Himself of every opportunity to train His apostles for their future mission. With them in particular he insisted on the great dangers connected with the possession of worldly riches,‡ and among the special rewards He promised as a return for their generous giving up of everything to follow Him He reckoned the privilege of undergoing persecutions for His sake.§ During this same journey He gave them that divine form of prayer which is so familiar to us under the name of the Lord's Prayer, and which ever suggested to Christ's followers the proper frame of mind in which to address God in prayer. ‖ For their own special benefit He

---

* LUKE x. 1-16.   † LUKE x. 17-24.   ‡ MARK x. 23-27.
§ MARK x. 27-30.   ‖ LUKE xi. 1-4; MATT. vi. 9 sq.

delivered several parables well calculated to inspire them with the various feelings which should animate them in the discharge of their future apostolic duties.*

If from the disciples of Jesus we turn to the multitudes which gathered around Him it is easy to notice that in His passage through Peræa Our Lord produced a deep impression upon men, of whom probably only a few had already seen and heard Him. Thus after He had cast out an evil spirit they began to consider Him as the Messias, and to expect—despite the calumnious charges of His enemies—that He would soon give the great sign which, according to their notions, was to usher in the Messianic era.† They were most desirous to listen to His words, and hence they crowded around Him in very large numbers ; ‡ indeed, on one occasion " they trod one upon another " in their eagerness to hear Him.§ They admired the depth of His doctrine, ‖ recognized His perfect uprightness,¶ and they all rejoiced at the miracles He performed and at the victories He won in His contest with the Pharisees.**

As might naturally be expected, these enemies of Christ kept on His track during His journey through Peræa and did their utmost to undermine His popularity. But Our Lord, who was perfectly safe on a territory outside of the direct influence of the Jewish rulers, denounced on every occasion their hypocritical doctrines and practices. It seems, therefore, very probable that when some of them reported to Jesus that Herod Antipas (on whose territory He then was) had a mind to kill Him they simply wanted Him to hasten His passage into Judæa, because they felt it a hopeless task to check the growth of His influence in the country beyond the Jordan.††

A last prominent feature of this journey of Our Saviour through Peræa is connected with the fate which awaited

* Luke xi. 5 ; xii. 58.   † Luke xi. 14-29.   ‡ Luke xi. 29.   § Luke xii. 1.
‖ Luke xi. 27.   ¶ Luke xii. 13.   ** Luke xiii. 17.   †† Luke xiii. 31-33.

the Jewish nation, and to which Jesus repeatedly alluded as He advanced towards the province of Judæa.*   He knew that the nation would not profit by His invitation to penance—nay, more, would even put to death its only Saviour,† and the contemplation of the coming ruin of the Holy City drew from His loving heart the most tender expressions of grief.‡

It was in this frame of mind that He continued His way to Judæa, unwilling to remain beyond the reach of His deadly enemies, because He had been sent to lay down His life for the sins of the world.§

* LUKE xi. 21-26 ; 49-51 ; xiii. 1-9 ; 29, 35.   † LUKE xiii. 32, 33.
‡ LUKE xiii. 34, 35.   § LUKE xiii. 32, 33.

SYNOPSIS OF CHAPTER XIV.

THIRD PART OF THIRD YEAR'S MINISTRY.

(December 29 A.D.—February 30 A.D.)

I.
IN BETH-
ANY:
{ The Village Described.

Jesus and His Friends.

II.
IN JERU-
SALEM:

The Feast of the { Why instituted ?
Dedication: { How celebrated ?

Our Lord in the { His claims to be " One with
Porch of Solo-   the Father."
mon: { His escape from the hands of
                  the Jews.

III.
BEYOND
THE
JORDAN:

Jesus and the Pharisees.

Jesus and the Classes despised by the Pharisees.

Our Lord and His Disciples.

IV.
IN BETHANY
AGAIN:
THE
RAISING OF
LAZARUS.

Narrative of the Miracle (John xi. 1-44).

Its Consequences (John xi. 45-54).

CHAPTER XIV.

1. In Bethany. After having crossed the Jordan Jesus followed the wild road from Jericho to Jerusalem, and while His disciples pushed up to the Holy City to prepare for the festival of the Dedication, now very near at hand, He stopped at the little village of **Bethany**, about 2 miles east of the Jewish capital. This hamlet, now called El 'Azarîjeh, consists at present of about forty hovels occupied by Mussulman inhabitants. It is surrounded by fig-gardens and terrace-walls, which present rather a pleasant aspect. In the centre of the village is a tall square tower rising above what is pointed out as the tomb of Lazarus, a deep recess cut into the rock, over which a church had been erected in the fourth century of our era. Bethany was for Our Lord a convenient place of rest and seclusion, because it was situated on the eastern slope of Mount Olivet, which shut it out from the busy city of Jerusalem, and also because it was the home of souls dear to His heart—Martha, Mary, and their brother Lazarus.

The visit of Jesus at this comparatively wealthy house was most welcome.* This is manifest not only from the care and trouble of Martha in preparing food for Our Lord, but also from the calm attitude of Mary, who, sitting at the

---

* In assigning to this particular time Our Lord's visit to His friends in Bethany we follow what seems to be the more probable order of events.

feet of Jesus, gave undivided attention to His words. In her anxiety to supply everything for Our Lord's comforts Martha complained to Him of the apparent inaction of her younger sister. The reply of Jesus was no less admirable for its delicacy than for its far-reaching import. He gently called the attention of Martha to the distraction which her great solicitude about material things caused her, and then He added these remarkable words: " But one thing is necessary. Mary hath chosen the best part, which shall not be taken away from her." *

2. In Jerusalem. From Bethany Our Lord proceeded to Jerusalem to attend the feast of the **Dedication.** This festival occurred in the beginning of winter, in the Jewish month corresponding to part of November and December. It was instituted (B.C. 164) by Judas Machabeus in commemoration of the cleansing of the Temple after it had been profaned by Antiochus Epiphanes. † It reminded the Jews of recent victories over the Gentiles, and accordingly it had become one of the favorite solemnities of the nation, now groaning under the hated yoke of pagan Rome. Although this festival could be kept everywhere throughout the land, yet crowds of patriots repaired yearly to Jerusalem for its eight days' celebration.

It was about two months since Jesus had last been in Jerusalem, and it was well known to the Jewish authorities that during a great part of that time He had acted as one seeming to claim the Messianic dignity, yet not explicitly declaring Himself. As soon, therefore, as the Jewish rulers saw Him walking " in the Temple, in Solomon's porch "— probably the eastern portico of the Court of the Gentiles —they came around Him and said, " How long dost Thou hold our souls in suspense ? If Thou be the Christ, tell us plainly." In His answer Our Lord pointed to His well-known miracles as a sufficient evidence for all men disposed

---

* LUKE x. 38-42.   † 1 MACH. iv. 54-59.   See Outlines of Jewish History, p. 341.

to hear, recognize, and follow Him. Then He went on, stating that His hand and the Father's hand are one, and finally He declared explicitly, " I and the Father are one." These last words of Jesus plainly amounted to a claim of the divine nature, and this the Jews understood so well that at once they took up stones to put Him to death, because of blasphemy, " and because that He, being a man, made Himself God. " *

Our Lord then argued with His enemies (1) that there was no blasphemy on His part in saying, " I am the Son of God," since the very name " *God* " was repeatedly ascribed in Holy Writ to God's created representatives ; (2) that the truth of His claim to intercommunion of nature between Himself and the Almighty was clearly evinced by the works of divine power He had so often wrought before their eyes. Their only reply was an attempt to seize Him, but He escaped out of their hands and withdrew from Judæa.†

3. **Beyond the Jordan.** Threatened with imminent death, Jesus hastened to go again beyond the Jordan into the safer province of Peræa, and He took up His abode in Bethany, beyond Jordan, where John had formerly baptized. The words which the holy precursor had uttered on several occasions about Our Lord's character and mission were still rumored in the district of Bethany, and many, having resorted to Jesus to ascertain whether He was indeed the Messias, believed in Him. ‡

To this period of the last year of Our Lord's ministry we may probably refer the various events which are recorded in Chapters xiv.–xvii. 10 of St. Luke. Several of these events show us how, on the one hand, the Pharisees continued their hostility against Jesus, striving to entrap Him (xiv. 1), to undermine His authority with the people (xv. 2),

---

* JOHN x. 23-32.
† JOHN x. 34-40. Cfr. EDERSHEIM, Life and Times of Jesus the Messiah, vol. ii., pp. 229-232.
‡ JOHN x. 40-42.

etc. ; and how, on the other hand, Our Lord unmasked their hypocrisy (xiv. 5, 6), rebuked their pride and their selfishness (xiv. 7 sq.), and opposed their false notion that because they were the first invited guests of the kingdom they were sure to obtain a place therein (xiv. 16–24). Very different, indeed, were the relations of Our Saviour with the classes despised by the Pharisees. They willingly drew near Him, knowing that they would find in Him a tender compassion for their manifold miseries ; and He, on His part, delivered several touching parables — such as the parables of the lost sheep, of the prodigal son — on their behalf. Meantime Jesus inculcated upon His disciples important lessons, such as the necessity of self-denial to follow Him, the duty of forgiveness, etc., etc.

4. **In Bethany Again.** Jesus had been for some considerable time beyond the Jordan when He received from Martha and Mary a message informing Him of the illness of their brother, Lazarus. The words of their delicate prayer touchingly indicate the affectionate intimacy existing between Our Lord and this family " Lord, behold, he whom Thou lovest is sick." *

Instead of uttering a word of power to heal His friend at a distance or of hastening to Bethany Jesus " remained still in the same place two days," knowing that this illness of Lazarus was to be the occasion of great glory to " God " and to the " Son of God."†

On the third day Our Saviour proposed to His disciples to go into Judæa again, and they, learning from His mouth that their common friend Lazarus was actually dead, agreed to their Master's proposal, despite their fears lest His enemies should apprehend Him and put Him to death.‡

Lazarus had died on the very day his sisters sent their anxious message to Jesus, and his burial had, according to Eastern customs, taken place a few hours after his death.

* JOHN xi. 1-3.   † JOHN xi. 4-6.   ‡ JOHN xi. 7-16.

As Our Lord started only after a two days' delay, and spent a day to cross the Jordan and reach Bethany, he found at His arrival that His friend " had been four days already in the grave." It was therefore in the midst of the seven days of mourning, and the friends of the family had come from Jerusalem, only about 2 miles distant, to pay the customary visit of condolence to the two sisters.*

On the news of Our Saviour's approach spreading through the village, Martha rushed out to meet Him, while Mary remained in the house. The words of Martha betrayed at once her faith and her sorrow : " Lord," she said, "if Thou hadst been here, my brother had not died ;" then she ventured to mention her hope that He, even now, would do something for them. This was followed by the sublime words of Jesus, " I am the resurrection and the life ; he that believeth in Me, although he be dead, shall live," and by the wonderful act of faith of Martha, " Yea, Lord, I have believed that Thou art Christ, the Son of the living God, who art come into this world."†

Upon Mary's arrival in tears, and accompanied by weeping friends, the scene became so moving that Jesus, weeping in His turn and groaning in spirit, inquired where they had laid the dead.‡

They repaired to the sepulchre, which was a cave, the mouth of which was closed with a large stone. At the bidding of Jesus, and despite the expostulations of Martha, the stone was removed, and after a brief prayer of thanksgiving to His Father, the Son of God uttered these three simple words " Lazarus, come forth ! " The summons was obeyed, and Lazarus, soon freed from the garments of death which were wound round his body, walked out of the sepulchre. §

This was, indeed, a work of divine power, and many Jews who had witnessed this raising of a man from the corruption of the tomb believed in Jesus, while others, probably

* John xi. 17-19.   † John xi. 20-27.   ‡ John xi. 28-34.   § John xi. 35-44.

enraged at what had occurred, reported it to His enemies. Alarmed by this news, the chief priests and the Pharisees hastily convened a meeting of the Sanhedrim, at which the high priest Caiphas presided, and in which they debated what was to be done. This great miracle of Our Lord could not be denied any more than those He had already performed during His public career, and it was generally felt in the council that if He was allowed to continue His ministry the people at large would believe in His Messianic claims, rebel against the Roman power, and thereby bring about the ruin of Jerusalem and its Temple ; for in the eyes of His enemies it was self-evident that Jesus was not the man who, in the event of a popular uprising, could cope successfully with the legions of Rome.*

At length the high priest, arising, declared with disdain that his colleagues "knew nothing at all," and then he cruelly advised them to put Jesus to death. "It is expedient for you," he said, "that one man should die for the people, and that the whole nation perish not." This language of Caiphas was, as the sacred writer tells us, a wonderful though unconscious prediction of Our Lord's sacrificial death, and from this time forward it was a settled resolve with the highest council of the nation, that the public safety required the death of our divine Saviour, and all that was deliberated upon in the following meetings of this same assembly was how the sentence of death could be best carried out.†

Knowing the criminal designs of His enemies, Jesus withdrew to a safe distance from the Jewish capital and went secretly to Ephrem, where He was soon rejoined by His disciples. In this secluded place—about 16 miles north of Jerusalem—He eluded the furious search of His enemies, and probably spent the time preparing His disciples for His coming death. ‡

* JOHN xi. 45-48.   † JOHN xi. 49-53.   ‡ JOHN xi. 54-56.

SYNOPSIS OF CHAPTER XV.

THE GOSPEL MIRACLES OR SUPERNATURAL FACTS RECORDED DURING THE PUBLIC MINISTRY OF CHRIST.

I. SUPERNATURAL CHARACTER OF THE GOSPEL MIRACLES

- Suggested by
  - their various names in the sacred narrative.
  - the harmony of the Gospels with the other parts of Holy Writ.
- Clearly Implied in
  - the moral integrity of Our Lord's character.
  - the substantial integrity of the Gospels.

II. THEIR MANIFOLD OBJECT:

1. The World of Nature (Variety and Importance of this first Kind of Miracles).
2. Man:
   - Cures.
   - Knowledge of thoughts.
   - Resurrections.
3. Spirit-World: Possessions (Reality; Connection with Natural Diseases).
4. Future Events: Prophecies.

III. THEIR CHIEF CHARACTERISTICS:

1. Appropriateness as Proofs of Divine Mission and Character.
2. Perfect Mastery over All Things.
3. Marvellous Simplicity.
4. Commonly Inspired by Compassion for Others.
5. Never Wrought for Self.

171

CHAPTER XV.

Up to recent times it has been universally felt that the miracles of Our Saviour are both the most salient feature of His public career and the most convincing proof of His divine mission. Contemporary rationalists, however, discard entirely the miraculous element of the Gospels while professing to retain their doctrinal teachings. Even outside this radical school, there are many who show a tendency to neglect the supernatural features of Our Lord's life as of secondary importance. As a consequence, before concluding this rapid study of Our Lord's public ministry, we shall examine, however briefly, (1) the supernatural character of the miracles recorded in the Gospels, (2) their manifold subject, (3) their chief characteristics.

1. **Supernatural Character of the Gospel Miracles.** That the extraordinary events recorded in the Gospels were *real* miracles, that is, actual and observable events which must be referred to a special intervention of God, may easily be inferred from the names of "*wonders*," "*powers*," "*signs*" and "*works*" which they bear in the sacred narrative. These various names clearly describe them as striking facts, requiring the exercise of superhuman power for their pro-

* For this chapter, see BACUEZ et VIGOUROUX, Manuel Biblique, vol. iii., n. 234 sq.; BOUGAUD, Christianisme et Temps Présents, part translated by C. L. CURRIE, under the title, An Argument for the Divinity of Jesus Christ, chap. iii.; TRENCH, On Miracles; BRUCE, The Miraculous Element in the Gospels; SEELEY, Ecce Homo, chap. v.; WESTCOTT, Characteristics of the Gospel Miracles, etc.

duction, and granted by Heaven as credentials of a divine mission. This inference is all the more natural, because these are the very names under which the works of *divine* power are designated in the Old Testament and in the writings of the New Testament distinct from the Gospels the identity of names points to an identity of nature. Furthermore, if both before and after Our Lord's time the supernatural character of the mission of the prophets and of the other messengers of God had to be evidenced by real miracles, the record of which is preserved in the sacred Scriptures, it is only natural to think that the divine character of the much more important and difficult mission of Our Lord had also to be evidenced by real miracles, by such miracles as those we find described in the Gospel narratives.

Thus, then, the reality of the Gospel miracles is *suggested* by their various names in the sacred narrative, and by the harmony of the Gospels with the other parts of Holy Writ; but from other considerations it is possible to go much farther. It may be shown, for instance, that the reality of the miracles recorded in the Gospels is necessarily implied in the **moral integrity of Our Lord's character.** Jesus professed to work miracles ; He gave them as God's testimony in His favor and as signs of His Messianic dignity ; He vindicated their divine character when they were ascribed to the agency of the Evil One ; He was not only believed by His followers to be endowed with the power of working miracles, but He professed to impart a similar power to His twelve apostles and next to His seventy-two messengers; and after they had themselves exercised these miraculous powers, He confirmed them in their belief that He and they worked real miracles. He so acted that His very enemies could not help believing that He actually wrought miracles, and on several occasions He uttered awful woes against flourishing cities and against the Jewish rulers, because, despite the stupendous miracles He had worked to convince them of His divine mission and character, they had persevered in their rejection of His claims. From all this, it is plain that the veracity of Our Lord absolutely requires that we should admit that He worked real miracles, such miracles as those with which the Evangelists make us acquainted.

The reality of these same miracles is no less clearly implied in the substantial integrity of the Gospels. Whatever their differences, the four Gospels agree in representing the public life of Jesus as an almost unbroken series of miracles. Hardly a day is described in them at any length without the record of one or several miracles of Our Saviour. Again, throughout the Gospels, Our Lord's miracles are represented either as the occasion or as the subject-matter of His discourses; they are given as the chief reason why His enemies pursue Him as a Sabbath-breaker, and also why many believe in Him and the multitudes follow Him everywhere. In a word, to the attentive reader of the Gospels it must appear self-evident that the removal of the miraculous element from the Gospel narrative would destroy the connection, the strength and even the meaning of what would remain.

2. **Manifold Subject of the Gospel Miracles.** The first sphere of Our Lord's miracles is the **world of nature,** which in a variety of ways felt the effect of His unlimited power. At His will a substance was changed into another, as at Cana of Galilee, or was almost indefinitely increased, as in the twofold multiplication of loaves. At other times the laws which govern the physical universe seemed deprived of all force in His presence, as when He walked freely upon the sea or stilled the storm. This first kind of miracles had a great influence upon the minds and feelings of Our Lord's contemporaries. The witnesses of these wonderful deeds felt at once that they were in the presence of

a truly divine power, and this feeling led them to praise God and to ask themselves whether Jesus was not indeed the expected Messias.

A second class of miracles comprises those which had man for their object. Apparently every great form of bodily infirmity—blindness, leprosy, issue of blood, deafness, etc.—was brought before our merciful Saviour, who was never known to deny a miracle of healing to the expressed or silent prayer either of the sufferers or of their friends. In point of fact, he perceived the secret wish for relief no less distinctly than the most explicit and open appeal to his power of healing, for " He knew what was in man." This knowledge of men's intimate thoughts, whether of His enemies or of His friends, or of those with whom He came in contact, Jesus evinced in a thousand ways, and He ever used it to the best advantage either of the surrounding multitudes or of those who were made aware that their innermost feelings did not escape His all-seeing eye. Finally, it is recorded that on three several occasions the lifeless remains of man felt the effect of His power over death, and these three great miracles were well calculated to convince all that He was indeed "the resurrection and the life."

A third class of miracles has reference to the spirit-world, and in this connection Jesus exerting His miraculous power appeared as the Holy One of God who had come to destroy the empire of Satan. Despite all the theories advanced to disprove the reality of demoniacal possessions, it must be admitted that a careful study of the Gospel narrative proves that in this respect the Evangelists and Our Lord Himself shared and approved the belief of their contemporaries. For them, as for all those around them, demoniacal possessions were a form of disease distinguishable from all others, and expulsions of evil spirits were events of real and frequent occurrence.

The last subject of Our Lord's miracles we wish to mention here consists in the **future events** which He distinctly foretold.   He spoke with the confidence of one who is perfectly acquainted with the future respecting His own person, His church, His disciples, His enemies, Jerusalem and other cities of His country, etc., and we all know with what absolute accuracy His predictions have been fulfilled.

3. **Chief Characteristics of the Gospel Miracles.** One of the leading characteristics of the miracles recorded in the Gospels is their appropriateness as proofs of Our Lord's divine mission and character.   Not only were they actions making exception to all the laws of nature, they were also the very deeds which the prophets of old * had led Our Lord's contemporaries † to regard as the credentials of the future Messias.   Performed in the full blaze of the mid-day sun, in the streets, in the public places, in the presence of immense crowds, they appealed powerfully to the imagination of the people at large, as well as to the reason of thoughtful observers.   No wonder, then, that Jesus repeatedly pointed to His miracles as clear signs of His divine mission and character, and that unbiased men, whatever their rank in society, feeling that these were not the deeds of one leagued with Beelzebub, as the Jewish leaders affirmed, were led to recognize Jesus as a prophet, as the Son of David and the expected Messias.

A second and no less striking characteristic of Our Lord's miracles is the perfect mastery over all things which they evince.   As stated above, the subject of His miracles is coextensive with all creation : all the elements of nature, all the diseases of the body, however inveterate, death itself and the powers of hell, are subject to His command; men's most intimate thoughts do not escape His notice, and the future has no obscurity for His mental vision.   He, indeed, moves in this world as the supreme Master of all things.

* Isai. xlii. 1 sq.   † John vii. 31.

Unlike the prophets of old, and the holy servants of God through ages, He performs miracles in His own name with the greatest ease, and as men are wont to do their simplest actions. He has only to will, to say the word, and the effects, however astonishing, come to pass; and as His is not simply a delegated power, He can impart it to whomsoever He wills, and thereby cause his numerous messengers to perform similar wonders in His name.

Intimately connected with this perfect mastery over all things is the marvellous simplicity with which it was exercised. Examine the Gospel miracles one after another and you will find none performed as a mere display of power. They all arose naturally out of their occasions, they all served a useful purpose in connection with Our Lord's personal mission, and neither before nor after their performance can the least trace of ostentation or self-satisfaction be discovered on the part of Jesus. Viewed from this standpoint, Our Lord's miracles offer the most striking contrast to the puerile, extravagant, grotesque, not to say absurd, character of the miracles ascribed to Him in the Apocryphal Gospels : * the former are manifest proofs of divine wisdom, the latter are but the play of human fancy.

But the miracles of Jesus appear much more deeds of His merciful love and tender compassion than works of His wisdom and power. As has been beautifully said by a contemporary writer, " This power which he wielded so royally, which He held back so mightily, so that no provocation, no danger, no treason, no contempt could induce Him to use it in His own defence, seemed to escape from His control when there was question of doing good to others. Let Him meet the poor or the sick, and swift as lightning this divine power escaped from His heart in acts of love. Sometimes

---

* Cfr. the Gospel of JAMES, chaps. xviii., xxii., xxiv. ; the Gospel of THOMAS chaps. ii., iv.,v. ; the Gospel of Pseudo-MATTHEW, chaps. xxvi., xxix. ; the Arabic Gospel of the Infancy, chaps. xxxviii., xxxix., xl.

it would almost seem as though He were no longer the Master of it, as in the incomparable history of the poor woman who approached Him humbly from behind, saying, ' If I can but touch the hem of His garment I shall be cured.' On certain occasions He even gave way to tears and groanings, and unwonted trouble, which bore witness to the intensity of His love. Who does not recall the impulse of mercy which touched Him at Naim, by the side of the bier of the only son and the sorrowing mother ?   .
How shall we forget the unwonted agitation which He manifested at the tomb of Lazarus !"* Almost all the miracles of Jesus were prompted by His compassion for the needs of others, and this is why St. Peter, reminding his hearers of what had been the most constant and the most salient feature of Our Lord's public life, said that Jesus "went about doing good and healing all that were oppressed by the devil."†

A last characteristic to be mentioned here in connection with Our Lord's miracles consists in this: they were never wrought for self. Search the Gospels and you will find that while Jesus multiplies His miracles in behalf of others, He acts towards Himself as if He were absolutely powerless to supply His own wants in a miraculous manner. Rather than to resort to His power of performing miracles, He prefers to suffer hunger and thirst, to be absolutely destitute of the things of this world, to flee from His enemies as long as His own hour has not come, and then to be arrested, tried and sentenced to the most ignominious and cruel death of the cross. Indeed, no clearer proof could be given than all He voluntarily endured, and that during His entire mortal life He was the divine victim sent to atone for the sins of the world.

---

* Cfr. BOUGAUD (transl. C. L. CURRIE), An Argument for the Divinity of Jesus Christ, pp. 54, 55.
† ACTS x. 38.

SYNOPSIS OF CHAPTER XVI.

THE LAST DAYS OF CHRIST'S PUBLIC MINISTRY.

I. FINAL JOURNEY TO JERUSALEM:

1. From Ephrem to Jericho:
   - The road followed: why chosen?
   - Jesus and the Pharisees.
   - Our Lord and the twelve.

2. Through Jericho:
   - The two blind men healed.
   - Zacheus, a son of Abraham.

3. At Bethany:
   - Anointing of Our Lord.
   - Conspiracy of the chief priests against { Lazarus and Jesus.

II. BEGINNING OF PASSION WEEK: (April 2–5, A.D. 30.)

1. Palm Sunday: Triumphal Entry into Jerusalem.

2. Monday:
   - Cursing of the fig-tree: its meaning.
   - Second cleansing of the Temple.

3. Tuesday:
   - In the Temple:
     - The parables delivered: their significance.
     - Vain attempts of all the sections of His enemies to ensnare Jesus.
   - On the Mount of Olives: last prophecies and parables.
   - Plot against Jesus. The traitor's covenant.

Wednesday: Seclusion at Bethany.

CHAPTER XVI.

THE LAST DAYS OF CHRIST'S PUBLIC MINISTRY.

§ 1. *Final Journey to Jerusalem.*

1. From Ephrem to Jericho. After a seclusion of several weeks Our Lord left Ephrem and started on His final journey to Jerusalem. As He intended soon to make His triumphal entry into the Holy City at the head of great multitudes, He so directed His steps as to meet the caravans which from the north and from the east were already moving towards Jerusalem on the approach of the Paschal celebration. Accordingly He went northward through Samaria, and next eastward on the border-land between that province and Galilee, to meet in the plain of the Jordan the Galilean caravans. Then He crossed the Jordan and kept along the river-banks, where He was joined by the Jewish caravans coming from the east, and together with them He recrossed the Jordan at a ford nearly opposite Jericho.*

Scarcely had Jesus re-entered public life, when the Pharisees reappeared, pursuing Him. With mockery they inquired of Him when all His preparatory preaching of the Messianic kingdom would be at an end, and the new kingdom begin. Our Lord's answer was a complete condemnation of the manner in which His enemies thought the Messianic kingdom should appear. He affirmed in opposition to their views that no great external signs would usher it in,

* LUKE xvii. 11; MATT. xix. 1; MARK x. 1. Cfr. FOUARD, vol. ii., p. 131, footnote 1.

and that no magnificent court would surround the new King, so that no throng attracted by His apparel could say : "He is here ! He is here !" Indeed, the kingdom they still expected had already begun in their midst, and they were not aware of the fact.* However humbling to their pride Our Lord's condemnation of their Messianic views may have appeared in the eyes of the Pharisees, His words in several other circumstances were still more calculated to wound their sensibilities.†

Meantime, Jesus was actively engaged in training His disciples for their apostolic mission and for His near departure from them. Among the special instructions He gave them during this period, we may notice in particular His teachings about celibacy, as about a special calling in life higher in its nature than that of matrimony.‡ His main efforts, however, were plainly directed towards preparing their minds and feelings for His coming passion and death.§ Yet their preconceived notions about the victories of the Messias over the enemies of the Jews, and about His glorious earthly rule, prevented them from realizing the plain import of Our Lord's words.‖ In fact, as various troops of pilgrims fell in with the crowds which already surrounded Jesus, and as they greeted Him with enthusiasm, the apostles shared the common belief that at length their Master would very soon begin His glorious rule.¶ This explains to us how, only a few hours after one of His most explicit predictions of the ignominious treatment He was to suffer at the hands of the Gentiles, two disciples of Jesus, James and John—probably instigated by Salome, their mother—laid an open claim on the highest honors of Our Lord's kingdom. The jealousy of the other apostles was at once aroused by this ambitious request of

---

* LUKE xvii. 20, 21. † Cfr. LUKE xviii. 9-14 ; MATT. xix. 1-9 ; MARK x. 1-9.
‡ MATT. xix. 10-12. § Cfr. LUKE xvii. 25 ; xviii. 31 ; MARK x. 32.
‖ LUKE xviii. 34. ¶ LUKE xix. 11.

the two brothers, and Jesus profited by this new outburst of their love of superiority and power, to teach them a lesson most important for themselves and for their successors in the holy ministry. He plainly told them that, however it might be among the rulers and leading men of the world, greatness among his disciples was to be attained only by the humble and faithful discharge of their arduous mission, "as the Son of Man also," He added, "came not to be ministered unto, but to minister, and to give His life a redemption for many." *

2. **Through Jericho.†** Having crossed the Jordan, Jesus soon arrived at Jericho, an important town 5 or 6 miles west of the Jordan and between 15 and 20 miles northeast of Jerusalem. In connection with this town the Synoptists agree in recording a miracle of healing as performed by Our Lord at its gate, but they seem to be at variance on the two following points : (1) while St. Matthew states that *two* blind men received their sight from Jesus, St. Mark and St. Luke speak only of *one* man ; (2) St. Matthew and St. Mark affirm that the miracle was performed on Christ's departure *from* Jericho ; St. Luke says, on the contrary, that it occurred when " *He drew nigh* " that city.‡

Whatever may be thought of these discrepancies, it was certainly at but a few miles from Jerusalem that Jesus accepted again the Messianic title of "Son of David," publicly given Him by the blind men of Jericho, and that in imparting to them the special blessing they asked for, He proved Himself to be the Messias predicted by the prophets

---

* MARK x. 35-45.   † MATT. xx. 29-34; MARK. x. 46-52; LUKE xviii. 35; xix. 28.

‡ The three narratives resemble one another so closely that it is difficult not to admit, with MALDONATUS and other commentators, that the Evangelists describe but one and the same event (cfr. MALDONATUS, in Matt. xx. 30). The only reason to think otherwise is the difficulty of reconciling their statements. The discrepancies which have been noticed are met differently by scholars, according to the views they hold as to the amount of accuracy of detail required by inspiration (cfr. BRUNEAU, Harmony of the Gospels, p. 89 sq.; KNABENBAUER, in S. Matthæum ; ANDREWS, pp. 417, 418 ; see also LAGRANGE, l'Inspiration et les Exigences de la Critique, Revue Biblique, Oct. 1896).

of old. * It is true that in the eyes of many His conduct towards Zacheus, the despised chief of the publicans of Jericho, appeared at first unworthy of one claiming to be the holy King and mighty deliverer of the Jews ; yet when they noticed the conversion of Zacheus and heard Our Lord's assertion that He had come to reclaim the lost sons of Abraham, they were satisfied that Jesus had acted in a manner worthy of the Messias whom they expected. Nay more, their hopes about Him ran so high, under the circumstances of the time, that " they thought that the kingdom of God should immediately be manifested." It was to counteract these wild expectations of His immediate enthronement in Jerusalem, that before leaving Jericho Our Lord delivered the significant parable of the Pounds, wherein He suggested that He must first take His departure from the midst of His own people, and that only on His glorious return He would treat both friends and foes according to their deserts.

3. At Bethany. † While the pilgrims who had already reached Jerusalem debated among themselves whether Jesus would come for the Paschal festival, Our Lord left Jericho and proceeded towards the Holy City. On the sixth day " before the Pasch " He arrived in Bethany and repaired to the house of Martha and Mary, which He intended to make His home during the last week of His mortal life. At the end of the next day (probably Saturday, April 1, 30 A.D.) a supper was prepared for Him and for His disciples. Lazarus was there, and Martha served. As they were at table, Mary came behind the couch on which Jesus reclined, and poured on His sacred head and feet a most precious ointment, the sweet odor of which filled the house. This costly offering, prompted by her love, greatly displeased the avaricious Judas, who openly murmured against it as a waste, and whose view about the

* Cfr. Isai. xlii. 1-7.   † Matt. xxvi. 6-13 ; Mark xiv. 3-9 ; John xi. 55 ; xii. 11.

matter was shared by some others of the disciples. But the action of Mary was highly praised by Our Saviour, who saw in it a loving homage especially connected with His approaching death and burial.

Meanwhile the news of Our Lord's arrival at Bethany had spread through the Holy City, and a great multitude of Jews hearing it, went to Bethany to see Him and also Lazarus, whom He had raised from the dead. Whereupon the chief priests, who had already decided upon the death of Jesus, took it into serious consideration whether Lazarus also should not be put to death, because as long as he should live he would be the means of inducing many to believe in Christ, who had restored him to life.

§ 2. *Beginning of Passion Week* (*April* 2–5, 30 A.D.).

1. **Palm Sunday.** *   On the first day of the week of His passion—known as Palm Sunday—Jesus left Bethany about mid-day to effect His triumphal entry into Jerusalem. Attended by His disciples and other pilgrims, He probably followed the usual road for horsemen and caravans, and which is the southernmost of the three roads connecting Bethany with the Holy City. Soon **Bethphage** was in view, and according to His directions, two of Our Lord's disciples brought to Him an ass and a colt, whereon, as predicted by Zacharias (ix. 9), Jesus wished to make His Messianic entry into Jerusalem. This appeared to some of His disciples the signal that He would at length assume the rank and title which they believed to be His ; and placing their outer garments on the yet unbroken colt, as a kind of saddle, they set Jesus thereon, and accompanied Him with joyful acclamations.

Thus they moved on towards Jerusalem, Lazarus and the apostles near Jesus, and a great multitude following Him.

* MATT. xxi. 1–17 ; MARK xi. 1–11 ; LUKE xix. 29–44 ; JOHN xii. 12–19.

This multitude shared in the enthusiasm of Christ's disciples, and in their joyful transports strewed their outer garments and palm branches in the way of our divine Saviour. Many of them had been witnesses of the raising of Lazarus, and they proclaimed, as they advanced, this wonderful deed of Jesus.*

When the long and triumphant procession reached the point of the road where first begins "the descent of Mount Olivet,"† the multitudes caught the first view of the Jewish capital, and this sight drew from them shouts of triumph "Hosanna to the Son of David ! Blessed be the King who cometh in the name of the Lord: Hosanna in the highest !" It was indeed as a king that on that glorious day Jesus presented Himself to the Holy City and to its rulers. But the future was not hidden from His eyes, as it was from the eyes of all those who surrounded Him, and hence, when a short while after the multitudes had begun their hymns of triumph, the road allowed Our Saviour to contemplate the whole city in all its splendor, He wept over it, and described the awful fate which awaited it and its inhabitants.

Probably as they descended the Mount of Olives, crowds from Jerusalem and its neighborhood met them, attracted by the shouts of Our Lord's followers. They, too, were bearing branches of palm-trees, and turning round, they fell in with the procession and preceded Jesus, joyfully proclaiming Him the King of Israel.

St. Luke informs us that among this ever-growing multitude there were Pharisees who would have had Jesus silence His partisans. Instead of rebuking His disciples as requested by the Pharisees, Our Lord declared that this public proclamation of His Messianic dignity was so entirely in conformity with the divine designs, that "if these should hold their peace, the stones would cry out."

When the triumphant procession entered Jerusalem the

---

* JOHN xii. 17.   † LUKE xix. 37.

whole city was moved ; and the Pharisees in their impotent
rage were reduced to say among themselves : " Do you see
that we prevail nothing ? behold the whole world is gone
after Him ! " while the Saviour of the world was led to the
Temple.   There the procession dispersed, the Jewish customs not allowing the pilgrims to come near the sanctuary
in travelling clothes and with dusty feet.

It was late, and Our Lord simply visited the Temple,
" viewing all things round about," as if He would observe
whether all was done according to His Father's will, and
then He returned to Bethany with the twelve to spend the
night.*

2. Monday.†   The next morning Our Lord returned to
Jerusalem, and on His way thither He saw at a distance by
the wayside, a fig-tree which had an appearance of bearing
fruit.   He went to it, but finding nothing but leaves, He
doomed the tree to perpetual barrenness in the hearing of
His disciples.‡   In this action of Our Lord we cannot help
recognizing a figure of the decay to which Israel was henceforth and forever doomed, because Jesus had found in the
Jewish nation nothing but the appearances of righteousness.

Entering the city He went to the Temple, the desecration of which He had noticed the evening before.   The old
abuses against which He had energetically protested at the
beginning of His public life had crept in again—nay more,
they were apparently greater than at the time of the first
cleansing of the Temple by Jesus.   He therefore cleansed
a second time the house of His Father, and then proceeded to exercise in its purified courts His public ministry
of teaching and healing.   His doctrine caused the admiration of the whole multitude around Him, and His wonderful deeds of healing moved the children, who may have been

---

* MARK xi. 11.

† MATT. xxi. 12-22 ; MARK xi. 12-26 : LUKE xix. 45-48.

‡ For further details in connection with this cursing of the fig-tree, see FOUARD, vol.
ii , pp. 171, 172 ; TRENCH, On Miracles ; FILLION, St. Marc, p. 162.

members of the choir of singers employed in the Temple, to re-echo the joyful *Hosannas* of the preceding day. The chief priests and Scribes in their displeasure demanded that He should put a stop to these acclamations, but in presence of His popularity they did not feel able to proceed farther with their murderous designs. At evening Our Lord returned to Bethany.

3. **Tuesday.*** The next day Jesus appeared again in the Temple, where He was soon met by an official deputation from the Sanhedrim. These deputies inquired of Him the *nature* and *origin* of His mission, pretending thereby that they were competent judges of His claims to a divine mission. But Our Lord showed clearly to them, that if— as they affirmed themselves—they were not able to decide whether the baptism administered by John was of heaven or not, He had a perfect right not to consider them competent judges of the character and origin of His own mission. Then He proceeded to tell them in parables, whose meaning they could not help realizing, that since they had rejected all the divine warnings, they in turn would be rejected, together with their capital and nation, to give place to a new theocratic people yielding fruits worthy of God's kingdom.

Never had the words of Jesus been calculated to wound more deeply the personal and national pride of the different sections of the Sanhedrim that had been deputed to Him, and this is why Pharisees, Sadducees and Scribes attempted in turn to ensnare Him by their captious questions. To the Pharisees who asked Him whether it was lawful to give tribute to Cæsar, Our Saviour answered that they could not have accepted the coins of the emperor without recognizing his sovereignty and thereby declaring it lawful to pay him tribute. The question put to Christ by the Sadducees betrayed their disbelief of a future life, and He clearly

---

* MATT. xxi. 20; xxv. 46; MARK xi. 20; xiii. 37; LUKE xx. 1; xxi. 38; JOHN xii. 20-50.

showed that their frame of mind had no other basis than their ignorance of the infinite power of God and of the exact meaning of the Mosaic Law.   After this direct and precise answer of Jesus to one of the standing difficulties of the Sadducees against the popular belief of a future resurrection, one of the Scribes was deputed to ask Him, with a view to ensnare Him, " Which is the great commandment in the Law ? " He also received a fully satisfactory answer, the wisdom of which he even acknowledged with genuine admiration.

But Our Lord had been long enough upon the defensive. He therefore proceeded to put to a test the knowledge of His adversaries by one single question.   He inquired of them how the Messias could be the son of David, and yet be called " Lord " by David himself, speaking under the inspiration of the Holy Ghost.   This was a topic about which the leaders of the Jews should apparently have had a ready and distinct answer, yet " no man was able to answer Him a word," and this is why " no man durst from that day forth ask Him any more questions."   In consequence of this avowed ignorance of the Sanhedrists, Jesus was fully justified in the eyes of all to denounce the blindness and pride of His deadly enemies, and then He gave vent to the tender feelings of His compassionate heart about the coming ruin of Jerusalem and its sanctuary, hurried on by the guilty leaders of the Jewish nation.

As Our Lord left the Temple He foretold again its utter destruction, and this led some of His disciples to inquire " privately " about the *time* and *signs* of this awful calamity. It is probably when seated on the Mount of Olives, opposite the Temple, that Jesus uttered His last prophecies concerning the ruin of the Holy City and the end of the world, and that in this connection He delivered the parables of the Ten Virgins and of the Talents to impress upon the minds of His hearers the constant duty of watchfulness and faithfulness. To this He added a description of the last judgment, and He concluded by a prediction of the *occasion*, the *manner* and the *very day* of His sufferings and death.

While Our Saviour was thus predicting to His disciples that He was to suffer and to be crucified during the Paschal festival, the chief priests and ancients of the people, in a meeting at the palace of Caiphas, had resolved not to arrest Him during the feast for fear of the multitudes. But Our Lord's prediction was fulfilled in a way His enemies were far from anticipating. Judas, one of the twelve, came to them and offered, for money, to betray Jesus secretly into their hands. Great indeed was the joy of the leaders of Israel at this unexpected offer, and they covenanted to give Judas thirty pieces of silver (about $18.70), while he, on his part, agreed to watch for a favorable opportunity to betray his Master to them.

Our Lord's public ministry closes with Holy Tuesday (April 4th), for He does not seem to have returned to Jerusalem the following day, which He probably spent in seclusion at Bethany.

SYNOPSIS OF CHAPTER XVII.

THE LAST PASCH CELEBRATED BY OUR LORD.

I. PREPARATIONS FOR THE PASCHAL MEAL:

1. By Whom and In What Place Made.
2. On What Day? Thursday Afternoon ⎰ Nisan 14. ⎱ April 6.

II. THE LAST SUPPER:

1. The Jewish Paschal Meal in the Time of Our Lord.

2. Particulars of Our Lord's Last Supper:

  Arrival: ⎰ Placing of guests. ⎱ Contention as to rank.

  First cup and washing of feet. References to betrayal. Departure of Judas. Institution of the Holy Eucharist.

3. After the Last Supper: ⎰ Our Lord's lengthened discourse and closing prayer. ⎱ Departure from the supper room.

190

THIRD PERIOD:

THE PASSION AND RESURRECTION.

CHAPTER XVII.

THE LAST PASCH CELEBRATED BY OUR LORD.

§ 1. *Preparations for the Paschal Meal.*

1. By Whom and in What Place Made. Leaving aside the traitor Judas, who was ordinarily in charge of such affairs,* Our Lord selected Peter and John to make the necessary preparations for the Paschal supper. He bade them go to the Holy City and enter a house, which He pointed out to them only in general, though sufficient, terms, for He did not wish to indicate this house or its owner in a clearer manner in the hearing of His betrayer. They were to ask the owner of this house for a very humble apartment, but as Jesus predicted, he would place at their disposal an *upper room*, that is, the most honorable place of his house, and which he had already furnished and made ready in view of the Paschal celebration. † It was, then, to this upper room that Peter and John had to carry the lamb after they had slain it in the Temple, and to bring the unleavened cakes, bitter herbs, wine, etc., required for the Paschal supper. ‡

---

* JOHN xii. 6; xiii. 29.

† In the present day, a minaret rises above the Cœnaculum or hall pointed out by tradition as the upper room used by Our Lord for His last supper. The hall is some 50 feet in length by 30 in width.

‡ LUKE xxii. 7–13 ; MATT. xxvi. 17–19; MARK xiv. 12–16.

2. On What Day was this Last Pasch Prepared?

The answer to this question depends on the day we must admit for the last supper of Our Lord, for it is beyond doubt that Jesus ate His last supper on the evening of the day on which it was prepared by St. Peter and St. John. Now, if we consult the Evangelists, we shall find that there is an apparent contradiction between the Synoptists and St. John, concerning the day on which Our Lord ate His last supper. The former state plainly* that Our Lord's last supper took place on the legal day for the celebration of the Pasch (Thursday, Nisan 14th, April 6th); the latter, on the contrary, seems to say that this last supper occurred one day before the Pasch was celebrated by the Jews,† and consequently that the legal day for the Paschal celebration was only Friday evening, April 7th.

It is impossible to detail and examine here the various theories which have been advanced in connection with this difficult question. Suffice it to say, (1) that we should reject every theory which holds that Jesus ate His last supper before the 14th of Nisan, for in such case Christ's last supper would not have been a *Paschal* meal, contrary to what we read in St. Luke (xxii. 15); (2) that a careful study of the sacred text shows that two of the passages of St. John above referred to ‡ must be understood as referring to the same day as the Synoptists, while the other two § can easily be interpreted in the same harmonious manner. We therefore admit that St. John agrees with the first three Evangelists in placing Our Lord's last supper on Nisan 14th, Thursday, April 6th; so that the preparations for this last supper must have been made in the afternoon of the same day. ||

* MATT. xxvi. 17; MARK xiv. 12; LUKE xxii. 7.
† Cfr. JOHN xiii. 1, 29; xviii. 28; xix. 14.
‡ JOHN xiii. 29; xix. 14.   § JOHN xiii. 1; xviii. 28.
|| Cfr. ANDREWS, pp. 452-481; VIGOUROUX, Dictionnaire de la Bible, art. Cène; BRUNEAU, Harmony of the Gospels, p. 110; HASTINGS, Bible Dictionary, vol. i., p. 410 sq.

§ 2. *The Last Supper.*

1. **The Jewish Paschal Meal in the Time of Our Lord.** The Paschal supper which Jesus had longed so ardently to celebrate with His disciples * was probably conducted as follows by His Jewish contemporaries : The party, varying in number between ten and twenty persons, met in the evening and reclined on couches disposed along three sides of a low, Eastern table. The supper opened with a cup of wine mingled with water, which the master of the household or the person who presided had prepared and blessed, and of which all present partook. Thereupon all washed their hands, another blessing being at the same time pronounced. The different dishes of the feast, the lamb, the unleavened bread, the bitter herbs and the thick sauce (called the **Charoseth**), were next placed on the table, and the president, dipping some of the bitter herbs into the Charoseth, ate of them and gave to others. Then the person who presided explained the meaning of the festival, and the whole party, sharing in his gratitude to Jehovah, sang the first part of the **Hallel**, that is, Psalm cxiii. and part of Psalm cxiv., after which prayer was offered and the second cup drunk.

The head of the party washes his hands for the second time, breaks one of the cakes of unleavened bread, blesses it, and all partake of it, dipping the portions of it with the bitter herbs into the Charoseth. The flesh of the lamb was now eaten, and another blessing pronounced, when the third cup, or **Cup of Blessing,** was handed round. This was succeeded by the fourth, called the **Cup of Hallel**, because the second part of the **Hallel** (Psalm cxiv., second part; Psalms cxv.–cxvii.) was now sung, and this concluded the supper.

With these details before our minds we can easily under-

* LUKE xxii. 15.

stand several particulars of Our Lord's last Paschal supper, as recorded in the sacred narrative.

2. Particulars of Our Lord's Last Supper. It was probably in taking their places on the couches around the table that the contention as to rank arose among the disciples. They wished (following probably in this the custom of the Pharisees of the time) to recline at this important meal according to their rank, and this contest for precedence drew from Our Lord's lips a well-deserved rebuke. * The contest once over, St. John occupied the place on Our Lord's right, so that his head could easily repose on the bosom of Jesus ; St. Peter, stung by his Master's rebuke, had probably rushed with his ordinary impetuosity to take the lowest place at the other end of the table, opposite St. John, to whom he could therefore easily beckon to ask who the traitor was ; † finally, Judas occupied very likely the place immediately on Our Lord's left, as is suggested by several particulars of the Gospel narrative.‡

The disciples having reclined at table, Jesus, as the head of the party, "took the chalice, gave thanks and said, Take and divide it among you." § This was the *first cup* of the Jewish Paschal supper, and when it had passed round, the next ceremony was the *washing of hands*, which St. John probably records as transformed by his divine Master into the *washing of feet*. For this menial office, usually performed by slaves, Jesus left aside His garments, poured water into the basin, placed as usual at the end of the table, and came first to Peter, the nearest of all, and over whose resistance He finally prevailed. He washed in succession the feet of all, not without, however, making an obscure allusion to the betrayal of Judas : " You are clean, but not all." ‖   Then He resumed His garments, took His

* LUKE xxii. 24-30.   † JOHN xiii. 23-25.
‡ MATT. xxvi. 23, 25 ; JOHN xiii. 26-28. See EDERSHEIM, Life of Jesus, vol. ii., p. 494 sq.
¶ LUKE xxii. 17.   ‖ JOHN xiii. 10.

place again at table, and as the Jewish meal proceeded He
explained to His disciples the meaning of so mysterious an
action : He had given them an example of humility which
they should imitate so as to secure to themselves eternal
bliss. *

One of them, however, would be by his own fault
excluded from the promised reward, and this is why Jesus
added, " I speak not of you all "; and He then referred to
the prediction made long centuries before, that He would
be betrayed by one of His disciples. † But the apostles did
not heed this new reference to the betrayal, probably
because of their joy while singing the first part of the
Hallel and drinking the *second cup*. But Our Saviour was
far from rejoicing ; indeed, " He was troubled in spirit,"
and when He made a new and more explicit reference to
the betrayer, " Amen, Amen, I say to you, one of you shall
betray Me," all the disciples remained at first amazed, and
next asked, " Lord, is it I ? " ‡ Our Lord's answer left still
the special person undetermined, but He added an awful
woe against the betrayer.   Judas, in his turn, repeated, " Is
it I ? " and Jesus gave him an affirmative answer, which the
traitor alone could hear because of his nearness to Our
Lord. § Unable to discover otherwise who was to betray
his Master, St. Peter beckoned to the beloved disciple, who
then, changing a little his posture, leaned back on the sacred
bosom of Jesus, asking Him who was to be the betrayer,
and received as a sign the giving of the *sop* which probably
followed the *second cup*. This sop consisted of a morsel of
the Paschal lamb, together with a piece of unleavened bread
and some bitter herbs, and it was first handed to Judas by
Our Lord, who then added, " That which thou dost, do
quickly." Judas " went out immediately," for as he had

---

* JOHN xiii. 1-17.   † JOHN xiii. 18-20.
‡ MATT. xxvi. 21, 22 ; MARK xiv. 18-21 ; LUKE xxii. 21-23 ; JOHN xiii. 21, 22.
§ MATT. xxvi. 23-25 ; MARK xiv. 20, 21.

eaten the Pasch he could now leave for business purposes or for giving alms to the poor, so that "no man at table knew" the reason of his departure. The precise time at which Judas left the upper room has ever been a matter of discussion in the Church, yet it seems very probable that he went out *before* Our Lord instituted the Holy Eucharist. *

The departure of Judas was manifestly a great relief to the Saviour, † and He soon proceeded to give to His faithful disciples the supreme pledge of His love by the **institution of the Holy Eucharist.** ‡ The eating of the flesh of the lamb was now completed, after which nothing more was to be eaten; but here Our Lord anticipated a later rite, that of breaking and eating bread after the Paschal supper. § He "took bread, and blessed and brake and gave to His disciples, and said, Take ye, and eat: THIS IS MY BODY"; and by these all-powerful words of the Son of God the bread was actually changed into the body of the Lord: into that very body which was soon to be crucified for man's salvation. Then "taking the chalice," the *third cup*, or "*Cup of Blessing,*" as it is called by St. Paul, ‖ " He gave thanks and gave to them, saying : Drink ye all of this; for THIS IS MY BLOOD of the New Testament, which shall be shed for you." By virtue of the same divine power, these words of Jesus changed the wine of the chalice into His most precious blood soon to be shed on Calvary for our redemption. Nor was this mysterious transformation of bread into the Lord's body, of wine into His blood, to take place only once, for He entrusted the power to effect it to His apostles and to their successors in the priestly office : " Do this for a commemoration of Me."

3. After the Last Supper. Our Lord's last supper was practically over ; yet He remained at table a little

---

* This is the view admitted by such recent Catholic scholars as DEHAUT, FILLION, LE CAMUS, CORNELY, TROCHON, FRETTÉ, BRUNEAU, etc.

† JOHN xiii. 31, 32. ‡ Cfr. MATT. xxvi. 26-29; MARK xiv. 22-25; LUKE xxii. 19, 20. § Cfr. EDERSHEIM, vol. ii., p. 511. ‖ 1 COR. x. 16.

longer time, during which He imparted to His disciples His first consolatory words, * then predicted to Peter his three-fold denial, † and addressed again words of comfort to His apostles.‡ Then rising from the supper table, He said the **Hymn**—probably the second part of the **Hallel**§—and delivered the beautiful discourse recorded in chapters xv. and xvi. of the fourth Gospel. This long discourse Jesus closed with a prayer which He addressed to His Father, and in which He spoke as the great High Priest of the New Law. ‖

After these words Jesus went forth from the supper room with His disciples. ¶

* JOHN xiii. 33-35.   † JOHN xiii. 36-38 ; LUKE xxii. 31-38.
‡ JOHN xiv.   § Cfr. MATT. xxvi. 30 ; MARK xiv. 26.
‖ JOHN xvii.   ¶ JOHN xviii. 1.

SYNOPSIS OF CHAPTER XVIII

THE ARREST AND TRIAL OF JESUS.

I.
THE ARREST:
{ 1. Time and Place.
{ 2. Actors and Incidents.

II.
THE TRIAL BEFORE THE RELIGIOUS AUTHORITIES:

1. The Preliminary Examination (Annas and Caiphas).

2. The First Session of the Sanhedrim: Condemnation to Death: { Its legality.
{ Its only ground.

3. The Second Session of the Sanhedrim: The Sentence of Death Formally Ratified.

III.
THE TRIAL BEFORE THE CIVIL AUTHORITIES:

1. Jesus before Pilate: { Site of the prætorium.
{ An artifice of the Jews eluded by Pilate.
{ Accusations against Jesus declared groundless.

2. Jesus before Herod: How Received, Treated, and Sent Back to Pilate?

3. Jesus before Pilate again: { The weak policy of Pilate a failure.
{ The people choose Barabbas; demand Our Lord's crucifixion.
{ Jesus is scourged and presented to the people.
{ The Jews declare that { Jesus "ought to die, having made Himself the Son of God."
{ To release Him is to be the enemy of Cæsar.

The Final Sentence: "Ibis ad Crucem."

CHAPTER XVIII.

THE ARREST AND TRIAL OF JESUS.

§ 1. *The Arrest.**

1. Time and Place. It was probably between ten and eleven at night when Jesus, leaving the Cœnaculum, went with His disciples towards **Gethsemani**, an olive orchard east of Jerusalem. On His way thither His main concern was to prepare His apostles for what was now at hand. He predicted to all their common desertion, and to Peter, the loudest in his protestations of fidelity, He foretold again his threefold denial.

Meanwhile they crossed the deep ravine of the Cedron, and soon reached the garden of Gethsemani, not far distant from, if not identical with, the present enclosed space pointed out by tradition as the scene of Our Lord's agony. This garden was well known to Judas, for it was a place to which Jesus often resorted to pray. On this night His prayer lasted long, and meantime His soul was sorrowful unto death, His body covered with a sweat of blood, and His heart wounded by the insensibility of His three chosen disciples, Peter, James and John. But at length Jesus, comforted by a heavenly messenger, lovingly accepted the chalice of His passion, and bade His apostles be ready to face those who, at that very moment, were approaching the garden to arrest Him. As Our Lord's walk from the Cœnaculum to Gethsemani, together with His prayer and

---

* MATT. xxvi. 31-57; MARK xiv. 26-xv. 1; LUKE xxii. 39-54; JOHN xviii. 1-13.

agony in the garden, took probably more than one hour,[*] His arrest is most likely to be placed about midnight.

2. Actors and Incidents. The chief actor in the arrest was one of the twelve, the traitor Judas. This night, during which all were busily engaged at the Paschal meal, had appeared to him the most favorable time to betray his Master, and hence it was probably understood between him and Our Lord's enemies [†] that he should leave the Paschal table immediately after he had eaten the Pasch, and lead without delay those in charge of the arrest, to the exact place where Jesus was reclining with His disciples. It is in this way that Judas became "the leader of them that apprehended Jesus," [‡] that is, of "a multitude" made up (1) of soldiers and servants from the chief priests and ancients of the people ; (2) of a part of the Roman cohort under one of its captains, in case a disturbance should arise ; (3) of chief priests and ancients to direct the proceedings. Thus accompanied, the betrayer went first to the upper room, but finding it empty, he went next to the garden of Gethsemani, where he suspected his Master might still be in prayer.

Judas had calculated aright, and upon his arrival at the other side of the Cedron he soon found Jesus, who, with the eleven apostles, had come forth from the garden to meet His betrayer. According to an arrangement, calculated, it was thought, not to cause any suspicion among Our Lord's followers, Judas left those who accompanied him a little behind, and "coming forward" saluted Jesus with the usual salutation, to which he added the kiss of peace. Scarcely had Our Saviour received this sign of friendship, now transformed by Judas into an act of treachery, when He went towards the multitude and asked them, "Whom seek ye ?" "Jesus of Nazareth" they replied, to which Our Lord answered, "I AM HE." At these simple words of Jesus they went backward and fell to the ground, the Son

---

[*] MATT. xxvi. 40 ; MARK xiv. 37.   [†] Cfr. JOHN xiii. 27.   [‡] ACTS i. 16.

of God proving thereby that had He so willed, no power on earth would have been able to arrest Him.

But as Our Lord's second question and reply to the multitude, together with His request that they should allow His followers to escape unmolested, implied His willing surrender of Himself, they proceeded to seize Him. At this moment, Peter, drawing his sword, intervened and cut off the ear of Malchus, the servant of the high priest. But Our Lord rebuked him, healed the ear of Malchus, and affirmed explicitly His resolve not to defend Himself, protesting, however, against the unworthy conduct of the Jewish leaders He then noticed among the crowd. Jesus was then seized and bound, while in the midst of the confusion His disciples took to flight.[*]

§ 2. *The Trial of Jesus before the Religious Authorities.*[†]

1. **The Preliminary Examination.** From Gethsemani, Jesus was led first to Annas, one of the most influential men of the time,[‡] and whose house was probably nearer the place of the arrest than that of Caiphas, his son-in-law and the actual occupant of the high priesthood. Furthermore, Annas, having been the official high priest during about eight years, had been deposed by the representative of a foreign and heathen power, the Roman procurator, Valerius Gratus, so that in the eyes of the Jews he was still their lawful high priest, bearing the title and wielding the influence of his former office. It was only natural, therefore, that immediately on His arrest, Jesus should be brought to him, the more so because he would greatly rejoice at the success of the plot against Our Lord. However this may be, we have no record in the Gospel of a trial to which An-

---

[*] As to the incident recorded in St. MARK (xiv. 51, 52) regarding the young man who followed Jesus, "having a linen cloth cast about his naked body," see EDERSHEIM, vol. ii, pp. 544, 545.

[†] MATT. xxvi. 57; xxvii. 1; MARK xiv. 53; xv. 1; LUKE xxii. 54–71; JOHN xviii. 13–27.

[‡] JOSEPHUS, Antiq. of the Jews, book XX., chap. ix., 1.

nas would have subjected Jesus, and we are simply told that he "sent Him bound, to Caiphas the high priest."

Soon the house of this official high priest of the Jews was reached, but as some interval would necessarily elapse before the members of the Sanhedrim could be assembled, Caiphas asked Jesus some questions about His disciples and His doctrine. This was but a preliminary examination, since "there was no formal accusation, no witnesses, no sentence pronounced." (Andrews.) In His answer Our Lord reminded the high priest that as an accused person, He should not be expected to criminate Himself. At these words of Jesus, an officer of Caiphas, knowing that he would thereby please his master, smote the face of the Son of God for what he called an irreverent answer to the high priest; but Our Lord patiently bore this outrage, mercifully expostulating however with that man to open his eyes to the injustice and baseness of his action.

Meanwhile, Peter and John, having recovered from their panic, had followed their Master to the house of the high priest and had been introduced by the portress, and it is probably during Our Lord's preliminary examination by Caiphas, that the first two denials of Peter occurred.*

2. **The First Session of the Sanhedrim.** At length —between two and three in the morning—the Sanhedrists met in a large room of the high priest's palace, and the result of their first sitting was a sentence of death against Our Lord, the illegality of which can easily be perceived. It is clear, for instance, that the most elementary forms of justice were not observed in the case of Jesus; before His trial His death had been agreed upon by His judges;† at the trial, no one appeared for Him as advocate, no witnesses were called to testify in His favor, and when the witnesses against Him could not agree in their testimony, He Himself was put under oath and compelled by the high priest to

---

* FOUARD, ii., p. 280 sq.; ANDREWS, p. 517 sq.   † JOHN xi. 47-53.

criminate Himself; again, the trial took place before sunrise, in opposition to Jewish law, and the ill-treatment both before and after the trial proves that Our Lord's judges were in reality His cruel and implacable enemies. A further proof of the illegality of this sentence is found in the fact that it was pronounced although the charges brought against Jesus could not be proved by witnesses.*

The time came during this iniquitous trial when the witnesses were so manifestly untrustworthy that Our Lord declined to answer their various charges, and then it was that His declared enemy, the high priest Caiphas, resorted to a manœuvre apparently reserved for the emergency. He arose, put Jesus under oath, thereby obliging Him to speak, and bade Him declare whether He was "the Christ, the Son of the blessed God." Our Lord answered affirmatively, and then added a few words which implied a claim on His part to equality in power and dignity with Jehovah Himself. In the eyes of the high priest and of the Sanhedrists present the declaration of Jesus amounted to an open blasphemy, and this is why, dispensing with further witnesses, they at once pronounced the sentence, "HE IS GUILTY OF DEATH!" Then the Sanhedrim suspended its session to meet again at daybreak.†

It was during this first session of the Sanhedrim, or at its close, that the third denial of Peter occurred, upon whom Jesus then cast a look of mercy and who, "going forth, wept bitterly." We must also mention here the awful scene of ill treatment to which our divine Saviour was subjected between the two meetings of the Sanhedrim, and the general features of which are recorded in the Synoptists. ‡

3. **The Second Session of the Sanhedrim.** In holding a second meeting at the earliest possible moment after

---

* Cfr. MATT. xxvi. 59 sq.; MARK xiv. 55-59.
† Cfr. FOUARD, ii., pp. 278, 279.
‡ MATT. xxvi. 67, 68; MARK xiv. 65; LUKE xxii. 63-65.

sunrise * the Sanhedrists wished to comply with one of the strict rules of the court forbidding capital trials at night. This second session was held, like the first, in the house of Caiphas † and lasted but a short time, for it was simply devoted to secure from the lips of Jesus a most explicit statement of His claim to the divine nature and authority. Our Lord's judges began with a question about His Messiahship, to which He apparently refused to answer. But as He soon repeated the very words which in their first meeting the Sanhedrists had considered as implying a claim to equality in power and dignity with Jehovah, they asked Him with one accord, " Art Thou then the Son of God ? "

Plainly all the circumstances of the case gave to this question of Our Lord's judges but one meaning. They wanted Him to commit Himself to a formal declaration that He was no less truly God than Jehovah Himself, whom He claimed as His Father. This was their meaning and Jesus fully realized it ; and this is why He answered by the rabbinical formula, " You say, that I am," whereby He endorsed as His own affirmation the full intent of the question put to Him. By this formal declaration of Our Lord the Sanhedrists had fully reached their object. They themselves " had heard it from His own mouth " that He claimed to be equal to God, and therefore the sentence of death already pronounced against Him was at once ratified by the highest tribunal of the Jews.

Judas soon learned this issue of His Master's trial, and having returned the money to the chief priests and ancients, he went and hanged himself, despairing that his deliberate perfidy could be forgiven him.‡

* The sun rises at Jerusalem in the month of April about 5 o'clock.
† Cfr. JOHN xviii. 28.
‡ MATT. xxvii. 3 sq.

§ 3. *The Trial of Jesus before the Civil Authorities.*

1. **Jesus before Pilate.**[*] There now remained for the Jewish rulers to obtain from Pilate the ratification of their sentence of death against Jesus, for without the approval of the Roman procurator they had no power to carry out a capital sentence. But this approval they hoped easily to wrest from the weakness of Pilate, and in consequence they hurriedly led Our Lord to the fortress Antonia where, as is very probable, this Roman official now resided.

Arriving at the **prætorium**—for so were called the headquarters of the procurator wherever he happened to be—the Sanhedrists refused to enter this heathen house, lest they should incur a legal defilement which would have prevented them from eating the **Chagigah**,[†] as they were expected to do on that very day, Nisan 15th. Pilate therefore came out to give them audience, and he at once demanded they should proffer grounds of accusation against their prisoner. The Jewish officials remonstrated in order that their sentence should be confirmed without inquiry into the matter, but Pilate stood firm and compelled them to bring forth definite charges of which he would feel bound to take cognizance. "They therefore began to accuse Jesus, saying : We have found this man perverting our nation, and forbidding to give tribute to Cæsar, and saying that He is Christ the King." These charges directly affected the Roman power, and hence Pilate, entering the prætorium, began to inquire into them. As, however, they could be summed up in the charge of setting up a kingdom in opposition to that of Cæsar, Pilate questioned Jesus about His title of King of the Jews. To this fair inquiry of His judge, Our Lord answered that He was indeed a King, but that His kingdom, being not of this world, could

[*] MATT. xxvii. 1, 2 ; 11-14; MARK xv. 1-5; LUKE xxiii. 1-6; JOHN xviii. 28-38.
[†] See the able discussion of this point in EDERSHEIM, vol. ii., pp. 566-568.

not clash with the Roman power. This reply of Our Lord fully satisfied the susceptibility of the Roman official, and in consequence Pilate, going out with Jesus, declared to the Jews, "I find no cause [that is, ground for condemnation] in Him."

Our Lord's enemies were little prepared for such a public and unhesitating acquittal of Jesus, and this made them all the more earnest in repeating their charges : "He stirreth up the people," said they, "teaching throughout all Judæa, beginning from Galilee to this place"; and St. Mark adds : "and the chief priests accused Him in many things." Amid this storm of accusations Jesus remained silent, and this perfect self-command on the part of his prisoner astonished the procurator. As Pilate's ear had caught the name of Galilee among the clamors of the multitude as the province wherein Jesus had excited the people to revolt, this suggested to the Roman official an expedient to relieve himself from all responsibility in connection with Our Lord. Having assured himself that the accused was a Galilean, he sent Him to Herod Antipas, now in the Holy City, as one to whose jurisdiction Jesus naturally belonged.

2. **Jesus before Herod.*** Accompanied by the Roman soldiery and by a delegation of the Sanhedrim, Jesus left the prætorium on Mount Moria, crossed the bridge which spans the Tyropœon valley, and soon reached the palace of Herod on Mount Sion. The Galilean ruler had long wished to see the prophet whose fame had reached his ears, and it was with a firm hope that Our Lord would perform some miracle to secure his patronage, that he saw Jesus standing before his tribunal. This, however, Jesus refused to do ; nay, more, He even remained silent both to the numerous questions of Herod and to the vehement accusations of the chief priests and the Scribes. Herod was irritated, and in scorn of Our Lord's claims he arrayed

* LUKE xxiii. 7-12.

Him in the white garment of a candidate to royalty, and sent Him back to Pilate.

This interchange of civilities restored the broken friendship between the Roman procurator and the Galilean tetrarch.

3. Jesus before Pilate Again.* With Our Lord's return to the prætorium, Pilate felt that all the responsibility he had wished to shift upon Herod had come back to him. He was thoroughly convinced of the innocence of Jesus, and accordingly having called together "the chief priests and the magistrates and the people," he took his place on the judgment-seat, intending to proclaim Our Lord's innocence and to end the trial. Through his weak policy, however, instead of authoritatively putting an end to the trial, he suggested a compromise, calculated, as he thought, to satisfy all parties. It was customary at the Paschal festival to release any prisoner for whom the people had a special desire, and now Pilate proposed that since the charges against Jesus had appeared groundless to Herod and to him, he would simply have Our Lord "chastised" and then released.

Pilate's policy was a lamentable failure. The priests, of course, could not be satisfied with anything but the capital punishment of Jesus, and the people, reminded of their right to the release of any prisoner they asked for, rejected the idea that the Roman procurator should limit their choice to Jesus. Pilate was thus led to allow the multitude to choose between Our Lord and Barabbas, and to this he agreed the more readily because he felt sure that Jesus would be the object of their preference, since a few days before they had received Him with enthusiasm into Jerusalem.

While the people deliberated about the choice of a prisoner, the procurator received from his wife a message to the

* MATT. xxvii. 15-31; MARK xv. 6-20; LUKE xxiii. 13-25; JOHN xviii. 39; xix. 16.

effect that during the night she had been greatly troubled
in a dream about the just man now standing before her
husband's tribunal ; she therefore advised him not to inflict
upon Him the least punishment.   This, of course, made
Pilate more anxious to end the trial ; but to his great astonishment, he soon discovered that, following the perfidious
suggestions of their leaders and their own national feelings
in favor of one who, like Barabbas, had fought against the
Roman yoke, the multitude had agreed upon asking for the
release of Barabbas and for the crucifixion of Jesus.   In vain
did the Roman procurator remonstrate with the people ; the
multitude persisted in choosing Barabbas and clamoring for
Our Lord's crucifixion.*

At last Pilate yielded and ordered that Jesus should be
scourged, this being the usual preliminary to crucifixion.
The soldiers therefore stripped Our Lord to the waist, tied
Him to a low pillar that, bending over, He might better receive the blows of the instrument of torture, viz., a leather
thong often loaded with lead or iron.   There is no doubt
that this scourging of Jesus was of the severest kind : the
victim was of the hated Jewish race, and the Roman soldiers could inflict any number of lashes.

After this cruel scourging, another awful scene took place
in the inner court of the prætorium.   There, before the
assembled cohort, the soldiery arrayed Jesus in purple,
crowned Him with thorns, placed a reed in His right hand,
and paid a derisive homage to Him as the King of the Jews,
smiting at the same time His sacred head with the reed, and
spitting upon His august face.

When Pilate beheld Jesus in this pitiable condition, he
was moved with compassion, and presented Him to the
multitude, hoping that this sight would be sufficient to
touch the hearts of all.   In fact, in presence of such meek-

---

* The principal reasons which may be given to account for this great and rapid change
in public feeling in regard to Our Lord are well stated by ANDREWS, pp. 537, 538.

ness and suffering the people were touched, and only " the
chief priests and their servants " cried again for Our Lord's
crucifixion. Pilate was angry at this implacable hatred of
the Jewish rulers, and realizing that he had gained ground
over the people's mind, resolved not to put Jesus to death.
" Take Him you," said he, " and crucify Him : for I find
no cause in Him."

It is at this juncture, that to regain their hold upon the
multitude, the Jewish rulers charged Our Lord publicly with
the crime of blasphemy, which must needs be punished with
death. " We have a Law," they exclaimed, " and according
to the Law He ought to die, because He made Himself the
Son of God." Hearing this, Pilate greatly feared, submitted
Our Lord to a new interrogation, and even took an open
step towards His release. But the Roman procurator was
no match for the crafty Sanhedrists. They now threaten
him with the vengeance of Tiberius for releasing a man
accused of treason against the emperor. Pilate, doubtless,
remembered how in one of his former conflicts with the
Jews, that emperor had pronounced against him, and he
knew well that to the suspicious mind of Tiberius the simple
accusation of indifference to his imperial interests would be
equivalent to conviction. Trembling for his very life, Pilate
now prepared to give the final sentence, not without, however, protesting his own innocence by washing his hands
before all ; then he ordered that Jesus be taken away and
crucified. As Our Lord came forth, Pilate presented Him
to the Jews as their King, and as such, the representatives
of the Jewish people rejected their Saviour, declaring that
they had no king but Cæsar.

The form of the final sentence is not given in the Gospel
narratives ; the usual form was " *Ibis ad crucem.*"

SYNOPSIS OF CHAPTER XIX.

THE CRUCIFIXION.

I. ON THE WAY TO CALVARY:

1. The Via Dolorosa.

2. Christ Bearing His Cross:
   - Shape of the cross; the title.
   - Simon of Cyrene.
   - Women of Jerusalem.

II. CALVARY:

1. The Execution:
   - General remarks on the punishment of the crucifixion.
   - The crucifixion of Our Lord described.

2. On the Cross:
   - Witnesses of the crucifixion.
   - The seven words of Jesus.
   - Death and accompanying circumstances.

3. The Burial:
   - The taking down from the cross, and embalming.
   - Further preparations for embalming the body of Jesus.
   - The sepulchre sealed and guarded.

CHAPTER XIX.

THE CRUCIFIXION.*

§ 1. *On the Way to Calvary.*

1. **The Via Dolorosa.** The road followed by Jesus to reach the place of the crucifixion is commonly called the **Via Dolorosa.** According to tradition its starting point was the fortress Antonia, where Pilate resided, and its terminus the place of the Church of the Holy Sepulchre. As, however, that church is within the city walls, while the Evangelists speak of the place where Our Lord was crucified as outside the city and " nigh unto it," many reject the traditional site of Calvary, and consider the hill lying without the present wall, a little to the northeast of the Damascus gate, as the place of Our Lord's crucifixion. But as it is agreed on all hands that the present city wall does not correspond exactly with the wall of Jerusalem in Our Lord's time, it is possible that the old city wall did not actually include the site of the Church of the Holy Sepulchre, and in point of fact, no conclusive argument, archæological or otherwise,† has yet been brought forward against the traditional place of Calvary. Admitting, therefore, that the general course of the road followed by Jesus is correctly indicated by tradition, the **Via Dolorosa** was about one-third of a mile in length.

2. **Christ Bearing His Cross.** After the final sentence had been pronounced, Our Lord was clothed again in

* MATT. xxvii. 31–66; MARK xv. 20–47; LUKE xxiii. 26–56; JOHN xix. 16–42.

† Cir. FOUARD, vol. ii., p. 316, footnote 1; ANDREWS, pp. 577–588; and also the article Calvaire, in VIGOUROUX, Dictionnaire de la Bible.

His own garments, and He soon started for the place of execution, called **Golgotha**, from its skull-like appearance. He was led by a Roman centurion—to whom tradition gives the name of Longinus—and was surrounded by four soldiers, in the same manner as the two malefactors who accompanied Him, and whose execution had been decided on, on this great festival, to inspire with awe the Jewish multitudes. After the Roman custom, Jesus had to bear His own instrument of torture, a cross, most likely the *crux immissa*, or Latin cross ✝, as represented in early paintings. Whether the *title*, or white wooden tablet bearing the superscription which stated Our Lord's offence, was borne before Him, hung upon His neck, or already fixed to the cross, cannot be defined.

Our Lord's cross was indeed of sufficient size and weight to support the body of a man, but it was not the lofty and massive object which we often picture to ourselves. Yet it soon proved too heavy a burden for the physical strength of Jesus, exhausted by His long agony in the garden, by the barbarous treatment He had endured between the two meetings of the Sanhedrim, and chiefly by the scourging and crowning of thorns of the early morning. Patiently and slowly He moved up to the western city gate, accompanied by a very large multitude; but there, as He sank under His burden, the soldiers caught sight of a certain Simon, a Cyrenian, who was just coming from the country, and whom they recognized as a stranger by his dress, and they at once compelled him to bear the cross after Our Lord. At this moment, also, the women who had followed with the populace coming closer to Him, raised their lamentations, but Jesus bade them not to weep over Him, but **over themselves and over their children.**

§ 2. *Calvary.*

1. **The Execution.** Finally Ca'vary was reached, where the Son of God was to undergo the most ignominious and most painful of punishments. Crucifixion was ever regarded by the nations among which it was in use, as a most shameful punishment, and among the Romans in particular, it was generally reserved for slaves and foreigners. In the eyes of the Jews, one dying on the cross was accursed by God,* and this is why Our Lord's enemies had been so anxious to secure for Him this punishment as a signal protest against His pretensions to the Messianic dignity. To this peculiar shame of the crucifixion were added sufferings of the most intense character, and which terminated always after many hours, often after several days of cruel agony. †

It was, in fact, to render these dreadful sufferings less unendurable that, according to existing custom, a draught of wine mingled with myrrh was offered to Our Lord before He was nailed to the cross; but Jesus refused to drink this stupefying potion, because He wished to experience fully the torments of His crucifixion. The crucifixion itself, being a mode of execution familiar to their contemporaries, is left undescribed by the Evangelists, but from various authors who speak of the execution of criminals by the cross, we may infer that Our Lord's crucifixion was carried out as follows: While the cross was being placed in the ground, Our Redeemer was stripped of His garments, and with only a linen cloth about His loins, was lifted up by means of ropes to the *sedile*, or little projection midway upon the upright post of the cross. Having sat upon the *sedile*, Jesus stretched out His arms to be tied with cords to the transom, and then His hands and feet‡ were nailed to the

* Cfr. DEUTER. xxi. 23.   † Cfr. SMITH, Bible Dictionary, art. Crucifixion.
‡ That both Our Lord's hands and feet were nailed to the cross is plainly inferred from St LUKE xxiv. 39, 40, and from a unanimous tradition applying to Jesus the words of PSALM xxi 17. Cir. FOUARD, vol. ii., p. 325, footnote 6.

cross, four nails being most probably used for the purpose. Of course a similar treatment was inflicted on the two male-factors who were crucified, the one on the right, and the other on the left of Jesus.

To complete Our Lord's crucifixion, there remained only one thing to be done, namely: to set up above His head the *title* written by Pilate in Latin, Greek and Aramaic, to indicate the nature of the offence for which Our Saviour was thus punished. The wording of this *title*, which apparently declared Jesus the true King of the Jews, was naturally objected to by the Jewish leaders, but to their remonstrances Pilate had simply replied by the legal for-mula: " What I have written I have written."

2. On the Cross. While the four soldiers in charge of Our Lord's execution divided among themselves His garments, the great body of the people seems to have re-mained silently gazing upon Him, and only those who had borne false testimony against Him now mocked at Jesus, shaking their heads and repeating their calumnious accusa-tions. Soon, however, the Sanhedrists chimed in, congratu-lating themselves with loud and scornful insolence upon their success; and they actually communicated their feel-ings of hatred and scorn not only to the ignorant Roman soldiers, but also to the people at large and to the very malefactors agonizing by the side of Jesus.* Apparently but a small group of those who witnessed Our Lord's agony on the cross, among whom of course were His mother and His beloved disciple, continued to sympathize with Him and to give Him external proofs of their intense grief.

Meanwhile Jesus had but feelings of compassion and love for those around Him, as is proved by three of the *seven words* placed on His dying lips by the inspired nar-

---

* As to the question whether both malefactors or only one of them reviled Our Lord, cfr. FOUARD, vol. ii., p. 332, footnote 3 ; ANDREWS, p. 556.

rators. The first was a prayer for forgiveness in behalf of His very enemies; the second held out a magnificent reward to the repentant malefactor, while by the third He tenderly entrusted Mary and John to their mutual loving care. It is probable that during the miraculous darkness which set in at noon* Jesus suffered in silence, and that He uttered the other four words only when it had ceased. The fourth word evidenced the incomprehensible anguish of His soul, and the fifth the intolerable thirst which consumed Him. By the sixth word He solemnly declared His redeeming work consummated, and in consequence, with the seventh, a final recommendation of His soul to His Father, "He gave up the ghost."

At this same moment, prodigies attested the dignity of the Person who had just breathed His last. The veil of the Temple—the one which separated the Holy from the Most Holy Place—was rent from top to bottom; the earth quaked ; the rocks were torn asunder ; the graves were opened, and "many bodies of the saints that had slept arose." No wonder, then, that in presence of the signs he witnessed, the Roman centurion exclaimed, "Indeed this man was the Son of God," and that the Jewish multitude "returned striking their breasts."

3. **The Burial.** While Jesus, the Lamb of God and the High Priest of the New Law, was consummating His sacrifice on Mount Calvary, the Jewish priests had been offering their usual sacrificial lamb on Mount Moria. As soon as their sacrifice was over, they hurried to Pilate, requesting him to hasten the death of the crucified that their corpses might be taken down before the beginning of the Sabbath, that is, before sunset. Pilate agreed at once

---

* The discrepancy between St. MARK xv. 25 (cfr. also MARK xv. 33; MATT. xxvii. 45; LUKE xxiii. 44), who places Our Lord's crucifixion at the third hour, and St. JOHN xix. 14, who speaks of the sixth hour when Pilate sat down to pronounce the final sentence, is closely examined by ANDREWS, pp. 545-547. See also FILLION, St. Jean, p. 348; RAMSAY, in the Expositor, March 1893; June 1896; etc.

to their request, for he was well aware that the Roman custom of leaving the bodies of crucified criminals without burial had been expressly modified in favor of the Jews, whose Law commanded that all such should be buried before night. According to his directions, the soldiers broke the legs of the malefactors who had been crucified with Our Lord, in order to hasten their death, but when on the point of doing the same to Jesus they found Him already dead, they did not break any of His bones ; one of them simply pierced Our Lord's side with his spear. Thus was the actual death of Our Saviour put beyond all doubt, for the inflicting of the wound was immediately followed by a flow of blood and water ; * thus also were fulfilled two prophetical passages of the Old Testament.†

Meantime, a disciple of Jesus and a man of wealth, the Sanhedrist *Joseph* of Arimathea—a town probably to be identified with *Ramleh*—had come to Pilate to obtain the body of Jesus. The Roman procurator had not the least objection to grant a private burial for a man whom he had so often proclaimed innocent ; but as crucified criminals survived much longer their execution, he made sure from the centurion in charge of Our Lord's crucifixion that Jesus was really dead, and then he freely granted the request of Joseph. Having purchased fine linen, Joseph repaired promptly to Golgotha, where he was joined by Nicodemus, one of his colleagues and fellow-disciples, who brought about a hundred pounds of spices wherewith to embalm the body of his Master. Together they took down the body, wrapped it in the linen cloth, the folds of which they sprinkled with myrrh, aloes and other spices, conveyed it hastily into a garden near the place of the crucifixion, and laid it in a new tomb hewn out of a rock, which belonged

---

* While most commentators regard this flowing of blood and water as supernatural, many prefer to explain it by the separation of the blood of the heart into its red and white parts, a separation which naturally takes place after death.

† NUMB. ix. 12 ; ZACH. xii. 10.

to Joseph; finally, having rolled a great stone to the entrance, they departed.

The holy women who had been devoted to Jesus during His lifetime, and who now witnessed His hasty burial, carefully remarked the place where He was laid, and return-ing promptly to the Holy City, they purchased spices and ointments for a more perfect embalming of Our Lord's sacred body after the Sabbath was past.

Apparently it was all over with the Messianic preten-sions of Jesus, whose remains now lay lifeless in the sepulchre. And yet His enemies, remembering His pro-phetic words about rising on the third day, preferred to take precautions against all possible contingencies. The very morning of their great Paschal Sabbath, they therefore repaired to Pilate and obtained from him permission that the sepulchre should be made secure until the third day. Accordingly, the door of the sepulchre was carefully sealed, and Roman soldiers entrusted with the charge of watching the tomb of Jesus.

SYNOPSIS OF CHAPTER XX.

THE RISEN LIFE (TIME: FORTY DAYS).

I. THE RESURRECTION:

1. Our Lord's Resurrection Entirely Unexpected.

2. The Visits to the Sepulchre:
   - The holy women.
   - Peter and John.
   - The soldiers report and are bribed by the priests and ancients.

II. SUCCESSIVE APPARITIONS OF JESUS:

1. On the Day of the Resurrection
   - to Mary Magdalen alone.
   - to the other women mentioned in St. Mark xvi. 1.
   - to Simon Peter alone.
   - to two disciples going to Emmaus.
   - to the apostles in the absence of Thomas.

2. Up to the Ascension:
   - In Jerusalem (a week later): to the apostles, in the presence of Thomas.
   - In Galilee:
     - to seven disciples.
     - To the eleven.
     - To 500 brethren.
   - In Jerusalem?
     - to James only.
     - to all the Apostles.

III. THE ASCENSION:

1. Time and Place.

2. Our Lord's Last Words and Actions.

Conclusion of the Life of Christ (John xx. 30, 31; xxi. 24, 25)

CHAPTER XX.

THE RISEN LIFE. (TIME: FORTY DAYS.)

§ 1. *The Resurrection.**

1. Our Lord's Resurrection Entirely Unexpected.
The day which followed the burial of Jesus was a day
of exulting triumph for His enemies. Without the least
popular tumult they had arrested, tried, and sentenced Jesus
and had caused Him to pass in the eyes of the public for a
blasphemer justly condemned to death by the highest authorities of the land. He had undergone a most shameful
and most cruel death hard by the walls of the Holy City,
and large multitudes had seen Him hanging upon the cross
as a criminal accursed by God. His immediate followers
were dispersed, and a Roman guard watched over His sealed
tomb. What appearance was there that He should be heard
of again except as "a seducer," that is, as one of the many
unsuccessful adventurers who had excited and disappointed
the hopes of a credulous people? In this frame of mind
Our Lord's enemies never entertained seriously the thought
that His words about His future resurrection could prove to
be true.

Meantime the disciples of Jesus were wholly disheart-
ened by the ignominious sufferings and death of Him whom

* MATT. xxviii. 1-15; MARK xvi. 1-11; LUKE xxiv. 1-12; JOHN xx. 1-18. The
differences noticeable between the four Evangelists in their accounts of Our Lord's resurrection offer considerable difficulty to those who hold a strict conception of inspiration
in regard to accuracy of details; but, admitting the differences here spoken of, to their
fullest extent, they by no means impair the historical value of the Gospel narrative.
Cfr. FOUARD. vol. ii., p. 395 sq.; FILLION, St. Matt., p. 562; PLUMMER, St. Luke,
p. 546

219

they had hoped should be the Redeemer of Israel.* During these hours of discouragement and stupor it never came to their minds that, since everything had so far come to pass as He had foretold, His arising from the tomb, so distinctly predicted by Him, would also come to pass. In point of fact they so completely lost sight of His prophetical words in this respect that when the first reports of Our Lord's resurrection reached them they treated them as "idle tales," unworthy of credence.† It is plain, therefore, that the disciples of Jesus did not expect His resurrection any more than His enemies, and that if later they believed in His resurrection they yielded assent only to the strongest and clearest evidence.

2. **The Visits to the Sepulchre.** The first to pay a visit to the tomb of Jesus, on the first day of the week, were the holy women who desired very much to complete the embalming of their Lord. They started from Jerusalem as early as possible on that Sunday morning,‡ not knowing that the sepulchre of their Master had been sealed during the course of the Sabbath and was guarded by the Roman soldiers, so that the only difficulty which occurred to their minds, in the way of accomplishing their pious designs, was that of removing the enormous stone they had seen rolled to the entrance of Our Lord's tomb. While they were on their way to the sepulchre the earthquake mentioned by St. Matthew took place, an angel descended and rolled the stone away, probably only to allow the holy women to enter, for Jesus had risen before the stone was removed.§ As they approached the sepulchre, they saw the stone rolled away, and one of them, Mary Magdalen, who naturally in-

* LUKE xxxiv. 20, 21.
† LUKE xxiv. 11.
‡ JOHN xx. 1 ; MATT. xxviii. 1.   It is most probable that in chap. xxviii. 1, St. Matthew refers not to Saturday *evening*, but to Saturday *night*, when that night was already well spent, and consequently towards daybreak on Easter Sunday. Cfr. FILLION, MEYER, and other commentators.
§ FOUARD, vol. ii., p. 352, footnote 3.

ferred that the body of her Lord had been taken away by the Jews, ran in deep excitement to announce it to Peter and John.

As at this moment the angel was not actually sitting on the removed stone, and the soldiers had already departed, the other women approached nearer and soon entered the sepulchre. There they met angels, one of whom, calming their fears, told them that Jesus was risen, and bade them announce that He would meet His disciples in Galilee ; whereupon the holy women left the sepulchre and, saying nothing to the strangers whom they met by the way, they hastened to find those for whom their message was intended.

Soon after their departure Peter and John, warned by Mary Magdalen, come running with all speed, soon enter the open sepulchre, examine everything, believe in Our Lord's resurrection,* and then return home, while Mary Magdalen, who had followed them back to Our Saviour's tomb, remained behind weeping.

Meantime the Roman guards, who at first had been struck with terror by the appearance of the angel who rolled the stone away from the door of the sepulchre, not only fled, but hastened to report to the chief priests their breach of duty, and in order to exculpate themselves, they detailed all that had occurred. At this news a meeting of the Sanhedrim was convened, wherein it was resolved to conceal by every means the miraculous disappearance of the body of Jesus. Accordingly the chief priests and ancients gave heavy bribes to the soldiers, who were thereby induced to affirm that while they were sleeping, Our Lord's body had been carried away by His disciples ; and this story, industriously spread by the Jewish leaders, soon obtained general credence among the Jewish multitude.

* See FILLION, St. Jean, p. 365 ; FOUARD, vol. ii., p. 354, footnote 2.

§ 2. *Successive Apparitions of Jesus.*

1. Apparitions on the Day of the Resurrection

The first of Our Lord's apparitions recorded in the Gospels occurred in favor of Mary Magdalen, whom an intense sorrow detained in the garden, and near the sepulchre of Jesus, even after the return of Peter and John to the Holy City. Absorbed in her grief, and not expecting to see our risen Saviour, she at first mistook Him for the gardener, but when Jesus pronounced her name, she at once recognized the well-known tones of His voice, and exclaimed, " My Master ! " In her transports of joy she wished to detain Him that she might express to Him all her feelings of loving gratitude, but Jesus would not allow it ; * He bade her go and say to His disciples, " I ascend to My Father and to your Father, to My God and to your God." †

The second apparition of Our Lord was granted to the other women mentioned in St. Mark (xvi. 1), who had the inestimable privilege of kissing His feet in mark of reverent worship, and to whom He gave this message : " Go tell My brethren that they go into Galilee ; there they shall see Me." ‡ It should be noticed that up to this time Jesus had appeared only to women, and that this was deemed by Our Lord's disciples quite sufficient to question the reality of His resurrection. §

We have no details respecting the third apparition of Jesus ; it is simply stated that He " appeared to Simon," and the fact seems to have been the starting point of the belief of some disciples. ‖

Our Lord's fourth apparition on this glorious day of His resurrection is, on the contrary, recorded quite at length by St. Luke (xxiv. 13–35). As two of His disciples were going

---

* About the various reasons assigned by commentators to this unwillingness of Jesus to be detained by Mary Magdalen, cfr. FILLION, St. Jean, p. 368 sq.

　　† JOHN xx. 11-17.　　　　　　　‡ MATT. xxviii. 9-10.
　　§ Cfr. LUKE xxiv. 24.　　　　　　‖ Cfr. LUKE xxiv. 33, 34.

to **Emmaus**—a town which cannot be identified with certainty in the present day, but which was about 7 or 8 miles from Jerusalem—Jesus joined them without being recognized by them. During the conversation which ensued, they stated their own discouraging views about the events of the preceding week and those of the present day, and then it was that Our Lord taught them from the Scriptures that the Christ should "suffer these things and so to enter into His glory." It was only when, being at table with them, " He took bread and blessed and brake and gave to them," that they recognized Jesus, who at the same moment vanished out of their sight. That very evening they returned to Jerusalem and told the apostles what had occurred.

" While they were speaking these things" Jesus appeared for the fifth and last time on the day of His resurrection. As He stood suddenly in their midst the ten apostles present—Thomas was then absent—were greatly disturbed, so that to convince them that they did not simply see a spirit He allowed them to see and touch His hands and feet and He ate before them ; then He gave them power to remit and retain sins.*

2. Apparitions up to the Ascension. A week elapsed, and Our Lord, appearing for the sixth time, found the apostles still in Jerusalem, probably in the upper room where He had celebrated the last supper. This time Thomas was present, and as he heard Jesus bidding him to examine for himself as he had desired to do he felt fully convinced of Our Saviour's resurrection, and he therefore exclaimed, " MY LORD AND MY GOD ! " This fervent act of faith in Our Lord's resurrection and divinity was praised by Jesus, who then added : " Blessed are they that have not seen, and have believed ! "†

At length, all the apostles being convinced that Jesus was truly risen, complied with His often-repeated directions to

---

* JOHN XX. 19-23 ; LUKE xxiv. 36-43.   † JOHN XX. 24-29.

repair to Galilee. The first recorded apparition of **Our Lord** in that province occurred by the lake of Genesareth. He appeared to seven of His disciples, who, in company with Peter, had spent the whole night in unsuccessful efforts to catch fishes, and He bade them cast their net on the right side of the ship. This they did, and their obedience was at once rewarded by an abundant draught of fishes similar to the one granted to them during Our Lord's mortal life.* The beloved disciple was the first to recognize Jesus, and he said so to Peter, who, with his usual impetuosity, cast himself into the sea and came to his Master without delay. It was also on this memorable occasion that Christ, having asked Peter three times, "Simon, son of John, lovest thou Me?" invested him with the supreme pastoral office in the Christian Church, and foretold to him the manner of his death, a thing which Jesus declined to do when this same disciple inquired about the future of St. John.†

Our Lord's next apparition in Galilee occurred on a mountain, which He Himself had indicated beforehand, but which is not named in the Gospel narrative. The eleven were present—probably with some other disciples—and they received from Him to whom "all power was given in heaven and on earth" their great commission to teach and baptize all nations, fully sure that their Master would be with them "all days, even to the consummation of the world."‡

The last apparition of Jesus before His ascension was granted to all the apostles, who were gathered together once more in Jerusalem, probably in the *upper room*. The festival of Pentecost was not far distant and they were bidden

---

* Cfr. LUKE v. 3 sq.

† Cfr. JOHN xxi. 1-23.

‡ MATT. xxviii. 16-20. The apparition of JESUS "to five hundred brethren at once," which is mentioned by St. Paul (1 COR. xv. 6), took place probably also in Galilee; the place where the apparition to St. James occurred mentioned only in the same Epistle (chap. xv. 7), is a mere matter of conjecture.

"stay in the city" till they should "be endued with power from on high." *

§ 3. *The Ascension* (*May* 18, A.D. 30).

1. **Time and Place.** For forty days our risen Saviour had lingered on this earth, appearing time and again to His chosen witnesses, and now the time had come when He was to withdraw entirely His visible presence from them. The place from which He chose to take His final departure was a spot on "the Mount of Olives," † apparently on its eastern slope in view of Bethany ‡ and about three-quarters of a mile from the Holy City.§ A very old tradition, however—it goes back to the second century of our era—places Our Lord's ascension on the western side of Mount Olivet and upon its central summit ; and this tradition is not yet entirely disproved.‖

2. **Our Lord's Last Words and Actions.** It was the feeling of the apostles when Jesus led them out of Jerusalem to the Mount of Olives that something great was at hand, and, as their national expectations of a Messianic temporal rule had revived with the certainty of their Master's resurrection, "they asked Him, saying : Lord, wilt Thou at this time restore again the kingdom to Israel ?" This question proves clearly how little they had realized Our Lord's teachings about the nature of His kingdom, and how much they needed the light of the Holy Spirit to understand the very nature of their own mission after the departure of their Master. The answer of Jesus was such as not to hurt their feelings, and yet such as to prepare their minds for their real mission ; the coming of His kingdom they had to leave to His Father's care, and

---

* LUKE xxiv. 44-49. With regard to the manner in which St. Mark and St. Luke seem to connect Our Lord's resurrection directly with His ascension cfr. ANDREWS, pp. 634-637.
　† ACTS i. 12.　　　　　‡ LUKE xxiv. 50.　　　　　§ ACTS i. 12.
‖ See V. GUÉRIN, La Terre Sainte, vol. i., p. 112 sq. ; FILLION, St. Luc, p. 415.

their own mission of witnesses of His resurrection, divinity, teachings, etc., they would courageously discharge for the benefit of all nations after they had received the power of the Holy Ghost.[*]

Meantime Our Lord had reached with them the Mount of the Ascension ; there, lifting up His hands, He rose from their sight and slowly disappeared in a cloud, "and was carried up to heaven,"[†] where "He sitteth on the right hand of God."[‡]

CONCLUSION.

With this narrative of the ascension we naturally bring to a close our summary account of Our Lord's life. Our study, however rapid, of the facts narrated in the canonical gospels proves to evidence that Jesus was not simply an extraordinary man, a wonderful teacher and a powerful worker of miracles : He was also "the Word made flesh," the very Son of God sent by the eternal Father to lay down His life for the redemption of the world. On the one hand, the circumstances of His birth, the miracles He performed, the title of "*Son of Man*" He so constantly assumed, His distinct claim to Jewish kingship and Messiahship, together with His perfectly sinless life, prove Him to be the long-expected Messias ; on the other hand, His repeated affirmations of equality with the Almighty, His own positive and solemn declaration before the Sanhedrim that He was the "*Son of God*" in the strictest sense of the word, and, indeed, His general attitude during His public life, demand that every candid inquirer into His life and character believe Him to be the Son of God, "that believing, he may have life in His name."[§]

---

[*] ACTS i. 6-8.   [†] LUKE xxiv. 50, 51.   [‡] MARK xvi. 19.   [§] JOHN xx. 31

PART SECOND.

THE APOSTOLIC HISTORY.

SYNOPSIS OF CHAPTER XXI.

APOSTOLIC WORK IN PALESTINE.

(Acts i.–xii.)

I. PENTECOST AND THE FIRST CONVERTS: (Acts i.–v.).	1. Pentecost:	The disciples gathered in the upper room. The descent of the Holy Ghost and the discourse of St. Peter.
	2. The First Converts:	Circumstances of their conversion. Their manner of life. The apostles before the Sanhedrim.

II. THE FIRST DEACONS: (Acts vi.–viii.).	1. Their Ordination, Names and Office. 2. Zeal and Martyrdom of St. Stephen. 3. The Work of St. Philip (Conversion of the Samaritans—Baptism of the Eunuch, etc.).

III. WORK OF ST. PETER OUTSIDE JERUSALEM: (Acts ix. 31 ; xi. 23).	1. Peter's Visitation of "the Saints":	"The peace of the Church." St. Peter at Lydda and Joppe.
	2. The Conversion of Cornelius: the fact and its importance.	
	3. St. Peter in Antioch:	Early introduction of Christianity into that city. Tradition as to St. Peter's residence in Antioch.

IV. PERSECUTION UNDER HEROD AGRIPPA I.: (Acts xii.).	1. Herod Agrippa I.: The Man and His Rule (A.D. 41-44). 2. Martyrdom of St. James. Arrest and Deliverance of St. Peter. 3. Tradition Respecting the Departure of the Apostles from Jerusalem.

CHAPTER XXI.

APOSTOLIC WORK IN PALESTINE (A.D. 30–44).

§ 1. *Pentecost and the First Converts.**

1. **Pentecost.**† It was in compliance with the parting recommendation of their risen Master that, leaving the Mount of the Ascension, the disciples of Jesus returned to Jerusalem. They carried with them the explicit promise that within a few days they should receive the Holy Ghost, and they instinctively felt the need to prepare for this heavenly blessing by cultivating a devout frame of mind. Day after day they were assiduous in the Temple at the time of the morning and evening sacrifices, and outside these sacred hours they gathered in the upper room— probably the one wherein their Master had celebrated His last supper—and "persevered with one mind in prayer with the women, and Mary the mother of Jesus, and with His brethren."

Soon they were joined by former disciples of Jesus, and one day, when there were about 120 gathered together, Peter, whose right of pre-eminence was unquestioned, invited those present to fill up the vacancy in the number of the apostles caused by the treachery and death of Judas.‡ The one finally selected for the apostolic office was Matthias, one of those who had best known Jesus during His mortal life. §

* ACTS i.–v. † ACTS i.–ii. 36.

‡ The discrepancy between ACTS i. 18, 19, and St. MATT. xxvii. 6-8, concerning the buying of the potter's field with the money of the traitor, is perhaps to be traced back to two different traditions embodied in the sacred records.

§ ACTS i. 15–26.

It was not long after the mystical number of twelve had thus been restored when the promised outpouring of the Holy Ghost was granted to the gathered disciples of Christ. This occurred on the fiftieth day after the Passover-Sabbath, under circumstances the miraculous character of which is clearly implied in the sacred narrative. But as might naturally be expected, this miraculous character was not realized by the Jewish multitudes which "out of every nation" had convened in Jerusalem for the celebration of the Pentecost festival : while most witnesses of the event simply wondered, saying one to another: "What meaneth this?" Many of a less serious turn of mind derided the ecstatic condition of the apostles and exclaimed : "These men are full of new wine." Whereupon Peter, again taking the lead, boldly addressed the assembled Jews. In what they witnessed he bade his hearers to see the fulfilment of ancient prophecy regarding the last days—that is, the days of the Messias ; and in that Jesus of Nazareth whom he called "a man approved of God among them by miracles, and wonders, and signs," and whom they had lately crucified and slain, he showed that they should recognize the true Messias whose death and resurrection had been foretold by the Royal Prophet. *

2. The First Converts. † Great indeed was the effect of this first public discourse of St. Peter. It brought home to his hearers the magnitude of the crime committed by their nation, and numbers among them, "about 3000 souls," pricked to the heart, willingly heard the further instructions of the apostle, believed his words, received baptism, and thus became the first converts to Christianity.‡

Similar results soon followed on the great miracle of the healing of the lame man at the **Beautiful Gate** of the Temple, which is detailed with such vividness in the sacred record, and after which St. Peter addressed a second dis-

* ACTS ii. 1-36.   † ACTS ii. 37-v.   ‡ ACTS ii. 37-47.

course to the Jewish multitudes. He reproached them with their great crime against "the Holy One and the Just" whom God had raised from the dead, and bade them to secure themselves against the day of Christ's second coming by a sincere conversion and by a heart-felt obedience to Jesus Christ as "the Prophet" predicted by Moses and all the prophets of old. Finally, he exhorted them, as the children of Abraham, that they should avail themselves of the divine blessing, of which Christ's resurrection was the pledge, first to them and next to all nations.*

These words—to which many unrecorded were added by Peter and John—sank so deeply into the minds and hearts of the listeners that, as the sacred text tells us, "many of them who had heard the word believed : and the number of the men was made five thousand."†

Converts made under the influence of such extraordinary events were naturally filled with the greatest ardor and generosity. Not only did they listen eagerly to the further instructions of the apostles, but they also carried them out earnestly in their daily life. All around them were struck with their faithful attendance at the public services of the Temple, and especially with their wonderful love for one another. In point of fact this brotherly love was, according to the wish of Christ, the feature which most distinguished the nascent church of Jerusalem, of which it is written that "the multitude of believers had but one heart and one soul." It united them every evening at a meal which to all appearances ended with the reception of the Holy Eucharist, and it led them to a real community of goods, not unlike that which had existed between Jesus Himself and His apostles, the wants of all being defrayed from a common purse.‡ Of course the selling of their property by the first converts, as well as their entrusting of the price to the apostles for the relief of needy brethren,

* Acts iii. 1-26.   † Acts iv. 1, 4.   ‡ Acts ii. 42, 44-47 ; iv. 32, 34, 35.

was a free act on their part, and the awful death which
befell Ananias, and Saphira his wife, was a chastisement
inflicted on them simply because of their sinful attempt at
gratifying their avarice while appearing to practise perfect
detachment from worldly goods. *

The admirable life of the first converts, together with
the numerous miracles performed by the apostles, contributed powerfully to increase the number of the believers,
and this in turn called forcibly the attention of the Jewish
authorities to the fact that the followers of Jesus of Nazareth had rallied—nay, even that they were making rapid
and numerous conquests in Jerusalem.   This was of course
a movement most unwelcome to the Jewish leaders, and
they resolved to check it without delay.   In consequence,
while Peter and John were still speaking to the people
after the healing of the lame man at the Beautiful Gate,
the priestly guardians of the Temple, together with the
Sadducees (these last being especially annoyed at the doctrine of the resurrection of the dead implied in the apostolic preaching of Christ's resurrection), arrested the two
apostles and put them into prison, intending on the morrow
to institute a formal trial.   The next day the Sanhedrim in
full meeting inquired of Peter and John : "By what power
or by what name have you done this ? "   Whereupon Peter
declared openly that the miracle had been wrought by the
name of Jesus of Nazareth, whom the Sanhedrists had
indeed crucified, but whom God had raised from the dead,
and who was the only Saviour ever to be expected.

This bold language astounded the Jewish authorities and
threw them on the defensive.   Unable alike to deny the
reality of the miracle, because patent to all, and to inflict
any punishment on its authors because praised for it by the
people at large, they were finally compelled to dismiss Peter
and John, threatening them, however, with severe punish-

* ACTS v. 1-11.

ments should they persevere in teaching in the name of Jesus.*

The first arrest was soon followed by another, which was also caused by the desire of the Jewish leaders to put a stop to the miracles of the apostles and to prevent the growth of the Church in Jerusalem. The news of the miraculous deliverance of the prisoners during the night after the arrest disconcerted, at first, the Sanhedrists who had hastily convened to judge the refractory apostles. But when the culprits appeared before their tribunal, and openly declared their preference " to obey God rather than men," and their firm resolve to continue their preaching of the resurrection and Messiahship of Jesus, the Jewish authorities, considering themselves despised, thought of putting the prisoners to death. But the more moderate view of the venerable Gamaliel prevailed in the council. His colleagues agreed with him that if the movement originated by the apostles was not of God it would soon come to nothing, in the same manner as the movement started some time before by Theodas,† and after him by Judas of Galilee, those two bold deceivers who, despite their great pretension and temporary success, had met with speedy destruction without the least intervention of the Sanhedrim. In consequence, the apostles were simply scourged, and then dismissed with the renewed injunction "that they should not speak at all in the name of Jesus," an injunction which was of course soon disobeyed by men who, like the apostles, " rejoiced that they were accounted worthy to suffer reproach for that sacred name."‡

* Acts ii. 47; iv. 1-23.

† Commentators are much perplexed as to the manner of reconciling Gamaliel's reference to Theodas with the statement of Josephus (Antiq. of the Jews, book XX., chap. v., § 1.), who places the death of this ringleader some twelve years later. (See Fouard, St. Peter, p. 35, footnote 1; Alford; Meyer; Crelier; etc.)

‡ Acts v. 12-42.

§ 2. *The First Deacons.* *

I. Their Ordination, Names and Office. As time went on and the Church greatly increased in numbers, the wonderful harmony of mind and heart which had hitherto prevailed among the believers was seriously endangered by the neglect which the **Hebrews** or Palestinian Jews charged with the care of the widows gradually showed in ministering to the needs of the widows of the **Hellenists**, or Greek-speaking Jews, born out of the Holy Land. Naturally enough, the apostles, to whose ears the murmurs of the Hellenists came, did not think it proper that they should restrict their preaching of " the word of God" to ascertain themselves that at table each and all received their due share. Desirous, however, of righting everything, they called on the body of believers to choose seven men of unexceptionable character, "whom they might appoint over this business."

All the candidates chosen bore Greek names, whence many have inferred that no Palestinian Jew was numbered among them. This, however, is at best a very questionable inference, inasmuch as Greek names were very frequent among Jews born in the Holy Land. Indeed, the reverse is much more likely; it is even probable that the two principal elements of the early Church—the Hebrews and the Hellenists—had an equal number of representatives among the future deacons, while its least numerous element, that of the proselytes, had only one representative, the candidate Nicolas, whom the sacred text distinctly calls " a proselyte of Antioch." However this may be, the apostles ratified at once the choice of the multitude. They prayed fervently to God, and then solemnly imposed hands upon the seven candidates, thereby consecrating them for the ministry of the Church.†

* ACTS vi.–viii.   † ACTS vi. 1-6.

The precise nature of the functions entrusted to the newly ordained deacons can hardly be defined in the present day. They were of course in harmony with the circumstances which attended this first step in Church organization, and in consequence they certainly extended to whatever was then intimately connected with the daily ministration at tables.* Whether preaching and baptizing are also to be counted among the regular functions of the first deacons does not appear.†

2. Zeal and Martyrdom of St. Stephen. Most happy results soon followed on this ordination of the first deacons. The holy ministration of these men, "full of the Holy Ghost and wisdom," restored promptly perfect harmony within the Church, and secured to the apostles all the freedom from material care, which they needed to push with renewed vigor and success the preaching of "the word of the Lord." In point of fact, Jews in great numbers became converted, and even "a large multitude of the priests obeyed the faith."

Conversions so numerous and so important were also caused, to a large extent, by the great miracles and fearless zeal of St. Stephen, the first and foremost of the newly ordained deacons. As a valiant champion of his faith, he did not hesitate to sustain a series of disputations with the Hellenistic Jews of five different synagogues, "his companions in race and birthplace." ‡ Unable to bear calmly their repeated defeats by the inspired disciple of Christ, and fearing the effect of his victories upon the people at large, several adversaries of St. Stephen resolved to compass his ruin. For this purpose they artfully spread the rumor that he had uttered blasphemous words " against Moses and against God," and when the public mind was sufficiently prepared for his arrest, they rushed upon him and

---

* Cfr. Acts vi. 1-3.
† Cfr. Art. Diacre in Vigouroux, Dictionnaire de la Bible.   ‡ Stanley.

dragged him before the Sanhedrim. There they set up false witnesses, who declared: "We have heard this man saying that Jesus of Nazareth shall destroy this place, and shall change the traditions which Moses delivered unto us."

Instead of a direct answer of the holy deacon to these calumnious charges, the sacred text records a long discourse, the general purport of which can alone be mentioned here. By means of an historical retrospect, St. Stephen exhorted his hearers to see in Jesus the Messias foretold by Moses and all the prophets, and not to show themselves imitators of the rebellious spirit which had ever animated their forefathers. His words were bold, nay, even aggressive, especially when he denounced his judges as "the betrayers and murderers of the Just One"; yet they afforded nothing to substantiate the charge of blasphemy brought against him and to justify a sentence of death. Not so, apparently, with his exclamation, "Behold, I see the heavens opened, and the Son of Man standing on the right hand of God!" for scarcely had he uttered it when "with one accord they ran violently upon him, and casting him forth without the city, they stoned him."

The book of the Acts clearly implies that no permission was asked from the Romans to put Stephen to death, and even that his execution was carried out without a formal sentence by the Sanhedrim. The place where Christ's first martyr died praying for his murderers is most likely somewhat to the north of the present Damascus Gate, and very near the grotto of Jeremias.[*]

3. **The Work of St. Philip.** With the death of St. Stephen began a most severe persecution of the faithful of Jerusalem, which led to the dispersion far and wide of a large number among them, and thereby contributed greatly to the spread of Christianity.[†]   The surviving deacons

---

[*] ACTS vi. 7-vii.   See also FOUARD, St. Peter, chap. iv.; and McGIFFERT, The Apostolic Age, p. 85 sq.

[†] ACTS xi. 19.

had fled also; and the successful work of St. Philip, one of them, is now narrated in the book of the Acts. We are told how, being on Samaritan territory, he made by words and miracles numerous converts, among whom was Simon the magician; how he was soon after directed to go and overtake the eunuch of the queen of Ethiopia, then on his return from Jerusalem, and how he converted and baptized him; finally, how, miraculously withdrawn from the sight of the eunuch, he was found in Azotus, whence he reached Cæsarea, preaching the Gospel to all the cities on his way.*

§ 3. *Work of St. Peter outside Jerusalem.*†

1. **Peter's Visitation of "the Saints."** In the midst of the general dispersion caused by the persecution then raging against the church of Jerusalem, the apostles had considered it their duty to remain firm in the Holy City, as the great capital of the Messianic kingdom. It is there that they heard the comforting news of the successful preaching of St. Philip in Samaria, and that, in their desire to strengthen the new converts, "they sent unto them Peter and John." Soon after their arrival the two apostles imposed their hands upon those who so far had only received Christian baptism, and by this rite—in which Catholic theology has ever seen the sacramental rite of Confirmation—imparted to them the Holy Ghost. Before returning to Jerusalem Peter and John availed themselves of their passage through the Samaritan territory to preach the Gospel in many villages.‡

The visit of the other districts evangelized by St. Philip was prudently postponed until the persecution should have abated, and, in point of fact, peace was restored to the Christian communities of Palestine not long afterwards. This occurred when the prolonged attempts of the Emperor

---

* ACTS viii.; cfr. also xxi. 8, 9.   † ACTS ix. 31; xi. 23.   ‡ ACTS viii. 1 *b*, 14–25

Caligula to have his statue set up and worshipped in the Temple of Jerusalem caused so much alarm among the Jews that they had neither time nor thought to continue their persecution of the disciples of Christ. Under these circumstances the postponed visit could be safely made, and it was now carried out by St. Peter alone.*

Of this visitation of "the saints," that is, of the baptized believers, only two miraculous incidents are recorded in the sacred text. The first was the healing of the paralytic Eneas, which St. Peter performed in the important town of Lydda, some 20 miles northwest of Jerusalem. The second was the raising to life of a pious widow named Tabitha, which he wrought soon after his arrival at Joppe, a seaport only 10 miles distant from Lydda. These two miracles were of considerable importance for the Christian Church outside Jerusalem: besides confirming the faith of those already converted, they won to the Gospel numbers of Jews whom the preaching of St. Philip had failed to convince.†

2. The Conversion of Cornelius. An event of still greater importance for the Church at large occurred not long afterwards : it is detailed in the inspired record of the Acts, and is in substance as follows. During the "many days" of St. Peter's abode in Joppe an uncircumcised centurion of Cæsarea, named Cornelius, in compliance with an angelic message, sent for the apostle, to learn from him the divine will in his regard. As the men dispatched by Cornelius approached the city on the following day, St. Peter was favored with a vision, the exact meaning of which he realized only after the messengers of the centurion made known to him the purport of their mission. The interview solicited took place, and while St. Peter was addressing Cornelius and the friends he had gathered around him

---

* Cfr. JOSEPHUS, Antiq. of the Jews, book XVIII., chap. viii., § 2 sq.
† ACTS ix. 31-42.

"the Holy Ghost fell on all them that heard the word";
whereupon the apostle ordered that these Gentiles, who had
visibly received the Holy Ghost in exactly the same manner ..s the Jews, should be baptized at once in the name of
the Lord Jesus Christ.*

This event marked a new and important stage in the development of the early Church. Hitherto the preachers of
the Gospel had addressed themselves only to their fellow
Jews or to the Samaritans, who might be considered as belonging to the same stock as Israel, or, again, to proselytes
already adopted into the Jewish people by the rite of circumcision; henceforth they will endeavor to make the Gentiles also disciples of Jesus and sharers in His Messianic
kingdom. As, however, St. Peter "had gone into men
uncircumcised and eaten with them," the Jewish Christians
found fault with such close fellowship, and were reconciled
with his line of action only when, upon his return to Jerusalem, he made it clear by his detailed recital of what had
happened, that from beginning to end he had acted by
divine commission.†

3. St. Peter in Antioch. It is not improbable that
this first admission of Gentiles into the Church without subjecting them to the rite of circumcision was considered by
the Jewish Christians of Jerusalem simply as an exception
granted by Heaven to Cornelius and a few of his friends;
and in point of fact, those of the Jewish Christians of the
Holy City who had been dispersed by the recent persecution, and had been preaching "as far as Phenicia, and
Cyprus and Antioch," continued to preach "to the Jews
only." ‡ Fortunately, a different view of the occurrence
was taken and acted upon by men less wedded to the old
Jewish notions. At their arrival in Antioch, men of Cyprus and Cyrene, treading in the footsteps of St. Peter,
preached the Gospel to the Gentiles of that city, and did

* Acts ix. 43–x.   † Acts xi. 1–18; xv. 7.   ‡ Acts xi. 19.

not impose upon their converts the obligation of being circumcised. Their conduct was wonderfully blessed by Heaven, and it soon afterwards received what may be considered the formal approval of the church of Jerusalem. This church, which still acted as the metropolis of the Messianic kingdom, sent Barnabas as far as Antioch, to inquire into the condition of the nascent Christian community of that city; and this official deputy approved heartily all that he noticed there, because he clearly recognized in it the effect of divine grace.*

It is difficult to state, in the present day, at what precise time the direct connection of St. Peter with the church of Antioch began. On the one hand, a tradition which goes back to the middle of the third century of our era affirms that the prince of the apostles was its founder and first bishop. On the other hand, the inspired book of the Acts clearly implies that a large and well-organized Christian community had been in existence in the capital of Syria long before St. Peter visited it in person.†

§ 4. *Persecution under Herod Agrippa I.*‡

1. Herod Agrippa I.: The Man and His Rule. With the accession of Claudius, the successor of Caligula, to the empire, the power of a grandson of Herod the Great, named Herod Agrippa I., reached the highest point, for to the territories already bestowed upon him by Caligula, the new emperor added those of Judæa and Samaria. The man who thus became king of "all Judæa," as Josephus puts it, had hitherto been a bold adventurer who showed himself wherever he went a crafty, frivolous and extravagant prince ; and of course, when he took possession of his new estates,

---

* Acts xi. 20–24.

† Cfr. Acts xi. 24 sq. ; see also Tillemont, Mémoires, tome i., art. xxvii ; Döllinger, Origines du Christianisme, vol i., p. 56 ; Fouard, St. Peter, chap. ix.

‡ Acts xii.

he did not think for a moment of seriously amending his evil ways. All that he cared for, in fact, during the three years of his rule, was to be well with the Pharisees, who then held the nation under their control. With this end in view he selected Jerusalem as his usual place of residence, carried out with punctiliousness the Jewish observances, and showed himself a zealous defender of the interests of Judaism at home and abroad.[*]

2. Martyrdom of St. James. Arrest and Deliverance of St. Peter.

It was simply in harmony with his constant Judaistic policy, that Herod Agrippa I. should sooner or later "stretch forth his hands to afflict some of the Church." The first victim of this new persecution—which apparently aimed at the heads of the nascent Church—was no less a personage than James, the brother of John, who formerly had asked Jesus to allow him to sit at His right hand in His kingdom, and who now was the first of the twelve to drink of His chalice.[†] James was beheaded, that is, suffered a death which was at that time regarded as most disgraceful by the Jews, and which, on that very account, was most welcome to the hatred of the Jewish leaders and people. This King Agrippa perceived, and was therefore encouraged to proceed farther. In consequence, Peter, the well-known leader of what was then considered as a sect, was arrested, and detained in prison with the utmost care, till the Paschal festivities, already begun, should be over. The intention of the tyrant was himself to sentence his prisoner to death in the presence of the countless Jewish multitudes which had gathered in Jerusalem from all quarters of the world for the Paschal festival, but his hope was frustrated at the last moment. The very night which was to precede the condemnation and death of the prince of the apostles was

---

[*] Cfr. JOSEPHUS, Antiq. of the Jews, book XIX., chap. vi. sq.; and SCHÜRER, division i., vol. ii., pp. 150–165.

[†] Cfr. MATT. xx. 22, 23.

marked by his miraculous deliverance, which is so graphically described in the inspired narrative.* The next
morning came, and as it was impossible to find Peter,
who had prudently betaken himself to a sure hiding place,
the mortification and rage of the king knew no limits ; the
keepers of the prison were tried and put to death, and the
king himself withdrew to Cæsarea.† There it was, that, while
delivering a solemn discourse, Agrippa did not object to the
blasphemous exclamation of the people : "It is the voice
of a god, and not of a man"; whereupon he felt himself
stricken with a frightful disease which soon carried him to
the grave. This sudden death of the king (A.D. 44) seems
to have brought the persecution to an end. ‡

The inspired narrative of Agrippa's death found in the
book of the Acts is in perfect harmony with the description
of the same fact in Josephus, § for while the main incidents
are identical, the differences are not greater than might be
anticipated between two independent narratives of the same
event.

**3. Tradition respecting the Departure of the
Apostles from Jerusalem.** Among the various traditions
connected with the early times of the Church, there is one to
which much credence has been given by several ecclesiastical writers. This tradition is recorded by Eusebius, who
tells us ‖ that one of the Christian apologists of the beginning of the third century, named Apollonius, mentions " as
handed down by the elders, that Our Saviour commanded
His disciples not to depart from Jerusalem for twelve years."
This length of time before the departure of the apostles
from the Holy City seems, indeed, required by the manner
in which the book of the Acts describes the events it re-

* Acts xii. 1–11.
† Acts xii. 12–19.
‡ Acts xii. 20–24.
§ Antiq. of the Jews, book XIX., chap. viii., § 2.
‖ Ecclesiastical History, book V., chap. xviii.

cords, and this was distinctly realized by Cardinal Baronius (1538–1607) ; but it is difficult to reconcile it with other traditions, which make St. Peter go to Rome before 42 A.D. and preach the Gospel to several Asiatic provinces before he arrived at the capital of the Roman empire.*

* Cfr. TILLEMONT, Mémoires, vol. i., art. xxvii., xxviii., and note 6, sur St. Matthieu; see also FOUARD, St. Peter, chap. xi., p. 190 sq.

SYNOPSIS OF CHAPTER XXII.

St. Paul's Life and Work before his First Missionary Journey.

I. His Early Life:
1. Date and Place of Birth (Tarsus "no mean city ").
2. Parentage and Home Training: { Religious and secular knowledge. Tent-making.
3. Education in Jerusalem : Rabbinical training under Gamaliel.
4. St. Paul's Celibacy.

II. His Conversion:
1. Share of Paul in the Martyrdom of St. Stephen.
2. Paul's Commission to Damascus (Acts ix. 1, 2).
3 The Conversion of St. Paul: (Acts. ix. 3–19, etc.) { Its threefold account. The vision of Christ.
4. Sojourn in Arabia (Galat. i. 15–17).

II'. His Work before his First Missionary Journey:
1. In Damascus: { The city described. Enmity encountered by St. Paul. His flight.
2. In Jerusalem: { Paul and Barnabas. Paul and the apostles. Paul and the Hellenists.
3. In Tarsus (Acts ix. 30; Galat. i. 21 sq.).
4. In Antioch: Successful Preaching of Paul and Barnabas. The Name of Christians.
5. In Jerusalem Again : Relief to the Poor of Judæa.

CHAPTER XXII.

§ 1. *St. Paul's Early Life.*

1. **Date and Place of Birth.** Saul, whose first hatred against the followers of Christ, and whose subsequent zeal for the spread of the Gospel, are so intimately connected with the early trials and triumphs of the Church in Palestine, was born in the first years of the Christian era. Although this is only an approximate date, and one inferred from indirect statements of Holy Writ,* yet, owing to the extensive information we possess about the history of the time, it is close and certain enough to allow us a distinct insight into the features of the period and the circumstances of the world at the beginning of St. Paul's life.

The place of his birth is known with greater accuracy, for we have his own explicit statement that he was "born at Tarsus in Cilicia." † This was, as St. Paul says, "no mean city." ‡ It had already given birth to several illustrious men, and had been made by Augustus the capital of Cilicia, one of the most important Roman provinces in the southeast of Asia Minor. It was situated in a wide and fertile plain, and was, in the time of St. Paul, a large commercial centre which communicated on the south with the Mediterranean Sea, by the navigable river Cydnus, while on the north it was connected with the central districts of the Asiatic peninsula, by two important roads which passed

---

* Cfr. ACTS vii. 57 ; ix. 1, 2 ; PHILEMON 9.   † ACTS xxii. 3.   ‡ ACTS xxi. 39.

through the defiles of the Taurus range. It was a free city,
possessed a Roman stadium and gymnasium, and one of the
three great universities of the pagan world, ranking next to
Athens and Alexandria in respect of literary fame. Unfortunately for its numerous and thriving population, Tarsus
was also noted for its moral and religious corruption, its
tutelary god being no other than the infamous Sardanapalus,
its supposed Assyrian founder.

2. **Parentage and Home Training.** Like all the large
and flourishing cities of the Roman Empire, the capital of
Cilicia counted among its citizens a multitude of Jews, who
gloried in their title of members of God's chosen people.
To these dispersed children of Israel belonged both the
father and the mother of the future Apostle of the Gentiles.
His father claimed descent from the tribe of Benjamin, and,
although a Roman citizen, was a strict Pharisee, who faithfully circumcised his child on the eighth day and trained
him early in the customs and prejudices of the Pharisaic
party. From infancy the young Saul—called also Paul, a
Latin name given him for public use and very proper in a
Roman citizen—repeated the words of the Sh^ema^c * and
of the Hallel, and when six years old became a day-scholar
at the school of some Jewish master. From a few quota-
tions from Greek authors which are found in his later
speeches and epistles, some have inferred that Paul received
his early education and acquired his knowledge of Greek
literature in the flourishing pagan schools of Tarsus. But
this is highly improbable, for his father, a strict Pharisee,
would not have allowed it.

In conformity with the custom of the time and the recommendations of the Jewish rabbis, Saul learned a trade.
That chosen for him by his parents was naturally connected
with the circumstances of the country where they dwelt.
viz., that of tent-making.† The term denotes the art of

---

*DEUTER. vi. 4-9; xi. 13-17; NUMB. xv. 37-41.   † ACTS xviii. 3.

making, from the hair of the Cilician goats, a coarse cloth used in preference to every other kind for tent covers.

3. **Education in Jerusalem.** It was apparently when still quite a youth[*] that Paul repaired to Jerusalem, where his sister seems to have been settled,[†] and where he could easily follow the course of instruction given to future rabbis; for he perhaps purposed from that early age to pursue their avocation in life. There sacred learning had ever been imparted by great masters, and at this particular time none taught the Law of Moses and the traditions of the fathers with greater success than Gamaliel, a Pharisee of unquestioned orthodoxy, although he was well known as a student of Gentile literature. Under this great teacher, Saul became intimately acquainted with Holy Writ and with the interpretations of the Jewish schools, as is evidenced by his frequent and characteristic use of the sacred text in his various epistles. It was also at this time, and not unlikely at the school of Gamaliel, that he acquired some knowledge of the Greek language and literature. But while his mind thus underwent the influence of the great Jewish teacher, his natural character was in no way affected by what seems to have been the liberal and tolerant spirit of Gamaliel. [‡] Saul gradually became a stern and impetuous zealot of the Mosaic Law, and it is likely enough that after having finished his studies at Jerusalem and returned to Tarsus, he soon began some extensive missionary journeys, after the example of the Scribes mentioned by St. Matthew (xxiii. 15).

4. **St. Paul's Celibacy.** St. Paul was all the more free to pursue such missionary journeys because he does not seem to have ever been married. [§] This fact has indeed been denied by many Protestants desirous to draw therefrom an argument against sacerdotal and religious celibacy. But an impartial study of history clearly proves that outside

---

[*] Acts xxvi. 4.
[‡] Cfr. Acts v. 34 sq.
[†] Acts xxiii. 16.
[§] I Cor. vii. 7.

two or three early ecclesiastical writers,* who based their view on a wrong interpretation of such passages as Philip. iv. 3, 1 Cor. vii. 8, the opinion that St. Paul ever married has no ground in tradition.   As to the reason more recently advanced, that he must have married because he was a member of the Sanhedrim, it can easily be disposed of.   It is only an inference from a passage of the book of the Acts (xxvi. 10), which may, and in fact must, be understood differently because of the little likelihood that "a Tarsian Jew, a Hellenist by birth and a comparative stranger in Jerusalem, would be admitted into the august body of the Sanhedrim." †

§ 2. St. Paul's Conversion (31 or 32 A.D.).

1. Share of Paul in the Martyrdom of St. Stephen. When Paul returned to Jerusalem the disciples of Jesus had greatly multiplied, and Stephen, the first and foremost of the newly ordained deacons, was boldly sustaining a series of disputations with the Hellenistic Jews of different synagogues, among which was reckoned that "of them of Cilicia." ‡ In this synagogue Saul of Tarsus would certainly be told the words of the holy deacon—if indeed he did not hear them himself—which could be construed into blasphemous expressions against Moses and against God, and with his burning zeal for the authority of the one and for the glory of the other, he openly rejoiced at, and probably shared in, the arrest of St. Stephen.   Although it does not appear, as some authors affirm, that Saul was one of the judges who sentenced Stephen to death, yet it cannot be denied that he was one of the most prominent instigators of the attack against him, and that he heartily consented to his execution, for we read in the book of the Acts that " the witnesses laid down their garments at the feet of a young man, whose

---

* CLEMENT of Alexandria, ORIGEN, EUSEBIUS.
† GLOAG, Life of Paul, p. 19.   ‡ ACTS vi. 9.

name was Saul," and again, that "Saul was consenting to the death of St. Stephen." *

2. **Paul's Commission to Damascus.** In the severe persecution which followed St. Stephen's death, the fiery zeal of Saul against the disciples of Christ made of him the very best instrument which the Jewish chief priests could desire. Armed with their authority " he made havoc with the Church, entering in from house to house, and dragging away men and women, committed them to prison." † " Oftentimes he punished the believers in every synagogue, and compelled them to blaspheme" the holy name of Jesus.‡ It was in the midst of such cruel deeds, perpetrated, however, with the most sincere desire to do what was right,§ that Saul heard that the so-called sect he hoped utterly to exterminate had actually gained a footing in the great city of Damascus, some 135 miles north of Jerusalem. At this news his rage knew no bounds, and he resolved at once to leave the Holy City, where many others could continue the persecution, and to repair to a place where there was as yet no one to carry on the work of destruction. He therefore went to the high priest, whose authority as the head of the Sanhedrim would certainly be recognized by the numerous Jews of Damascus, and easily got letters empowering him " to bring bound to Jerusalem " any men or women belonging to what he considered a most hateful sect. ‖

3. **Conversion of St. Paul.** It was on his way to Damascus and when very near the city—perhaps on the spot now occupied by ancient Christian tombs, to the southeast of Damascus—that Saul was favored with that wonderful apparition of Jesus, which transformed him from the deadliest enemy of Christ into His most fervent disciple. As he and his companions hastened on, suddenly at mid-day there

---

* ACTS vii. 57 b, 59 b. † ACTS viii. 3. ‡ ACTS xxvi. 10, 11.
§ ACTS xxvi. 9. ‖ ACTS ix. 1, 2.

shone round about him a great light from heaven, and Saul fell to the earth in terror, while a voice sounded in his ears: "Saul, Saul, why persecutest thou Me?" Whereupon followed the well-known dialogue between Jesus of Nazareth and His fear-stricken persecutor, which convinced Saul of the Messiahship of Jesus and of his own mistaken zeal against the followers of Christ. Blinded by the dazzling light,[*] he was led by his companions into Damascus, where "he was three days without sight, and did neither eat nor drink."[†] Ananias, a disciple who lived in the city, was informed in a vision of what had happened to Saul, and was sent to restore his sight and admit him by baptism into the Christian Church.[‡]

Of this wonderful event we have a threefold account in the book of the Acts: the first is given by the sacred historian himself ;[§] the second is found in an address of St. Paul to the people ;[‖] the third is also recorded in St. Paul's words, in his speech before King Agrippa II.[¶] A careful comparison of this threefold account discloses differences, which several rationalists have magnified and made out to be contradictions impairing the very substance of the facts narrated. But unbiased critics, both within and without the Church, while admitting important differences in the line of additions, omissions or even discrepancies, [**] have clearly shown that these differences cannot be supposed to "constitute a valid argument against the general truth of the narrative."[††]

Rationalists have also done their utmost to do away with the miraculous element which is clearly implied in the sacred narrative. They do not, indeed, deny that Paul believed that he had actually seen the Lord, but they suggest

---

* Acts xxii. 11.   † Acts ix. 9.   ‡ Acts ix. 10–16.
§ Acts ix. 3–19.   ‖ Acts xxii. 6–21.   ¶ Acts xxvi. 12–18.
** Cfr., for instance, Acts ix. 7, with Acts xxii. 9, and xxvi. 14.
†† Encyclopædia Britannica, art. Paul; see also T. Lewin, Life and Epistles of St. Paul, vol. i , p. 49, note 33 ; Fouard, St. Peter, p. 118, footnote 2.

many " explanations of the possible ways by which he may
have mistaken an inward impression for an objective fact."*
Perhaps the least fanciful of these explanations is that which
represents Saul as a man of exalted and enthusiastic temperament, who, even after his conversion, was in the habit
of seeing visions and falling into trances, and who consequently was most liable to confound the subjective impression for the objective reality, in connection with the first
vision which befell him on his way to Damascus, when in a
state of approaching frenzy. His excited imagination, we
are told, created the image of Jesus, and made him
fancy that he heard His voice saying : " Saul, Saul, why
persecutest thou Me ? " the voice which he heard being
nothing but the echo of his own conscience, which on the
occasion of a natural phenomenon, such as a thunder-storm
and a flash of lightning, upbraided him with all his past
cruelty towards the followers of Christ.

The best refutation of this supposed explanation will
ever be the simple perusal of the sources of information regarding the apparition of Jesus to Saul, for such a perusal
is amply sufficient to convince any unprejudiced mind that
the theory in question, far from accounting for, really dis-
torts, the best ascertained facts of the case.†

4. **Sojourn in Arabia.**‡ As we learn from his Epistle
to the Galatians, St. Paul withdrew from Damascus soon
after his conversion. He went to Arabia, whereby is meant,
not the peninsula of Sinai, but rather the country to the
east of the Jordan and not far from Damascus, a city which,
in St. Paul's time, bordered on Arabian territory and was under the government of an Arabian king. The exact length
of his sojourn is unknown. " He himself tells us that it was
not until three years after his conversion that he went up

* IVERACH, St. Paul, His Life and Times, p. 21 sq.
† For a detailed examination of the theory, see C. A. Row, Christian Evidences, 4th
edition, p. 404 sq.
‡ GALAT. i. 15-17.

to Jerusalem ; * and the probability is that the greater part
of these three years was spent in Arabia."† Nor do we
know for sure the kind of occupation to which he devoted
his time, although it is most likely that this was not for him
a period of missionary activity, but rather a season of seclusion and prayer, during which the risen Saviour favored
his new and fervent disciple with further light concerning
his future mission and the deep mysteries of faith he was
soon to preach to the world. ‡

§ 3. *St. Paul's Work before his First Missionary Journey.*

1. In Damascus. § Few cities of the Roman Empire
had a finer location than the city of Damascus, to which
St. Paul first preached the Gospel on his return from Arabia.
Situated at the base of the Anti-Lebanon range, in a circu-
lar plain about 30 miles in diameter, and rendered most
fertile by the waters of the Barada river, which runs directly
through the city, Damascus ever was a great centre of trade
between Assyria and the East generally, and Phenicia, Palestine and Egypt on the west. " The old city—the nucleus
of the present Damascus—is oval in shape, and surrounded
by a wall, the foundations of which are Roman, if not
earlier, and the upper part a patch-work of all subsequent
ages. Its greater diameter is marked by the **Straight
Street,** which is an English mile in length. At its east
end is **Bab Shurkey,** 'the East Gate,' a fine Roman
portal, having a central and two side arches. The central
and southern arches have been walled up for more than
eight centuries, and the northern now forms the only entrance to the city.   In the Roman age, and down to the
time of the Mohammedan conquest (A.D. 634), a noble
street ran in a straight line from the gate westward through
the city. It was divided by Corinthian colonnades into

---

* GALAT. i. 18.   † GLOAG, Life of Paul, p. 28.
‡ Cfr. GALAT. i. 11, 12 ; see also FOUARD, St. Peter, p. 124.   § ACTS ix. 19 b-25.

three avenues, opposite to the three portals. A modern street runs in the line of the old one, but it is narrow and irregular. Though many of the columns remain, they are mostly hidden by the houses and the shops." *

In St. Paul's time there were probably no less than 50,000 Jews in Damascus, and it is to them that the great Apostle fearlessly preached Jesus as "the Son of God," and "the Christ." It is easy to imagine the utter amazement of his hearers when for the first time they heard such declarations from the lips of one who, not long before, " had come hither for that intent that he might carry bound to the chief priests, those that called upon the name of Jesus." Next they argued with him, but they were clearly and repeatedly unable to withstand the powerful affirmations of Saul, who joined to a rabbinical learning far superior to theirs, the strong conviction of a recent eye-witness of Christ's glory. As time went on and simply brought the confusion of their defeats into stronger light, they resolved to take away his life. Using their influence with the governor of Damascus, under Aretas the king, they obtained from him soldiers whom they set at the gates, watching day and night lest Paul should escape. But their rage proved less successful than the devotion of the disciples, who, during the night, let him down the wall in a basket through a window of one of those houses which in Eastern cities overhang the city wall.†

2. **In Jerusalem.**‡ Driven from Damascus, St. Paul betook himself to Jerusalem in order "to see Peter," the head of the Church. His arrival in the Holy City caused much terror to the faithful, who still remembered his persecuting fury, and could not bring themselves to believe in the sincerity of his conversion. One of them, however, better informed about the events of the last three years,

---

* J. L. PORTER, the Giant Cities of Bashan, p. 349.   † Cfr. 2 COR. xi. 32, 33.
‡ ACTS ix. 26-30; GALAT. i. 18-20.

"took him and brought him to the apostles," that is, to Peter and James, as we learn from the Epistle to the Galatians.* This was Barnabas, whose generosity in selling his possessions had formerly edified the faithful of Jerusalem, and whose influence in the Church contributed now largely to remove the popular prejudice against St. Paul.

We have no means of knowing what took place in this first interview between Paul and the apostles Peter and James. From both, the future Apostle of the Gentiles naturally learned much about the person of Christ, whom he had never seen in the flesh, and about His teachings as they were then understood and preached; while they in turn heard with joy and profit from the mouth of this "vessel of election" the account of his conversion and of all that had followed on it. Whether the great question of the exact relation of Christianity to the Gentile world was one of the topics spoken of on this occasion, does not appear. Of course it had not yet assumed the distinct importance which we know it possessed at the time of a later visit of St. Paul to Jerusalem; † yet even at this early stage of his work this great question had perhaps already confronted the mind of the great Apostle of the Gentiles, for we read that during his first sojourn in the Holy City he spoke not only to the Jews, but also to the Gentiles.‡

The Jewish synagogues to which St. Paul had access in Jerusalem were naturally those of the Hellenistic Jews, his companions in race and birthplace, and in them the former persecutor of the followers of Christ did not fear to proclaim the Messiahship of Jesus. His opponents were worsted by his arguments in Jerusalem, as they had been in Damascus, and in their wrath against one whom they considered a dangerous apostate, "they sought to kill him." Whereupon the brethren, most anxious to preserve the life of one

---

* GALAT. i. 18, 19.   † GALAT. ii. 1 sq.   ‡ ACTS ix. 29.

whose testimony to Christ was of such importance, "brought Paul to Cæsarea, and sent him away to Tarsus."

Thus ended this short sojourn of St. Paul near St. Peter and St. James, false reports of which were later circulated by his enemies, and which compelled him to conclude his brief account of it to the Galatians with the solemn attestation: "Now the things which I wrote to you behold, before God, I lie not."

3. **In Tarsus.*** It may be inferred from his Epistle to the Galatians that in repairing to his native city, St. Paul, sailing from Cæsarea of Palestine, stopped at Seleucia, the port of Antioch, and there went on by land to Tarsus. This gave him an opportunity to preach Christ and to make in those parts of Syria and Cilicia which he then traversed, many converts, whom he revisited later on. †

This was the first time that St. Paul returned to his native town since he had become a follower of Christ, and it would be interesting for us to know the impression which his arrival and prolonged sojourn produced upon his family and upon his fellow countrymen. It has been surmised— and indeed not without probability—that he spent his time preaching the Gospel and preparing in various ways, notably by the culture of Greek language and philosophy, for his future labors among the Gentiles ; yet it must be confessed that we have no positive evidence to that effect.‡

4. **In Antioch.** § The next time we hear explicitly of St. Paul's work before his first great missionary journey is in connection with Barnabas, whom the church of Jerusalem had lately deputed to Antioch, and who, being desirous to secure for himself effective help in the great work to be accomplished in the capital of Syria, "went to Tarsus to seek Saul; whom, when he had found, he brought to Antioch." Barnabas had judged rightly in selecting St. Paul as

---

* ACTS ix. 30 ; GALAT. i. 21 sq.   † Cfr. ACTS xv. 41.
‡ Cfr. FOUARD, St. Peter, pp. 134, 135.   § ACTS xi. 25 sq.

his co-worker in what was at the time the largest as well as the most important city of the Roman Empire, after Rome and Alexandria. The population of Antioch was no less mixed than that of Tarsus, and its most numerous elements, the Syrians and the Greeks, while hardly less cultivated than those of the capital of Cilicia, even surpassed them in religious and moral degradation. Like Tarsus, also, Antioch counted many and influential Jews among its inhabitants, and their faithfulness to monotheism, combined with their highly moral character, had made many proselytes to Judaism long before Christ's religion was preached within the walls of the Syrian capital. It thus appears that the commercial, political, religious and moral condition of Antioch was pretty much, although, of course, on a larger scale, of the same character as that of Tarsus, so that from his very arrival in the great metropolis of the East, St. Paul was able to realize the various needs and aspirations of its citizens, and to pursue for their conversion the same course of action which he had already employed with success in his own native city. In point of fact, during the whole year which Paul and Barnabas " spent there in the church, they taught a great multitude."

Thus did it come to pass that the faithful of Antioch, rapidly increasing in numbers chiefly drawn from the ranks of the Gentiles and clearly distinguished from the Jews by their non-reception of the circumcision, could no longer be considered either by the civil authorities or by the public at large, simply as one of the many sects of the Jewish religion. A new name was therefore invented to designate a party so important in the Syrian capital, and as many other names given to the political or religious parties of the time (such as, for instance, the **Cæsariani**, the **Pompeiani**, the **Herodiani**, etc.), the new designation was formed by adding the Latin termination "anus" to the name which the believers frequently called upon, and which outsiders naturally considered as the founder or author of the new party, "so that at Antioch the disciples were first named **Christians**," (in Latin "**Christiani**").

5. **In Jerusalem again.** While Paul and Barnabas were thus busily and successfully preaching the Gospel in Syria, "there came prophets from Jerusalem to Antioch," that is, men endowed not only with the gift of foretelling the future, but also with that of adapting their exhortations to the needs of their hearers.* Their precise object in coming to so distant a city—Antioch is some 300 miles north of Jerusalem—is not expressly stated in the sacred narrative. It may be supposed, however, that the constant and pressing needs of the Christians of the Holy City had induced them to go and solicit in behalf of their fellow-citizens the charity of the wealthy believers of the Syrian capital, who, differently from those of Jerusalem, had retained the ownership of their estates.

Be this as it may, one of these prophets foretold to the Antiochian church "that there should be a great famine over the whole world, which came to pass under Claudius." Moved to compassion by this painful intelligence, the Christians of Antioch contributed generously towards the funds, which the coming famine would render so much the more necessary for the relief of the poor of Judæa, and the sums thus collected were entrusted to no others than "Barnabas and Saul."†

Thus was St. Paul brought back to Jerusalem, where he remained, together with Barnabas, till "they had fulfilled their ministry"; after which, bidding farewell to the much-tried church of Judæa, and "taking with them John, who was surnamed Mark," they returned to Antioch.‡

---

* Cfr. 1 COR. xiv. 3, 5. † ACTS xi. 27-30.

‡ ACTS xii. 25. See RAMSAY, Paul the Traveller, pp. 52, 61.

SYNOPSIS OF CHAPTER XXIII.

St. Paul's First Missionary Journey.

I. THE DEPARTURE (Acts xiii. 1–3).	1. The Ordination by the Church of Antioch. 2. Object of the Mission Entrusted to Paul and Barnabas. 3. John (Mark) accompanies them.

II. THE JOURNEY: (Acts xiii. 4; xiv. 25).	1. Cyprus:	Physical, political and religious condition of the island of Cyprus. Apostolic work in Salamis and Paphos.	
	2. Asia Minor:	Physical, political and religious condition of this peninsula. Successful preaching in, and return through	Antioch of Pisidia. Iconium. Lystra. Derbe.
	3. Duration of the Journey.		

III. EVENTS BETWEEN FIRST AND SECOND MISSIONARY JOURNEYS:	1. In Antioch : Important Controversy about the Circumcision of the Gentile Converts.	
	2. The Council in Jerusalem:	The discussions before and during the public meeting. The apostolic decree (how far a compromise ?)
	3. In Antioch : Paul's Contest with Cephas (Galat. ii. 11–23).	

258

CHAPTER XXIII.

§ 1. *The Departure.* *

1. The Ordination by the Church of Antioch.
Upwards of ten years had already elapsed since St. Paul's conversion, and during all that time he had been faithful not to anticipate the moments of Divine Providence, and had waited patiently for the day when his special calling to preach Christ to the Gentile world † should receive the solemn sanction of the Church. At length that day came, and brought to him, together with the long-desired leave to enter upon an extensive missionary journey, the greater fulness of the Holy Spirit needed to discharge successfully the duties of the apostolate. ‡

Of this memorable day in the history of Gentile Christianity only a few details have come down to us in the book of the Acts. We are simply told that, some time after the return of Barnabas and Saul to Antioch, the heads of the Christian Church in that city, officiating on a solemn occasion with which fasting was connected—a fact which has led some authors to think of the prolonged fast observed by the Jews as preparatory for the feast of Tabernacles—heard the voice of the Holy Ghost : " Separate me Saul and Barnabas, for the work whereunto I have taken them." Accordingly, " they having fasted and prayed, imposed their hands upon Saul and Barnabas and sent them away."

---

* ACTS xiii. 1-3.   † Cfr. ACTS ix. 15 ; xxii. 17-21, etc.   ‡ Cfr. ACTS xiii. 4.

2. Object of the Mission Entrusted to Paul and Barnabas. The sacred narrative does not state explicitly whether the " prophets and doctors" at the head of the Antiochian church were apprised of the exact kind of work to be accomplished by those upon whom they had to impose hands and confer the apostolic powers.* The expression "they sent Barnabas and Paul away" implies, however, that they thought them called to undertake some missionary journey to countries far from the confines of Palestine, as we see undertaken at once by the two new apostles.   There is also hardly any doubt—though this is not suggested by any expression of the sacred text—that they conceived of the future communities to be organized by Paul and Barnabas, as so many copies of the Antiochian church, that is, as made up of all those who would embrace the Christian faith, irrespective of their Jewish or Gentile origin.   It seems therefore very probable that the object of the mission entrusted to Paul and Barnabas was from the start to bring about the conversion of both Jews and Gentiles, although, as we shall soon have occasion to notice, the two missionaries preached first to the Hellenists, because the Jewish synagogues established through the various districts of the Roman Empire were places into which they were free to penetrate, and in which they knew they would be invited as strangers to address an exhortation to the assembled brethren.

3. John (Mark) accompanies Barnabas and Saul. The only companion spoken of in connection with the departure of the two apostles was a certain John, surnamed Mark, and a cousin of Barnabas.† On their return from the Holy City they had taken him to Antioch, and now he probably volunteered to follow them, with the hope, no doubt, to be helpful in their missionary labors, but also, not unlikely, with the desire to visit the island of Cyprus, to which they

* Cfr. Acts xiv. 13.   † Colos. iv. 10.

first directed their course, and which was the home of Barnabas, and consequently also of several relations of Mark. In point of fact, it is worthy of notice that the departure of the apostles from Cyprus to evangelize other countries was speedily followed by Mark's return to Jerusalem.[*]

As to the kind of services John-Mark rendered to Paul and Barnabas while he was with them, we have no positive information. It has been surmised, however, with a fair amount of probability, that as they would be very busy preaching the Gospel, he would be useful to them in baptizing their numerous converts. [†]

§ 2. *The Journey.* [‡]

1. **Cyprus.** Leaving Antioch, Paul and Barnabas went to Seleucia, some 16 miles distant, and from this fine harbor of the Syrian capital they soon set sail for the island of Cyprus, about 100 miles to the southwest. This island, the third largest in the Mediterranean Sea, was still at the time one of the famous spots in the world for the beauty of its forests, the fertility of its plains, and especially the importance of its copper mines. Although deprived of natural ports, it had long been a flourishing and populous island, and in the apostolical age it numbered several important towns, two of which, **Salamina** and **Paphos**, are named in the sacred narrative.[§]

Cyprus, like all the islands of the Mediterranean, enjoyed no longer its autonomy, and for well-nigh a century had been subjected to Roman rule. It was only of late, however, that, ceasing to be an imperial province, that is, one depending directly on the emperor, it had become a senatorial province, whereby was meant one whose rule was directly in the hands of the Roman senate, and whose affairs were administered by a magistrate bearing the title of

---

* ACTS xiii. 13. † Cfr. 1 COR. i. 14, 17.
‡ ACTS xiii. 4; xiv. 25. § ACTS xiii. 5, 6.

proconsul, as is accurately stated in the bock of the Acts (xiii. 7).

Nor is the sacred narrative less accurate when, speaking of several Jewish synagogues in the single city of Salamina, it gives us to understand that Cyprus counted a large number of Jews among its inhabitants, for it is well known from other sources that the children of Israel had gone thither in great numbers, attracted chiefly by advantageous leases of the copper mines. They lived side by side and apparently in perfect harmony with the Greek population, a fact which did not prevent them from remaining faithful to the strict monotheism and high morality of their ancestors. Indeed, the immoral worship of Aphrodite or Venus in its most degrading form, which prevailed throughout the island, was doubtless calculated to strengthen their attachment to the pure worship of Jehovah.

Paul and Barnabas landed in Salamina, the eastern port and ancient capital of Cyprus, and "preached the word of God in the synagogues of the Jews." Thence, going "through the whole island," from east to west, preaching most likely in the various towns they met on their way, they reached Paphos, at the southwestern extremity of Cyprus. This was the residence of the Roman proconsul, Sergius Paulus, a man of noble lineage and not unlikely to be identified with the personage of the same name spoken of in Pliny, and with the "proconsul Paulus" mentioned in a Cypriote inscription recently discovered. The preaching of Paul and Barnabas soon came to the notice of this "prudent man," who, being desirous to hear them, sent for the apostles of the new faith. Near him, however, was a false prophet, whose name was Bar-Jesu, and who, feeling he would lose much of his own influence if the proconsul should become a Christian, did everything in his power to "turn him away from the faith." But this very opposition of the false prophet became the occasion of a striking miracle,

which St. Paul performed in presence of the proconsul and
which convinced him of the truth of Christianity.

It is from the time of this journey to Cyprus that the
book of the Acts designates Saul under the name of Paul,
which naturally enough became most current in the Christian churches which were founded among the Gentiles.*

2. Asia Minor. We are not told how long Paul and
Barnabas remained in Paphos and its vicinity after the conversion of Sergius Paulus, and before setting sail for the
western part of the Asiatic continent, to which, since the
fifth century of our era, the name of Asia Minor is very
commonly applied. This is a peninsula washed by three
seas—the Black, the Archipelago or Ægean, and the Mediterranean, and connected on the east with Armenia and the
rest of the continent by a tract of land, which presents no
natural boundary simply because Asia Minor is nothing but
the western continuation of the high table-land of Armenia,
with its border mountain-ranges to the north and to the
south. Its principal chain of mountains is Mount Taurus,
some points of which reach an altitude of 12,000 feet, and
its best-known rivers are the Cydnus, the Mæander and the
Halys. The total area of the peninsula is not far from
300,000 square miles, or a little more than four times the
area of the New England States.

This vast extent of territory, no less varied in its productions than in the races of which its population was made up,
was covered with "numerous communities ruled partly by
Roman prefects and partly by petty kings and potentates,
feudatories of the empire. The dominion of Rome
over these parts had been established for more than a
century, and the political divisions introduced by Rome,
which were quite independent of nationalities, had tended
strongly to break down the barriers of race and fuse the

---

* For further details concerning St. Paul's preaching in Cyprus, see FOUARD, St. Paul
and his Missions, chap. i.; LEWIN, i., chap. viii.; RAMSAY, St. Paul, chap. iv.

heterogeneous materials into one consistent mass. But though much had been done in this way, the distinctive features of the discordant peoples were still in the main preserved.

"The entire peninsula was given to idolatry, and the several component states varied only in the particular objects of worship. The prevalent religion appears generally to have come from the East, but Greek and Roman influences had so modified the primitive systems, that in the first century of the Christian era the idolatry in vogue was scarcely distinguishable from that of Greece and Rome."[*]

The Jews, however, who formed a considerable element of the population, were a noble exception to that general rule, and in the synagogues they had erected in the principal towns, they courageously persevered in the monotheistic worship of their ancestors.

Such, then, was the general condition of Asia Minor when Paul and "they that were with him" landed in Pamphylia, the imperial province, on the west, and next to Cilicia, the native country of St. Paul. Although the Christian missionaries had probably intended to preach at once in the towns on the seashore, and in Perge, the capital of Pamphylia, which was also built in the lowlands between Mount Taurus and the Mediterranean Sea, it seems clear from the sacred narrative, that, for reasons left unrecorded, they did not at this time announce the Gospel there. Perhaps, as some have conjectured, this conduct of Paul and Barnabas may be ascribed to the fact that, having reached the alluvial plains of Pamphylia in the early summer, that is, at the time when the inhabitants of those parts had already withdrawn to the mountains to escape the fevers and other maladies usually entailed in the low region by the advent of the hot season, the two apostles resolved at once to push forward,

---

[*] Lewin, i., p. 131 sq.

and preach the word of God in the districts north of the Taurus range. *

It was through most insecure roads † that Paul and Barnabas—now deprived of the help of John-Mark, who had left them at Perge to return to Jerusalem—made their way northward to Antioch, "a prominent city of Phrygia, and the political centre of the southern half of the Roman province of Galatia." ‡   Here, as in every important city of the peninsula, the Jews had built a synagogue, to which the two apostles soon repaired on a Sabbath day, and in which they gladly availed themselves of the invitation extended to them to address the assembled brethren.   The recorded discourse of St. Paul on this occasion began, like that of St. Stephen, with an historical retrospect which led up to Jesus as the descendant of David, as the Saviour promised to the Jewish race, and whose rejection by the authorities at Jerusalem, and resurrection by God from the grave, fulfilled old prophecies and proved Him to be the true and only Messias in whom all should believe.   The effect produced by these words was very great : the apostles were invited to come and preach on the next Sabbath, and many of their hearers—Jews and proselytes—were actually won over to the faith. §

The next Sabbath day crowds flocked to the synagogue to listen to the Christian preachers, but this concourse excited the jealousy of the Jewish leaders, who began to argue against St. Paul, and who next uttered blasphemies against Jesus.   Whereupon the two apostles, seeing that further discussion would be of no avail, took a bold stand, and announced publicly that henceforth they would leave the Jews in their unbelief and preach to the Gentiles.   This they did, and with such success that the Gospel was soon spread throughout the whole region.   It is easy to imagine

---

* Cfr. FOUARD, St. Paul and his Missions, chap. ii. ; RAMSAY, St. Paul, chap. v.
† Cfr. 2 COR. xi. 26.   ‡ McGIFFERT.   § ACTS xiii. 13–43 ; cfr. McGIFFERT, p. 186.

the rage of the Jews at a success which all their efforts had
not been able to prevent, and to understand how, under the
pressure of their influence, the public authorities drove Paul
and Barnabas "out of their coasts." *

Expelled from Antioch, the apostles went to Iconium, a
city some 50 miles distant, and regarded by many as the
capital of a small tetrarchy under the suzerainty of Rome.
Here also great success attended their preaching, but
although their words were often confirmed by "signs and
wonders," the opposition of the Jews finally succeeded in
rendering their life so insecure that they fled into that part
of Lycaonia which was under Roman rule and comprised
the two cities of Lystra and Derbe, together with their surrounding territory.† The ministry of the apostles in this
district is not recorded in detail (except, however, what is
connected with the healing of a man crippled from his
birth, in Lystra), but there is no doubt that it was crowned
with success, and, in point of fact, we are told that Paul and
Barnabas "taught many" in Derbe. ‡

Having thus reached the very borders of the kingdom of
Antiochus, which limited on this side the Roman territory,
the apostles retraced their steps to Antioch of Pisidia,
through the cities of Lystra and Iconium.   They profited by
their return through these communities, to strengthen them
in the faith and to establish them on a permanent basis, by
setting over them men having grace and power to promote
their spiritual welfare.   Leaving Antioch, Paul and Barnabas
passed through Pisidia and came into Pamphylia, in the
capital of which they now preached the Gospel.   Finally
they went to Attalia, the most frequented seaport of the
coast of Pamphylia, and thence sailed to Antioch of Syria,
"whence they had been delivered to the grace of God, unto
the work which they accomplished." §

* ACTS xiii. 44–50.   † Cfr. RAMSAY, St. Paul, p. 110 sq.
‡ ACTS xiii. 51; xiv. 20.   § ACTS xiv. 20–25.

3. **Duration of the Journey.** It is impossible, in the present day, to give with anything like certainty the duration of this, St. Paul's first missionary journey, for Holy Writ nowhere states explicitly how long it lasted, and at no stage of it supplies sufficient data to determine accurately its duration. Combining, however, all the more or less indefinite marks of time which we notice in the book of the Acts as having a bearing on the point in question, together with the approximate extent of territory travelled over by the two apostles, it does not seem improbable that this journey covered a period of about two or three years, and is to be placed between 44 and 46 A. D. *

§ 3. *Events between First and Second Missionary Journeys.*

1. **In Antioch.** †   Soon after their return to the capital of Syria, Paul and Barnabas assembled the Church, and related joyfully "how great things God had done with them, and how He had opened the door of faith to the Gentiles." This was, of course, most gratifying news for the faithful of Antioch ; and they all rejoiced heartily that the mission entrusted to the two apostles had brought about the establishment of several churches after the model of the Antiochian church, that is, of Christian communities in which, on the one hand, the Gentile converts were not bound to receive circumcision, and on the other hand, the Jewish converts were allowed free intercourse with their uncircumcised brethren.

Unfortunately, this most legitimate joy of the church of Antioch was not of long duration.   The news of the return of the two missionaries and of their great success among the Gentiles had speedily reached Jerusalem, and had aroused there the greatest opposition to the teaching of Paul and Barnabas, who, it was understood, did not require of their Gentile converts that they should submit to the Mosaic

* Cfr. LEWIN, i., p. 156, footnote 1   † ACTS xiv. 26; xv. 2.

rite of circumcision and to all that it implied. The more extensive the success of Paul and Barnabas was reported to have been, the more strongly also was it felt by many Jewish Christians persuaded of the ever-binding character of the ritual Law of Moses, that it was necessary to combat without delay a doctrine which, in not imposing the rite of circumcision, set aside a mark which Holy Writ plainly described as absolutely required to become a member of God's chosen people, which Christ Himself had borne in His flesh, and which the apostles who had lived with Jesus had hitherto imposed. In consequence, some of these Jewish Christians started for Antioch, and apparently also for the churches of Galatia, and proclaimed loudly to the Gentile converts : "Except you be circumcised after the manner of Moses, you cannot be saved."

Great indeed was the excitement caused in the Antiochian church by this drastic teaching, and Paul and Barnabas found it difficult in the eyes of many to vindicate the orthodoxy of their doctrine, since it was in direct opposition to the positive teaching proclaimed by those who came from Jerusalem, the cradle and headquarters of Christianity. Their present authority, their future usefulness, the reality of the divine gifts bestowed upon their uncircumcised converts,* the utter impossibility of winning the nations to the Christian religion if the despised and hateful yoke of the circumcision and other Mosaic observances was to be put upon them, etc., made it incumbent upon Paul and Barnabas to meet with powerful arguments the bold assertions of their adversaries. But it soon became evident that the matter could not be settled in Antioch, and accordingly it was decided that Paul and Barnabas "and certain others on the other side should go up to Jerusalem to the apostles and priests about this question."

* Cfr. GALAT. iii. 2, 5, etc.

2. The Council of Jerusalem.* It must have been gratifying for the defenders of Gentile freedom to notice on their way through Phenicia and Samaria the great joy with which the news of the conversion of the nations was received from their mouth "by all the brethren." More gratifying still was it for them, when, reaching Jerusalem, they were welcomed "by the Church and by the apostles and ancients," and witnessed the favorable impression which their declarations of "how great things God had done with them" produced at once upon the bulk of the assembled Christians. Their joy, however, was much tempered by the emphatic protests of representatives of the Jewish Christian party, who soon openly declared that the Gentiles "must be circumcised, and be commanded to observe the Law of Moses." †

Then it was most likely that the private interview of St. Paul with the ecclesiastical authorities of Jerusalem, viz., Peter, James and John, took place, during which he exposed in detail his views, and obtained their explicit approval of his doctrine. It seems, however, that, as he was accompanied by Titus, an uncircumcised convert whom he had taken with him to Jerusalem, he was asked with a view to allay more easily the opposition, to have Titus circumcised; but to this Paul and Barnabas rightly and successfully objected, for their yielding on this point would have of course been construed into a condemnation of their own position.‡

In the public meeting held soon afterwards there was at first much disputation; but the discourse of St. Peter, who powerfully argued against putting an unnecessary and unbearable yoke upon the necks of the Gentile converts, silenced the opposition and settled the main question. Then followed a recital by Paul and Barnabas of the "great signs and wonders which God had wrought among

* 45 or 46 A.D.   † ACTS xv. 3-5.   ‡ GALAT. ii. 1-5.

the Gentiles by them," and which were so many striking proofs of God's approval of their own doctrine and conduct. But what completed the defeat of St. Paul's adversaries was the address of St. James, who, as the brother of the Lord and a strict Jew, wielded much power over the Jewish Christians of the Holy City. It had ever been the divine purpose, he said, that the Gentiles should be introduced into the Church in the manner in which this had been of late revealed to Simon Peter; he was therefore of the mind "that they who from among the Gentiles were converted to God, should not be disquieted." As, however, Mosaic regulations regarding some special points had been from time immemorial read publicly in the synagogues, he proposed that a letter should be sent to the Gentiles prescribing a line of action concerning those points.*

This proposal was unanimously accepted, and the letter prepared at once for "the brethren of the Gentiles that were at Antioch, and in Syria and Cilicia." After a clear disavowal of the teachers who had caused all the trouble, and an explicit approval of the doctrine and conduct of Paul and Barnabas, it was laid down by the church of Jerusalem that those to whom the letter was addressed "should abstain from things sacrificed to idols, and from blood, and from things strangled, and from fornication." "No farther burden was to be laid upon them," and the letter was entrusted to Paul and Barnabas, to whom Judas and Silas, two men of the greatest authority in Jerusalem, were joined to attest by word of mouth the genuineness of the letter.†

Such was that important decree of the assembly of Jerusalem. Perhaps it appeared to many, at the time when it was framed, a compromise between St. Paul and his opponents, a middle course between setting aside altogether the Mosaic Law, and imposing it in all its details. In reality it was a full vindication of the authority and doctrine

* ACTS XV. 6-21.   † ACTS XV. 21-29.

of St. Paul, and the actual giving up of the whole ritual law of Moses, since the regulations purely Mosaic contained in the decree were enjoined only upon the Christian communities nearest to Judæa.[*]

3. In Antioch. Paul's Contest.

Great indeed was the joy of the faithful of Antioch when on the return of Paul and Barnabas, accompanied by Judas and Silas, the official deputies of the church of Jerusalem, they heard the contents of the apostolic decree, and learned that James, Cephas (Peter) and John had approved the teaching of Paul and Barnabas without restriction, and "given them the right hands of fellowship."[†]

Peace and union had scarcely been restored in the Syrian capital when an event occurred which threatened again division for the Antiochian church. On a visit to Antioch St. Peter had first freely associated with uncircumcised converts, but he withdrew from their company at the news that some Judaistic teachers had come down from Jerusalem. This he did, as we learn from the Epistle to the Galatians, through "fear of them who were of the circumcision," and his example betrayed into a similar "dissimulation" not only the Jewish converts of Antioch, but even Barnabas himself. Whereupon St. Paul, feeling it was necessary to stop without delay what might easily become the cause of great disturbance in the church of Antioch, came boldly forward and rebuked Peter for his inconsistency. Owing to this valiant opposition of the Apostle of the Gentiles, Peter was adduced to side openly with him against the Judaistic teachers, and to proclaim in action that which he fully admitted in theory, viz., that "what God hath cleansed, no one should call common."[‡]

---

[*] Cfr. FOUARD, St. Paul, p. 75; RAMSAY, St. Paul, p. 173.

[†] ACTS xv. 30 sq.; GALAT. ii. 6 sq.

[‡] ACTS x. 15, 28; GALAT. ii. 11-21.

SYNOPSIS OF CHAPTER XXIV.

St. Paul's Second Missionary Journey.

(Acts xv. 36; xviii. 22.)

I.
THE
DEPARTURE:

1. Purpose of Second Missionary Journey.
2. The Com- Neither Barnabas, nor John panions of (Mark), but Silas first, Timothy St. Paul next, and Luke last of all.

II.
THE JOURNEY:

1. Visitation of Churches
In Syria and Cilicia.
In Southern Galatia (Derbe, Lystra, Iconium).

2. Foundation of Churches
In Northern Galatia? Two theories. Which more probable?
In Macedonia: Philippi. Thessalonica. Berea.
In Achaia: Athens. Corinth.

III.
THE RETURN:

1. By way of Ephesus, Cæsarea and Jerusalem.
2. Duration of St. Paul's Second Missionary Journey.

CHAPTER XXIV.

ST. PAUL'S SECOND MISSIONARY JOURNEY.

§ 1. *The Departure.*

1. Purpose of Second Missionary Journey. While peace and harmony prevailed in Antioch, and the efforts of Judaistic teachers against Gentile freedom were fully met there by St. Paul's unswerving courage, it seems probable that his adversaries were active and only too successful in disturbing and influencing the minds of the Christian communities which he and Barnabas had recently founded and organized in southern Galatia. To counteract this pernicious influence he first wrote to them, not unlikely from the Syrian capital, the epistle which is addressed " to the Galatians," from the name of the Roman province in which lay these various communities. To vindicate his apostolic authority he narrated to them all that had come to pass of late in Jerusalem and in Antioch, of which they had as yet heard nothing, and to confirm his own doctrine he appealed to powerful arguments within the reach of their intelligence. But although this letter should have been more than sufficient to restore the Galatians to right views about men and doctrines, the Apostle of the Gentiles still feared the influence of the Judaistic teachers who resided in the midst of his converts, and finally resolved to visit them in person. Antioch was at the time well supplied with Christian ministers, so that his presence and that of Barnabas could be easily dispensed with in the Syrian capital; he therefore said to Barnabas, his former fellow-worker in Galatia: "Let us return and visit our brethren in all the cities wherein we have preached the word of the Lord, to see how they do." *

2. **The Companions of St. Paul.** At first Barnabas accepted joyfully Paul's proposal to start together on a visitation tour through the countries they had already evangelized; yet he was not to be the actual companion of the Apostle of the Gentiles during this, his second missionary journey. He was naturally attached to John-Mark, his near relative, and now expressed the wish that he should accompany them. To this St. Paul objected positively, unwilling to have in his company a man on whose services he could not rely implicitly; hence a "dissension" arose between the two apostles, which, as Barnabas would in no way part with Mark, resulted in the separation of the former fellow-workers, and also in the formation of two apostolic bands instead of one; for while Barnabas sailed for Cyprus with Mark, St. Paul started by land through Syria and Cilicia, with Silas, one of the official deputies of the church of Jerusalem, who had become much attached to him.†

At an early stage of this second missionary journey another man, who soon became the dearest and surest friend of the great Apostle, joined Paul and Silas. This was Timothy, a young Christian of Lystra, whom St. Paul willingly accepted as his companion because of the high esteem in which he was held by the faithful of Lystra and Iconium, and who, "as a son with a father, served with Paul in the Gospel." ‡

The third and last companion of St. Paul to be mentioned is no other than the writer of the book of the Acts, who through modesty does not give his own name, but simply introduces himself as one of the missionary band by

---

* ACTS xv. 35, 36; see also McGIFFERT, pp. 226–230.
† ACTS xv. 37-41.
‡ ACTS xvi. 1 sq.; PHIL. ii. 20, 22.

using the first person "*we*" in the sacred narrative,* and
whom Christian tradition has ever considered as identical
with the Luke spoken of in the epistle to the Colossians †
in these affectionate terms : "Luke, the most dear physi-
cian, saluteth you." He seems to have joined Paul and
Silas about the middle of this missionary journey, at Troas,
and to have accompanied them only up to Philippi.‡

§ 2. *The Journey.* §

I. **Visitation of Churches.** Leaving Antioch to visit
the Christian communities already founded in Asia Minor,
Paul and Silas passed through Syria and Cilicia, carrying
with them the decree drawn up by the Council of Jerusalem. As the genuineness of this decree was put beyond all
doubt by the official testimony of Silas, and as its tenor
fully justified St. Paul's doctrine regarding the admission of
Gentile converts into the Christian Church, it is easy to
imagine the powerful effect produced by the presence and
words of the great Apostle upon the minds and hearts of
the faithful of those regions. The baneful influence of the
Jewish teachers, who had probably passed there some time
before on their way to the central districts of Asia Minor,
was more than counteracted and the great object of St.
Paul's visitation fully secured.‖

Encouraged by this happy beginning, the Apostle hastened
to cross the Taurus range, through the defiles known as the
Cilician Gates, and soon arrived at Derbe and Lystra, the
two cities he had visited last on his first missionary journey,
for he was now travelling in an opposite direction. Thence
he went to Iconium and other cities of southern Galatia,
making known to them the apostolic decree enacted at Je-

---

* Acts xvi. 10, 11, etc.   † Col. iv. 14.
‡ Acts xvi. 8-40. Regarding the authorship of the passages which contain the pro-
noun " we," see CRELIER, Actes, Préface, p. vii.; McGIFFERT, p. 236 sq., etc.
§ Acts xv. 40; xviii. 17.   ‖ Acts xv. 40, 41.

rusalem, and turning it into account to vindicate his authority and effectively confirm the churches in the doctrine
he had formerly preached to them. The promulgation far
and wide of the apostolic decree had a twofold further result : the influence of the Judaistic teachers was destroyed
forever, and next the conversion of numerous Gentiles,
hitherto delayed for fear of the hateful yoke of the circumcision, was actually effected.

It was also in this district that St. Paul, fully aware of
the moral worth of Timothy, and realizing all the help he
might derive from his services, resolved to take him along
on his mission. As, however, it was well known that Timothy was the child of a mixed marriage between a Gentile
and a Jewess, the Apostle thought it better to have him
circumcised, in order not to arouse the ill feeling of the
Jewish communities he might have an opportunity to
address in Asia Minor.*

2. **Foundation of Churches.** Thus supplied with a
most helpful and faithful companion, the Apostle of the
Gentiles started for the foundation of churches in countries
as yet unvisited, and here we meet with two theories as to
the direction which St. Paul took soon after leaving the
southern part of the Roman province of Galatia, whose various churches he had just confirmed in the Christian faith. †
According to the older, and, indeed, as yet the more common, theory, the Christian missionaries, successively prevented by divine guidance from preaching in Asia and
Bithynia, the two Roman provinces adjacent to the province
of Galatia, went from the districts of southern to those of
northern Galatia, whose inhabitants they converted in large
numbers, and to whom St. Paul addressed later on the letter
known as the Epistle to the Galatians. The more recent
theory holds, on the contrary, that the great Apostle did not

---

* ACTS xvi. 1–5. Cfr. RENAN, St. Paul, p. 124 sq. (Paris, 1883).
† ACTS xvi. 5.

go to the northern parts of the province of Galatia when prohibited to preach the Gospel in Asia and Bithynia, but simply passed through the Phrygian part of the province of Galatia and the territory of proconsular Asia till he reached Troas, on the western coast of Asia Minor, so that the Epistle to the Galatians would have been written, not for the spiritual welfare of churches founded at this time in northern Galatia, but for the churches of southern Galatia, which, as we have seen, he had founded at the time of his first missionary journey.

Although this second theory is not free from all difficulties, yet it seems on the whole much the more probable, chiefly because many things noticeable in the Epistle to the Galatians * lead us to believe that the epistle was written some time before St. Paul's departure from Antioch for his second missionary journey, that is, at a time when he had as yet evangelized only the southern regions of the Roman province of Galatia.†

However this may be, St. Paul, as bidden by the Holy Spirit, traversed proconsular Asia without preaching in it at this time, and reached the town of Troas, on the Ægean Sea, about 4 miles from ancient Troy and 6 miles south of the entrance to the Hellespont (the modern Dardanelles). Here he was joined by Luke, and while still uncertain as to the place to which he should now proceed beheld at night, " in a vision," a Macedonian supplicating him to cross to Europe and preach the Gospel in Macedonia. Considering this as a divine summons, the Apostle and his companions sailed without delay from Troas " and pursued the usual track towards Macedonia. As they had a fair wind, they voyaged the same day as far as Samothrace (still called Samothraki),

---

* Cfr., for instance, the account given therein of the events connected with the Council of Jerusalem.

† Cfr. FOUARD, St. Paul, p. 44, footnote 4 ; RAMSAY, The Church in the Roman Empire, p. 74 sq., and St. Paul the Traveller, p. 194 sq.; J. B. LIGHTFOOT, Comm. on Galatians.

an island some 8 miles long and 6 miles broad, lying half·
way between Troas and the Macedonian harbor.   The next
day they sailed to Neapolis," * a town in Thrace, and from
that port journeyed overland to Philippi, some 8 miles distant.   In this important city, a Roman colony—whether the
actual capital of the first division of Macedonia at this time
does not appear—the Jews were but an inconsiderable element of the population, which was made up mostly of Greek
natives and Latin colonists, so that there was apparently no
Jewish synagogue in Philippi, but only a **Proseucha** or
place of prayer by the river-bank without the walls.   Con-
formably to his custom of addressing himself first to the
Jews, St. Paul went on the Sabbath day to their place of
meeting and preached the Gospel there.   The result was
the conversion of Lydia, " a seller of purple, of the city of
Thyatira," and a person of influence and position.   For several weeks the Apostle and his companions pursued their
missionary work, and apparently with considerable success,†
until he was imprisoned, with Silas, for having expelled "a
pythonical spirit " from a certain slave girl, thereby caus·
ing pecuniary loss to her masters, who had hitherto derived profit from her vaticinations.   The whole narrative
of St. Paul's imprisonment and release on this occasion be-
speaks the Roman character of the city organization, a fact
which explains why the Apostle demanded of the magistrates that they should offer him and Silas a public apology
for having scourged two Roman citizens " uncondemned."
It may also be noticed here that several features and details
of the narrative of St. Paul's journey to and sojourn in
Philippi concur in suggesting that the inspired writer had
long been a resident in that city.‡

Paul and Silas, parting from Luke at Philippi, and accompanied by Timothy, started for Thessalonica, about 100

* Lewin, vol. i., p. 199 sq.   † Cfr. Acts xvi. 40.
‡ Cfr. Acts xvi. 6–40. See also Ramsay, St. Paul, pp. 201–210.

miles distant, to the southwest. On their way they passed though the towns of Amphipolis and Apollonia, and finally reached Thessalonica, the capital of Macedonia **Secunda,** a populous city, supplied with a fine harbor, on the Ægean Sea, and governed by its own magistrates. In this large and flourishing centre of commerce the Jews had settled in great numbers and erected a synagogue, to which St. Paul repaired on three successive Sabbaths, and in which he argued with his hearers that Jesus was indeed the Messias, whose life, sufferings, death, and resurrection were foretold in the Scriptures. His efforts were crowned with such success that the Jews, filled with envy, stirred up the rabble and set the city in an uproar, for the raising of which they made Paul and Silas responsible before the magistrates. They also accused the Christian missionaries of treason against Cæsar, for they represented them as preaching " that there is another king, Jesus." The calmness and firmness of the magistrates appeased, indeed, the popular tumult ; yet, because of the hatred of the Jews, the faithful of the city "immediately sent away Paul and Silas by night into Berea." *

In point of fact severe trials befell the Christians of Thessalonica soon after the departure of the Apostle—so much so that they longed for Christ's second coming, and, as they imagined that it was near at hand, many among them became addicted to idleness, while others, seeing persons most dear to them dying before Christ's actual return, gave way to immoderate grief. This we learn from the epistles which, only a few months after he had left them, St. Paul felt it necessary to write for their consolation and instruction. In these same epistles to the Thessalonians we find also a few details which complete the narrative of the book of the Acts regarding the foundation of the church of Thessalonica. We learn, for instance, that the Thessa-

* Acts xvii. 1-10.

lonians received with great joy the Gospel as "the word of God," that the report of their conversion "from idols" soon spread throughout Macedonia and Achaia, and finally that St. Paul during his sojourn in their midst supported himself by working at his trade of a tent-maker, an avocation he could all the more easily pursue in Thessalonica because "one of the staple manufactures of the city was and is goat's-hair cloth." *

At Berea, "a secluded town," as it is called by Cicero,† the Jews, whom St. Paul addressed in their own synagogue, listened willingly to his words, and applied to the study of Holy Writ to ascertain whether the arguments drawn from the Old Testament records were conclusive. Many conversions both of Jews and Gentiles ensued; but, unfortunately, the bigoted Jews of Thessalonica, hearing of the great success of the Christian missionaries at Berea, hastened thither, and "stirred up and troubled the multitude." So great, in fact, was the fury of these bigots against one whom they considered as an apostate from the Law of Moses that, St. Paul's life being positively insecure in Berea, the Apostle had to depart hurriedly, while Timothy and Silas remained behind.‡

It was with feelings of deep regret for leaving his work so incomplete in Macedonia that St. Paul took ship for Athens, the first large city of the province of Achaia. He knew that God had called him to evangelize Macedonia, and, hoping that the obstacles to his return thither should soon be removed by God's providence, he longed for the moment when Silas and Timothy should bring him from Berea the welcome news that it was safe for him to go back and visit the Macedonian churches.§

Athens, the ancient capital of Attica, in which the Apostle was now waiting, had at this time lost much of its polit-

---

* DODS, Introd. to New Testament, p. 153.   † In Pisonem, 36.
‡ ACTS xvii. 10-14.   § Cfr. 1 THESS. ii. 17; iii. 6.

ical importance and literary prestige.   Yet it was still a free
city, governed by three distinct assemblies, to wit : the
Areopagus, a kind of senate or supreme court ; the **Boule,**
or council of six hundred ; and the **People.**   It also occupied a prominent place in the world of letters by its univer-
sity, which still ranked at least on a par with those of
Alexandria and Tarsus, although large crowds of students
frequented it less for literary than for athletic purposes.
Indeed, in St. Paul's time Athens presented to the eyes of
the visitor a much finer appearance than in bygone days,
when its **Agora** or " Market," where St. Paul disputed
" daily," had not yet its area between the *four hills of Athens*
(the Areopagus, or Mars' Hill, and the Acropolis on the
north, the Pynx on the west, and the Museum on the
south), crowded with the finest temples, statues, altars, and
public buildings.   Of course it may well be supposed that
the Apostle, who spoke of his native place as "no mean
city" and was anxious to "see Rome," was not indifferent
to the sight of so many masterpieces of Grecian art ; one
feeling, however, was paramount in his heart : that of indignant zeal against a city whose countless idols proved to
evidence that it was " wholly given to idolatry."

While waiting for the arrival of Silas and Timothy St.
Paul lost no opportunity to address the Jews and proselytes
to Judaism in their synagogue meetings, and disputed daily
in the market-place " with them that were there."   His
preaching about " Jesus and the resurrection " seemed very
strange to the Epicurean and Stoic teachers of Athens who
argued with him, and many of the witnesses of these disputations, desirous to hear more about " certain new things "
they had caught but imperfectly amid the noise and bustle
of the Agora, took him to the Areopagus, and thus gave him
a splendid opportunity to expose his doctrine before the
senate and people of the city.   The address of St. Paul
from the top of this rocky eminence began with a happy al-

lusion to one of the many altars "to an unknown god" which then existed in Athens. This unknown God, he declared, was no other than the One whom he preached, and whom he described as the almighty Father of the human race, and now desirous to bring all to a knowledge of Himself. Then he exhorted his hearers to give up idol-worship and prepare by penance for the day " wherein God would judge the world in equity by the Man whom He hath appointed," for of this He had given pledge and assurance to all by raising Him up from the dead.

The general line of thought followed by the Apostle and recorded in the book of the Acts was such as to keep up the interest of the Athenians ; but when he made mention of a resurrection some burst out into laughter, while others, apparently more polite, dismissed him with the words, " We will hear thee again concerning this matter." Whereupon the assembly dispersed, and a few only of his hearers (among whom were Dionysius, the Areopagite, and a woman named Damaris) embraced the faith.*

A day's sail brought St. Paul from Athens to Corinth, a city situated on the isthmus which connects the Peloponnesus with the rest of Greece and separates the Ægean from the Ionian Sea. This was at the time the capital of the province and the residence of the Roman proconsul of Achaia. No other Greek city could compare with it in commerce, wealth, refinement, and number of inhabitants ; and perhaps no city in the world could compare with it in licentiousness : Venus was its favorite goddess, and sensuality had taken the form of a religious rite. Its population, made up of people from all parts of the empire, comprised a large Jewish element, attracted thither by commerce, and swollen at this particular time by the numerous Jews expelled from Rome by the Emperor Claudius.† Among these refugees were a certain Jew named Aquila, born in Pontus,

---

* ACTS xvii. 16-34.　　　　　　† SUETONIUS, Claudius, 25.

and Priscilla, his wife, who had perhaps already embraced the Christian faith, and with whom St. Paul abode and worked, for Aquila was also a tent-maker.* As the Sabbaths came around they naturally all repaired to the Jewish synagogue, and St. Paul, availing himself of his great rabbinical learning, proved to his hearers—Jews and Gentiles—that Jesus was indeed the Christ, and made several converts to whom he refers in his First Epistle to the Corinthians.† It was, however, only after the arrival of Silas and Timothy, who brought to him the generous offerings of the Macedonian churches, that the Apostle, freed from temporal cares, powerfully seconded by his two devoted friends and greatly encouraged by a divine vision, effected a large number of conversions. Driven from the synagogue, he preached to all comers in the adjoining house of a proselyte named Titus Justus, who, with Crispus, the ruler of the synagogue, had believed in Christ. His success was very great, chiefly with the lower classes of the Gentile population, and this so incensed the Jews that on one occasion, the exact character of which is not recorded, " arising with one accord, they brought him to the judgment-seat " of the proconsul Gallio. But this Roman officer had hardly heard the only accusation they could proffer against St. Paul, viz.: " This man persuadeth men to worship God contrary to the Law," than he contemptuously refused to take up the matter, " drove them from the judgment-seat," and did not intervene in their behalf when they were mobbed by the multitude outside.

The Apostle was therefore allowed free scope to his zeal, and his long sojourn of one year and a half at Corinth resulted not only in the foundation of a large and flourishing community in the capital of Achaia, but also in the establishment of several churches within that province.‡ It was also from Corinth that St. Paul wrote his two epistles to the

---

* ACTS xviii. 1–3.   † 1 COR. i. 16; xvi. 15.
‡ ACTS xviii. 4–18; 2 COR. i. 1; ROM. xvi. 1, 16.

Thessalonians, to encourage and instruct them in their peculiar and trying circumstances already referred to.*

It is difficult in the present day to point out the reason of the Nazarite vow which St. Paul made before leaving Corinth, and in consequence of which he shaved his head in Cenchra, the eastern harbor of the capital of Achaia, from which he sailed "into Syria." † Perhaps he wished thereby to give public witness to his gratitude for his recent deliverance from the machinations of the Jews by the action of the Roman proconsul.

§ 3. *The Return.*

1. **St. Paul's Return by Way of Ephesus, Cæsarea, and Jerusalem.** The return from his second missionary journey was rapidly effected by St. Paul, who was anxious to be in Jerusalem for a festival, not otherwise specified in the Greek text (it is not even referred to in the Vulgate), but which has been supposed to be either the feast of the Passover or Pentecost, and which may have been connected in some unknown manner with the consummation of his vow in Corinth.‡ Sailing from Cenchra with Silas and Timothy, Aquila and Priscilla, he landed in Ephesus after a voyage of about thirteen or fourteen days, and started from it as soon as possible, notwithstanding the invitation to tarry which the Jews of the synagogue of that great capital of proconsular Asia had extended to him. He therefore simply promised soon to return to them "God willing," and, leaving behind Aquila and Priscilla, sailed for Cæsarea of Palestine, from which he went up to the Holy City, saluted the church of Jerusalem, and after a brief stay started for Antioch.

Duration of St. Paul's Second Missionary Journey. With St. Paul's return to Antioch of Syria closed one

---

* See p. 279.   † ACTS xviii. 18.
‡ Cfr. CRELIER, Actes, p. 224; PLUMPTRE, Acts, pp. 303, 304.

of the most important missionary journeys of the great Apostle. Besides confirming the faith of the churches already in existence in Cilicia and southern Galatia, he had, under the manifest guidance of Providence, crossed over to Europe and founded many important Christian communities in Macedonia and Achaia. It is generally agreed that this second journey took about three years, eighteen months of which were spent in Corinth : it extended probably from 46 to 49 A.D.*

* See, however, RAMSAY, St. Paul, p. 254.

SYNOPSIS OF CHAPTER XXV.

St Paul's Third Missionary Journey.

Acts xviii. 23 ; xxi. 17.)

I.
EARLY PART OF THE JOURNEY:

1. The Departure : Occasion ; Date ; St. Paul's Companions.
2. Visitation of the Galatian Churches.

II.
APOSTOLIC WORK IN PROCONSULAR ASIA:

1. Political and Religious Conditions of the Roman Province of Asia.
2. In Ephesus:
   - The city and its worship of Diana.
   - St. Paul's successful preaching.
   - The outbreak of the silversmiths.
3. The Other Churches in the Province of Asia.

III.
ST. PAUL'S WORK IN EUROPE:

1. Extensive Missionary Labors in Macedonia.
2. Sojourn in Corinth (Its Principal Object).

IV.
THE RETURN:

1. Through Philippi, Troas and Miletus.
2. The Voyage from Miletus to Cæsarea.
3. Arrival at Jerusalem.

CHAPTER XXV.

ST. PAUL'S THIRD MISSIONARY JOURNEY.

§ 1. *Early Part of the Journey.*

1. **The Departure.** It has been recently assumed [*]
that during his sojourn in Antioch at this time St. Paul received rather disquieting news about the churches of Galatia, and that this led him, first, to write his Epistle to the
Galatians, and, next, to start on his *third* missionary journey. It seems more probable, however, as stated in the
preceding chapter, that this painful intelligence had reached
the Apostle soon after the Council of Jerusalem, and had
then been followed by the writing of the epistle to the
Galatians and by St. Paul's departure for his *second* missionary tour. Of course he was glad when starting on his third
mission to the Gentiles to have the occasion of passing
through Galatia and of confirming in the faith the Christian communities of that province, but there is hardly any
doubt that his chief purpose was rather to fulfil his recent
promise to the Jews of the synagogue of Ephesus : " I will
return to you again, God willing." He tarried " some time,"
it is true, in the Syrian capital, but this was only natural
after a three years' absence from the Antiochian church, so
congenial and in many ways so dear to him, and a careful
reading of the sacred text seems to point to Ephesus,
where he actually remained upwards of two years,[†] as the
main object of his thoughts at this time. After a few months,
therefore, or even perhaps after only a few weeks, of stay

[*] RAMSAY, St. Paul, p. 189 sq.   [†] Cfr. ACTS xx. 31.

in Antioch St. Paul started for proconsular Asia, of which Ephesus was the large and flourishing capital.

Among the companions of the great Apostle on this third missionary journey we do not find Silas, who had probably remained in Jerusalem when St. Paul returned to Antioch, and whose presence near the Apostle of the Gentiles was in fact no longer so necessary as on the preceding journey, when he could bear official witness to the personal and doc-trinal authority of one whom the Judaistic teachers had slanderously represented as claiming a power which he did not possess. But we find with him Timothy, who most likely accompanied his beloved master from the beginning of the journey, and a certain Erastus, a Corinthian Christian, who had been with St. Paul on his voyage from Achaia to Jerusalem, and who appears at his side in Ephesus.* At what exact time the two Macedonians Gaius and Aristarchus, whom the book of the Acts calls St. Paul's "companions," joined him cannot be defined in the present day ; and the same must be said about Titus, a faithful disciple who has been already mentioned in connection with the Council of Jerusalem, and to whom the Apostle willingly entrusted important or delicate missions.†

2. **Visitation of the Galatian Churches.** St. Paul's third missionary journey opened, like the second, with a visitation of churches already founded. The exact route is not indicated, and in fact, of this early part of the journey, we are simply told that "he went through the region of Galatia and Phrygia, in order, confirming all the disciples," whereby we are given to understand that his visit, though rapid, was systematic and yielded abundant fruits.‡

While St. Paul was thus making all haste to Ephesus in fulfilment of his promise, a certain Jew named Apollo, a native of Alexandria, had succeeded him as a teacher in Ephesus, and by his eloquent preaching from the Scriptures,

* ACTS xix. 22.   † Cfr. 2 COR. vii. 6 sq.; viii. 6 sq.   ‡ ACTS xviii. 23.

which he interpreted in favor of the Messiahship of Jesus, was powerfully preparing the minds of the Jews of that city for the ministry of the great Apostle. Docile to the instructions of Priscilla and Aquila, who were then in Ephesus, this great and good man, who had hitherto known nothing of the Christian Baptism and simply given to those who believed his words the baptism of John, became a full-fledged Christian. He seems to have started for Corinth before all those to whom he had administered the baptism of the holy precursor had received the Christian Baptism, and we see from the sacred narrative that the test used by St. Paul after his arrival in Ephesus to discern between the two classes of believers was the question, " Have you received the Holy Ghost since you believed ? " *

§ 2. *Apostolic Work in Proconsular Asia.*

1. **Political and Religious Conditions of the Roman Province of Asia.** The western part of Asia Minor, the highlands of which St. Paul traversed on his way to Ephesus, was at the time a large senatorial province which comprised such important regions as Caria, Lydia, and Mysia, together with a considerable part of Phrygia. The chief representative of the Roman senate in the province was a personage who had been a consul at Rome, and who, with the title of proconsul, conferred annually, was allowed to display all the ensigns of his former consular office and given extensive civil and military powers. The officers under the proconsul were a quæstor, and three assessors or legates appointed also by the Roman senate, while near him there was a powerful procurator directly appointed by the emperor and having charge of the financial affairs of the whole province.

" Subject to this despotic dominion of the proconsul

* Acts xviii. 24 ; xix. 4.

qualified by the power of the procurator, the province governed itself. Matters of general interest were debated in Congress (**Sunedrion**), a council composed of representatives from the different states of which Asia consisted, and subordinate to this collective legislature were the separate governments of the cities which returned members to Congress." *

For judicial purposes the province was divided into assize districts, of which the proconsul made a yearly circuit, "sitting either in person, with the assistance of a jury, or nominating judges to act as his deputies," † and there is no doubt that law was generally administered with justice and equity.

Like the rest of the peninsula of Asia Minor, proconsular Asia was given to forms of idolatry which closely resembled those of Greece and Rome. It was in that province that some twenty-five years before Christ the worship of Rome and the emperor originated, and that soon afterwards not only in Ephesus, but also in Smyrna, Sardis, Laodicea, Philadelphia, etc., temples were built to the deified Cæsars. Each year delegates from the chief cities of the province elected a priest, among the wealthiest of Asia, and entrusted to him, with the titles of high priest and **Asiarch**, the presidency of the annual games celebrated by an assembly of the whole province in honor of Rome and the emperor. Unfortunately here also, as in the rest of Asia Minor, pagan worship approved of or even ordered immoral practices, and Ephesus, the political head of proconsular Asia, was also its worst city.‡

2. St. Paul in Ephesus. Of all the cities which St. Paul visited in his missionary journeys, Ephesus is the one in which he made the longest stay, owing probably to the

---

* Lewin, vol. i., p. 314. † Lewin, *ibid.*, p. 316.
‡ Cfr. E. Beurlier, art. Asiarque, in Vigouroux' Dictionnaire de la Bible; and De Pressense, Early Years of Christianity, p. 170 sq.

splendid opportunity he found therein freely to announce the word of God and to spread it through the whole province. In point of fact no other city of proconsular Asia could compare with Ephesus in respect not only of political but also of commercial, intellectual, and religious importance. Situated partly in a large and delightful valley at the foot of Mount Prion or Pion, partly on that mount and on Mount Coressus, it communicated with the Ægean Sea by an extensive lake turned into a broad harbor artificially embanked and connecting with the Kayster River by a large canal. This situation was favorable alike for maritime and for inland commerce, as it made of Ephesus a populous centre on the main road of traffic between the East and the West, and there is no doubt that the author of the Apocalypse, writing from the island of Patmos, well nigh opposite that great city, appealed to his recollection of the riches and commerce of this most flourishing metropolis of Asia to describe the riches and commerce of his Babylon or great mistress of the world.* Nor was the intellectual atmosphere of Ephesus less favorable to the spread of the Gospel than its commercial relations with the rest of the world. It was at the time one of the principal seats " of literary and scientific culture, where Greek philosophy and Oriental mysticism found eager and enthusiastic representatives, while every encouragement was given to eloquent defenders and expounders of the most curious views by a population whose natural temperament made them welcome, like the Athenians, the announcement of any new thing. . The variety of schools represented, as well as the reputation of individual philosophers and rhetoricians, attracted large numbers of young men from all parts of the world." †

There was, however, in Ephesus an influence at play which was likely to even more than counterbalance the advantages which the intellectual and commercial importance

---

* APOCAL. xviii. 11 sq.   † MACPHERSON, Epistle to Ephesians, p. 9.

of the city would offer for the preaching and spreading of Christianity. This was the wonderful influence which the worship of Artemis or Diana, the great deity of the Ephesians, exerted upon the cities and rural populations of proconsular Asia and of regions far beyond its limits. The magnificent temple of Diana " was to the Asiatics what the temple of Jerusalem was to the Jews." * Built at the joint cost of all Asia, out of the purest marble, adorned with 127 columns, each one the gift of a king, enriched with the most beautiful sculptures and paintings of Greek art and with the costliest offerings of Asiatic potentates, it was justly regarded as one of the seven wonders of the world. Nor did the rude and monstrous statue of Diana venerated in Ephesus appeal less powerfully to the imagination of its worshippers, for it was supposed to have fallen down from the skies, and the religious rites carried out in its honor by a numerous and wealthy priesthood were exactly suited to the sensual instincts of the degraded pagan populations. The whole month of May was consecrated to the honor of the goddess, and several cities, like that of Ephesus, gloried in the title of **Neocoros**, or humblest devotee of Artemis.

In truth the very attempt to undermine this sensual, national, and long-cherished worship of the Diana of Ephesus must have seemed even to St. Paul a bold undertaking, and it is not surprising that he should have remained something like three years in this great centre of paganism to rear the structure of a church "not having spot or wrinkle or any such thing, and that should be holy and without blemish," as he conceived the Spouse of Christ should be. †

In Ephesus the Apostle probably stayed with Aquila and Priscilla, for during his long sojourn in this metropolis he earned his support and that of his friends by manual labor.‡ As he had come to redeem his promise to the Jews of the

* GLOAG. Life of Paul, p. 61.   † EPHES. v. 27.   ‡ ACTS xx. 34.

synagogue, he naturally preached first to them the word of
God, but as after three months it was plain that his words
were no longer welcome, and that even his efforts to per-
suade his hearers gave occasion to public blasphemies
against Christianity, he withdrew with his converts, and
started a daily course of public instruction in the school of
a certain teacher named Tyrannus.   This he pursued during
two years with the greatest success, due to a large extent to
the numerous miracles which it pleased God to work out by
the hands of His servant ; conversions multiplied, and their
deep earnestness was evinced by the burning of magical
books to the value of fifty thousand pieces of silver, or
$9000.*

All these conversions, however, had not taken place without arousing in several quarters deep feelings of aversion
against St. Paul's doctrine and person.   This was the case in
particular with the silversmiths of Ephesus, for by his preaching against idolatry he had sensibly reduced the number of
those who formerly bought silver shrines of Diana (that is,
small models of her temple which contained an image of the
goddess) and had thereby greatly lessened the gains of those
artificers.   At length one of them, named Demetrius, so
wrought upon the angry feelings of his fellow laborers that a
frightful tumult ensued.   Fortunately the rioters did not
succeed in securing the person of the Apostle, who at first
had wished to venture among the multitude crowded in the
theatre and shouting, " Great is Diana of the Ephesians," but
who finally had been prevailed upon by his disciples and by
friendly Asiarchs not to expose himself " to the wild beasts
of Ephesus," as he figuratively called them later on.†   At
length the town-clerk of the city, a man of the greatest importance in Ephesus, succeeded by his skilful address to
the multitude in calming the popular fury and in dismissing
the assembly.

* Acts xix. 8-20.   † 1 Cor. xv. 32.

3. The Other Churches in the Province of Asia.

The chief reason which the silversmith Demetrius alleged to his assembled fellows to stir up their anger against St. Paul was that the Apostle had "drawn away a great multitude, not only of Ephesus, but almost of all Asia," from the worship of Diana. This was unquestionably the fact, for either by himself personally, or by his fellow-workers whom he had sent to the principal cities of the province, or even by the natural intercourse and influence of the Ephesian converts, large and flourishing Christian communities had been started in the leading cities of proconsular Asia before St. Paul left for Macedonia. It was at this time, for instance, that churches arose in Laodicea, Colossa, and Hierapolis, and most likely also in the other cities mentioned in the Apocalypse (i. 11).

It was also during this sojourn of St. Paul in Ephesus that he wrote his First Epistle to the Corinthians. Besides disclosing the trials or abuses peculiar to the church of Corinth, this letter makes us acquainted with the general temptations and doctrinal difficulties which naturally beset Gentile converts living in the midst of idolatrous and immoral populations, and with the tender, yet authoritative, manner in which the Apostle of the Gentiles deals with the various topics of which he had been apprised, either by letter or by men come from the capital of Achaia.

§ 3. *St. Paul's Work in Europe.*

1. Extensive Missionary Labors in Macedonia.

When St. Paul left Ephesus soon after the outbreak of the silversmiths he apparently intended to carry out at once his long-cherished project of visiting the churches of Macedonia. It seems, however, that the ship he took was bound for Troas, and that, once arrived in that city, he tarried long enough to found a church, which he revisited on his return from Greece.* Here also he anxiously waited for Titus, whom he had deputed to Corinth, but this faithful friend rejoined St. Paul only after he had sailed for Macedonia.† As the news brought by Titus was of a comforting kind about the condition of the Corinthian church, the Apostle felt free to remain long months in Macedonia, and was satisfied for the time being with writing his Second Epistle to the Corinthians.

Of this long stay of St. Paul in Macedonia we are simply told in the book of the Acts that "when he had gone over those parts, and had exhorted them with many words, he came into Greece." ‡ But it is very probable that, as in his second missionary journey he had already evangelized the three first districts of the province of Macedonia, he now visited the fourth or Macedonia, Quarta, for when he wrote not long afterwards to the Romans he could say : " From Jerusalem round about as far as unto Illyricum, I have replenished the Gospel of Christ." §

2. Sojourn in Corinth. At length St. Paul passed into Achaia, and, as he had promised to them in his first epistle, he remained long, perhaps the whole winter months, with the Corinthians. His chief object was evidently to set all things right in that weak, yet well-disposed, Christian community; and it seems that his presence and his admonitions at this juncture completed the good which his two epistles to the Corinthians had already so powerfully begun, for this much can be inferred with tolerable certainty from the words which St. Clement of Rome, writing to the same church some forty years later, uses concerning their past well-known brotherly love.‖

It was from Corinth that St. Paul, now about to retrace his steps without visiting Rome, wrote his Epistle to the

---

* ACTS xx. 1 ; 2 COR. ii. 12.   † 2 COR. ii. 13 ; vii. 5, 6.
‡ ACTS xx. 2.   § ROM. xv. 19.
‖ Epist. to Corinth., chap. xlvii.

Romans, first to excuse himself for not visiting them at this time, and next to announce to them his intended coming.

§ 4. *The Return.*

1. **Through Philippi, Troas, and Miletus.** By this time the collections for the Christians of Jerusalem which St. Paul had been making during his visit through the churches of Macedonia and Achaia were completed, and he now purposed to reach the Holy City before the Paschal festival. With this in view he was about to take a pilgrim ship carrying Jews from Achaia and Asia to the Passover, when the discovery of a Jewish plot against his life led him to give up his project and to pass into Macedonia, where he arrived in time to celebrate the Paschal festival in Philippi.

"It is clear that the plot was discovered at the last moment, when delegates from the churches had already assembled to carry the alms of their respective communities to Jerusalem. The European delegates were to sail from Corinth, the Asian from Ephesus, where doubtless the pilgrim ship would call. When the plan was changed, word was sent to the Asian delegates ; and they went as far as Troas to meet the others, for in ancient voyages it could be calculated with certainty that Paul's company would put in at that harbor." *

In point of fact after the Paschal celebration St. Paul and his companions—among whom was reckoned the writer of the Acts, who uses again the first person " we " in his narrative—sailed from Philippi, and reached Troas in five days. There they remained a week ; but in connection with this sojourn we are given an account only of what occurred on the last day before St. Paul's departure. We are told how on " the first day of the week " (our Sunday),

---

* RAMSAY, St. Paul, p. 287.

when the Christians had gathered "to break bread," the Apostle continued discoursing until midnight. Then, owing to the great heat of the upper room wherein the assembly was held, a young man named Eutychus, sitting on the window, was overcome by sleep, fell from the third story, and was taken up dead ; but the young man was restored to life by St. Paul, who, having spent the rest of the night conversing with the faithful of the place, so eager to listen to him, took leave at daybreak for Assos. This was a seaport of proconsular Asia, more than 40 miles distant by sea, but only about 20 by land, and the Apostle, for some unrecorded reason, chose to go thither on foot, while his companions sailed round the promontory of Lectum. At Assos St. Paul took to ship again with his companions, and, having touched at Mitylene, the capital of the island of Lesbos, and at Samos, a populous island off the coast of Lydia, reached Miletus, from which he intended to sail as soon as possible in order to arrive at Jerusalem for the feast of Pentecost.*

In thus coasting along the shores of Asia St. Paul had purposely omitted calling at Ephesus, lest he should be detained too long there ; but as his vessel had to remain a few days in Miletus, he profited by the comparatively short distance between the two cities to send word to " the ancients of the church" of Ephesus that they should come and meet him. When these were assembled, he delivered to them his celebrated farewell address, a touching model of paternal solicitude, and of apostolic zeal for their own welfare and that of their flock.† Finally the time came for parting, when all, falling on their knees, united in fervent prayer with St. Paul, and then surrounded him with the most sincere marks of attachment, chiefly because he had said "that they should see his face no more." ‡

---

* ACTS xx. 3-15.   † ACTS xx. 16-35.   ‡ ACTS xx. 36-38.

2. The Voyage from Miletus to Cæsarea. The second part of St. Paul's journey to Jerusalem was mostly by sea. The ship which carried him and his companions sailed first to the island of Coos, about 40 miles to the south of Miletus, and the next day to the island of Rhodes, and thence to Patara, the harbor of Xanthus, the capital of the Roman province of Lycia. There they changed ship, and took one which sailed direct to Tyre, in Phenicia. St. Paul spent a week with the Christians of Tyre, and, despite their predictions of the great dangers which awaited him in Jerusalem, went on board again, and finally reached Ptolemais (Acre), where the voyage by sea came to an end.*

The next day after landing, the Apostle and those with him were on their way to Cæsarea of Palestine, a city some 30 miles distant, and in which the deacon St. Philip lived with his household in the midst of an old and large Christian settlement. Of course the holy deacon welcomed most heartily St. Paul and his companions into his house, and the Apostle, on his part, accepted with joy and gratitude a lodging in a house so manifestly blessed by God, that the four daughters of St. Philip were endowed with the gift of prophecy. It was during this short sojourn in Cæsarea, that the prophet Agabus, who had formerly predicted the famine which occurred under Claudius,† came "from Judæa" to warn St. Paul of the danger he was running in going up to Jerusalem. Whereupon, the companions of the Apostle and all the Christians of Cæsarea besought him not to expose himself; but to all their words, accompanied by tears, the undaunted missionary simply replied: "I am ready not only to be bound, but to die also in Jerusalem for the name of the Lord Jesus."‡

3. Arrival at Jerusalem. About 70 miles separated Cæsarea from Jerusalem, and as the Pentecost festival drew near, St. Paul started for the Holy City in company

---

* ACTS xxi. 1-7.   † ACTS xi. 27 sq.   ‡ ACTS xxi. 8-14.

with several disciples of Cæsarea.   They had with them a certain Mnason of Cyprus, whose faith of long standing had proved him perfectly reliable, and who, possessing a house of his own in Jerusalem, was but too glad to place it at the disposal of St. Paul and his companions.   At his arrival in Jerusalem, the Apostle was joyfully received by those Christians who were made aware of his presence, and the next day "he went in unto James," with whom were gathered all the ancients of the Church.*

Thus terminated St. Paul's third and probably most important missionary journey, in respect both of the extent of ground covered and of the number of churches founded. It lasted four years or perhaps a little more, from about 49 to 53 A.D.

* ACTS xxi. 15-18.

SYNOPSIS OF CHAPTER XXVI.

ST. PAUL'S ARREST AND IMPRISONMENT.

I.
ARREST IN JERUSALEM:
(Acts xxi. 18; xxiii. 10).

1. Judaistic Opposition to St. Paul. **The Advice** of St. James.

2. The Arrest in the Temple: { The infuriated Jews. The address of St. Paul to the multitude.

3. St. Paul's Defence before the Sanhedrim.

II.
IMPRISONMENT IN CÆSAREA:
(Acts xxiii. 11; xxvi).

1. Paul sent Prisoner to Cæsarea.

2. He appears before Felix: { Character and administration of the Roman procurator. Charges of the Jews and St. Paul's defence. Two years' detention in Cæsarea.

3. St. Paul and Festus: { The new procurator. Date of his entrance into office. The trial before Festus ended by appeal to Cæsar.

4. St. Paul's Discourse before King Agrippa.

III.
JOURNEY TO ROME: (Acts xxvii.–xxviii. 16).

1. From Cæsarea to Malta: { The voyage and shipwreck. Minute accuracy of the sacred narrative.

2. Sojourn in the Island of Malta.
3. From Malta to Rome.

CHAPTER XXVI.

§ 1. *Arrest in Jerusalem.*

1. Judaistic Opposition to St. Paul. When, on the day which followed his arrival in the Holy City, St. Paul appeared before the formal assembly of the ancients of the Church under the presidency of St. James, he had not, in fact he could not have, any serious misgivings about their feelings regarding his own person and doctrine. What he had so far preached to the Gentiles had formerly received their distinct approval, and if slanderous reports had during his long absence caused in their minds something like doubt or even distrust as to his actual teachings to the Gentiles he knew that a straightforward account of the marvels which God had wrought everywhere through his agency, and to which his numerous companions were ready to bear witness, would be more than sufficient to dispel at once all traces of unfriendly feeling on the part of the heads of the church of Jerusalem. In point of fact we are told in the sacred narrative that, " having related particularly what things God had wrought among the Gentiles by his ministry, they hearing it glorified God." But in spite, or rather because, of their friendly dispositions towards St. Paul, the leaders of the church of Jerusalem felt they should take into account the state of excitement into which his presence was sure to throw his Judaistic opponents. By many Jewish converts he had ever been more less suspected of enmity to the Mosaic Law, and the late arrival of the Asiatic Jews, who, as we have seen, had plotted against his life at Corinth, and who had since their coming to the Holy City sedulously spread the rumor that he taught the Hellenistic Jews positive dis-regard of the Law of Moses, had wrought powerfully upon the feelings of the thousands of Jewish converts now in Jerusalem, and " all zealous for the Law." It seemed, there-fore, highly desirable that St. Paul should do something to destroy the effect of these calumnious reports on the Christian community, and at the same time disarm the hostility of the unconverted Jews. Accordingly the heads of the Jewish Church advised him to show to all in a prac-tical manner that he was no fanatic enemy of Mosaism. To this the Apostle readily agreed, for the particular conduct now suggested to him—that of taking part in the religious services of four Nazarites and of defraying the expenses which at-tended their purification—clearly involved no giving up of the great principle of Gentile freedom formerly promulgated in the Council of Jerusalem and ever since preached by him through the Roman Empire.*

2. **The Arrest in the Temple.** What St. Paul had consented to do was usually considered highly meritorious by all the Jews, but, under the circumstances of the time, his Asiatic enemies were so bent upon his destruction that what was best calculated to appease their anger simply furnished them with the opportunity of making an attempt upon his life. Towards the end of the seven days during which he had to appear in the Temple with the four Naza-rites, some of those bigots, meeting him within the sacred precincts after having seen him in the company of the Ephesian Trophimus some time before, called on others to help in arresting a great enemy of Judaism, and one who, moreover, as they affirmed, had brought Gentiles into that part of the Temple strictly forbidden to the uncircum-cised. An uproar ensued, during which the Apostle,

* ACTS xxi. 18-26.

dragged out of the Inner Court, would certainly have been beaten to death had not the tribune Lysias, informed of the riot, rushed down at once from the fortress Antonia with soldiers and centurions.   The tribune arrested the Apostle, whom he supposed to be an Egyptian impostor, who had lately caused a revolt, and had hitherto baffled the pursuit of the soldiers of Felix, the Roman governor.   But he was soon undeceived, for St. Paul, having been scarcely conveyed to the fortress, asked of him leave to address the people, affirming that he was " a Jew of Tarsus in Cilicia."

The recorded discourse of the Apostle under such unfavorable circumstances for an address is a model of skilful pleading calculated to secure and hold long—as we are told it did—the attention of most unfriendly hearers.   It is an historical retrospect of his life, in which the principal points are described so as to justify his words and conduct, but, still more, so as to please the popular fancy by setting forth every detail that could appear honorable to the Jewish Law and nation.   But, of course, the mention of his mission to the Gentiles had to be made, and when made it aroused at once the fury of the mob, and in their rage they clamored for his blood, " threw off their garments, and cast dust into the air." *

Witnessing this second outbreak, of which he could not make out the cause, for he did not understand the Aramaic language used by St. Paul, the tribune ordered that he should be examined by scourging ; but this was not carried out, the Apostle appealing at once to his Roman citizenship, which guaranteed exemption from such indignity.†

3. **St. Paul's Defence before the Sanhedrim.** The very next day Lysias, desirous to know what were the precise crimes laid to the charge of his prisoner, had him loosed and, under the guard of an escort of Roman soldiers, brought before the Sanhedrim.   The president of this

* See GLOAG, Life of Paul, p. 77.   † ACTS xxii. 1-29.

Jewish assembly was no other than the high priest **Ananias**, who belonged to the family of Annas, famous for its connection with the trial of Jesus, and who hastened to give evidence of his usual disregard of justice and of his deepseated hatred of Christianity. Hardly had St. Paul begun his address by affirming that he had ever been faithful to his conscience, when that infamous high priest ordered his servants who stood nearest to the Apostle, to strike him on the mouth. Whereupon St. Paul indignantly replied : "God shall strike thee, thou whited wall. For sittest thou to judge me according to the Law, and contrary to the Law commandest thou me to be struck ?" but being made aware that the one guilty of such unjust violence was no other than the high priest, he withdrew at once the expressions he had just used, and proceeded with his defence.

It seems that at this time the quarrel of long standing between Sadducees and Pharisees—the two principal elements of the Sanhedrim—with regard to the question of the resurrection had reached its hottest point, and St. Paul, who knew it full well, shrewdly exclaimed : "I am a Pharisee, the son of Pharisees ; concerning the hope and resurrection of the dead I am called in question." His device succeeded admirably, for there arose so great a dissension in the Sanhedrim that "the tribune, fearing lest Paul should be torn in pieces by them," ordered him to be taken from among them and brought back into the fortress.*

§ 2. *Imprisonment in Cæsarea.*

1. **Paul Sent Prisoner to Cæsarea.** Great indeed was the disappointment of the Asiatic enemies of St. Paul when they heard of the manner in which he had escaped condemnation by the Sanhedrim ; and in their rage some of them "bound themselves under a curse, saying, that they

* ACTS xxii. 30; xxiii. 10.

would neither eat nor drink, till they killed Paul." Their plan was that he should again be brought before the Sanhedrim as if to resume the inquiry so tumultuously interrupted, and that they would murder him on his way thither. But God watched over the life of one whom He destined to bear Him witness in the capital of the empire, and Paul's nephew, having become aware of the plot, found means to convey the information without delay to the Roman commander. Whereupon Lysias took instant and absolutely sure measures for the safety of his prisoner ; no fewer than 470 soldiers were to escort him that very night on the road to Cæsarea, the residence of Antonius Felix, the Roman procurator. At nine o'clock in the evening the escort started with Paul mounted on horseback, and it reached Antipatris, some 40 miles distant, in the early morning. As from hence to Cæsarea an ambuscade from the banditti who infested the district was no longer to be feared, the greater part of the escort returned to Jerusalem, while the rest hastened to deliver up the prisoner to the procurator, together with a short letter from Lysias which gave a substantially correct account of what had happened. Upon the reading of this letter Felix ascertained the province to which Paul belonged, and then promised to hear his case as soon as his accusers had come, ordering that meantime he should be kept in Herod's palace.*

2. **St. Paul before Felix.†** Few Roman officials have left after them a worse record than Antonius Felix, the procurator of Judæa, before whose tribunal St. Paul was soon to be confronted with his enemies. It is of that brother of Pallas, the freedman of Claudius, to whose influence in Rome Felix owed his actual continuance in office, that Tacitus says in his usual pithy manner : " He wielded the sceptre of a monarch with the soul of a slave." ‡ He rendered at first, it is true, some good service by putting

down the banditti who had infested Judæa under his pred ecessor; but he soon proved himself "artful and per- fidious, and stirred by revenge, even to the use of the assassin's knife, a votary of pleasure, and regardless of the feelings he wounded in the pursuit of it, ostentatious and extravagant, and feeding his wasteful indulgences by pecu- lation and extortion."*

After a few days of detention in the palace of Herod, which Felix actually used as his headquarters, St. Paul appeared before the procurator. The high priest Ananias had come down himself from Jerusalem, "with some of the ancients," to accuse the Apostle, and they had taken with them Tertullus, a hired advocate, to argue the case in the Greek language. In an artful speech Tertullus brought three distinct charges against the accused : first, that he had " raised seditions among all the Jews throughout the world," and was thus guilty of treason against the emperor ; next, that he was a ringleader of the "sect of the Nazarenes" ; lastly, that he had attempted to profane the Temple. The reply of St. Paul was a dignified answer to these charges. As the procurator could easily ascertain, the Apostle had in no way during his short sojourn of twelve days in Jerusalem provoked a sedition. He belonged indeed to the "sect " of the Nazarenes, who were considered by the Jews as heretics, but in becoming a member of it he had not given up belief in what is written "in the Law and the prophets," and since then he had most earnestly endeavored to live up to the dictates of his conscience. His coming to the Holy City, after many years of absence, was not only natural but even laudable, because prompted by his desire of bringing alms to his nation and of carrying out religious observances. Finally, his conduct before the Sanhedrim had been irre- proachable, and he challenged the present members of that

* LEWIN, vol. ii., p. 121 ; for details see JOSEPHUS, Antiq. of the Jews, book XX., chap. vii. sq.

assembly to gainsay that, standing before them, he had uttered but this one sentence : "Concerning the resurrection of the dead am I judged this day by you."

This was a vigorous defence, and as Felix, who for several years had already been procurator of Judæa, had had no reason to complain of the disciples of Christ, he put the Jews off with the pretext : "When Lysias the tribune shall come down, I will hear you." Meantime he ordered the centurion to whom he entrusted the guard of St. Paul that he should treat him with kindness, and not prevent any of his friends from visiting and ministering to him.

A few days elapsed, and, possibly at the request of his consort Drusilla, a sister of King Agrippa II., and a woman of abandoned character, Felix "sent for Paul and heard of him the faith that is in Christ Jesus." With fearless courage, like that of John the Baptist in almost identical circumstances, the Apostle attacked the vices and crimes of the procurator, and by his warnings of the judgment to come terrified without, however, converting him. Oftentimes, it is true, during St. Paul's two years' detention in Cæsarea the procurator held converse with his prisoner, but it was mainly, if not solely, to give him an opportunity of offering money for his release. At the end of two years Felix was succeeded by Portius Festus in the procuratorship of Judæa.

3. St. Paul and Festus. The new procurator, though probably a freedman like his predecessor, was very different from him. He combined justice and energy, together with a natural desire to ingratiate himself with the leading men of the nation under his government, so that, notwithstanding the many causes of friction constantly at play between Jewish susceptibilities and Roman rule, he succeeded during the whole time of his administration in giving no serious offence to the Jewish leaders.

The exact date at which Festus took upon him the charge

of procurator has been of late the subject-matter of a lively discussion among biblical scholars, owing to the fact that the date admitted, whatever it may be, has an important bearing upon the whole chronology of the book of the Acts, and upon early traditions concerning the work of St. Peter in Rome, the journey of St. Paul to Spain, etc. They all, indeed, agree as to the fact that Festus was the immediate successor of Felix in the procuratorship of Judæa ; but, because of a remarkable contradiction between Josephus and Tacitus, they disagree as to the date when Felix entered upon and was removed from office. Many scholars, abiding by the statements of Josephus, admit that Felix became procurator only after Cumanus had been deprived of that charge in 52 A.D., and that he filled that office until 60 A.D. Other scholars, on the contrary, standing by the authority of the Roman historian, hold that Felix began his career as procurator of Judæa at the same time as Cumanus became procurator over Galilee, and that both thus continued simultaneously in office, from 48 to 52, when, because of trouble between the Samaritans and Galileans, Cumanus was banished and Felix made procurator alone over the whole province, which he then administered up to the year 55. While, therefore, the former scholars admit that Festus entered into office as late as 60 A.D., the latter affirm that he became procurator in 55 A.D.

This is indeed a difficult question of chronology and one which should not be decided very positively either way ; yet a careful weighing of the arguments on both sides leads us rather to think with Baronius, Patrizi, Kellner, Ramsay, etc., that Tacitus was better informed than Josephus, and that consequently 55 A.D. is the preferable date for the entrance of Festus into office.*

* Cfr. JOSEPHUS, Antiquities of the Jews, book XX., chap. v.–viii.; Wars of the Jews, book II., chaps. xii., xiii. ; TACITUS, Annals, book XII., chap. liv. ; book XIII., chaps. xiv., xv.; EUSEBIUS, Chronicle, in Migne's Lat. Patrol., vol. xxvii., col. 584; see also The Biblical World for February and March, 1898; and The Expositor, February.

When Festus reached Cæsarea he hastened to pay a visit to Jerusalem to ingratiate himself with the heads of the Jewish people, and they at once thought it a favorable occasion to ask of the new procurator that Paul should be brought to Jerusalem, "laying wait to kill him in the way." As, however, the Apostle was already in Cæsarea, whither he himself intended to return very shortly, Festus denied the request, but invited the most influential among them to go down with him and set forth their charges against St. Paul. The trial was opened eight or ten days afterwards in Cæsarea, but, as the Jews could not prove their case, the procurator, anxious to show kindness to the Jewish leaders who had accompanied him, asked Paul whether he was willing to go up to Jerusalem and there be judged by the Sanhedrim, in his presence. Of course the Apostle could not agree to a proposal, which, while clearly implying his innocence, practically left the decision of his case in the hands of his sworn enemies. He therefore rejected the offer of Festus, and, exercising the right of every Roman citizen, appealed to Cæsar. The appeal was admitted, the Jews dismissed, and the Apostle remanded to prison.*

4. St. Paul's Discourse before King Agrippa.

Some days elapsed, after which, on the occasion of a friendly visit to the new procurator by Agrippa II., the king of the tetrarchies formerly under Philip and Lysanias, and the son of that Herod whose terrible death is recorded in the book of the Acts,† St. Paul appeared before Festus, his guest King Agrippa and his wife Bernice, and a numerous gathering of tribunes and principal men of Cæsarea. At the courteous invitation of the procurator to set forth before the king his peculiar religious views and the points of divergence between him and the Jews, the Apostle delivered a long discourse covering pretty much the same ground as the address he had delivered to the people immediately after

* ACTS XXV. 1-12.   † ACTS xii. 23.

his arrest in Jerusalem two years before. He spoke of his "education according to the strictest requirements of the Jewish law";* of the sincere zeal with which he formerly persecuted the disciples of Christ "even unto foreign cities"†; of the vision granted to him on his way to Damascus, and of his commission to preach the Gospel to Jews and Gentiles‡; and lastly of unceasing endeavors to carry out this commission, which had brought upon him the enmity of the Jews, though his teaching was in strict accordance with the Jewish Scriptures, and their predictions of the coming of a Messias who should suffer and rise from the dead. §

All this appeared sheer nonsense to Festus, who interrupted with a loud voice : " Paul, thou art beside thyself ; much learning doth make thee mad." The reply of the Apostle to the procurator was simple and dignified, and followed by a powerful appeal to King Agrippa's belief in the prophecies which were contained in the Old Testament records, and the fulfilment of which was manifest in the public life, passion and death of Jesus of Nazareth. Then Agrippa said to Paul : " In a little thou persuadest me to become a Christian," words which have been variously considered as giving expression to sincere conviction, bitter irony or courtly jest, but which plainly told the Apostle that his words had not worked the conversion he longed for and drew from his heart this fervent exclamation : " I would to God, that both in a little and in much, not only thou, but also all that hear me this day, should become such as I also am, except these bands."

Whereupon the king arose, satisfied with having seen and heard this great preacher of a new religion ; and when alone with the Roman procurator declared openly that Paul had " done nothing worthy of death or of bands " and that

* ACTS xxvi. 4-8.   † ACTS xxvi. 9-11.   ‡ ACTS xxvi. 12-18.
§ ACTS xxvi. 19-23.   MACLEAR, New Testament History, p. 501.

he " might have been set at liberty, if he had not appealed to Cæsar." *

§ 3. *Journey to Rome.*

I. **From Cæsarea to Malta.** Soon after this discourse of St. Paul before King Agrippa, he and several prisoners, together with Luke and Aristarchus—who probably passed and acted as the slaves of the Apostle during the voyage †—were delivered over to the charge of Julius, a centurion of " the band Augusta," an expression the exact meaning of which cannot be defined in the present day. This was a courteous officer, who throughout the voyage surrounded St. Paul with special marks of regard, ‡ and this most naturally, for the Apostle was not a man already sentenced to death like the other prisoners, simply shipped to Rome for amusing the people by their death in the arena, but a Roman citizen against whom no charge had been proved.

As in the harbor of Cæsarea there was no convenient ship about to start for Rome, the centurion and his prisoners set sail on a vessel which was going on a voyage along the coasts of proconsular Asia, and which would therefore touch at places where some other ship bound for the west would most likely be found. The first stopping place was Sidon, where St. Paul was allowed to visit his friends and receive their affectionate care. At the next harbor, that of Myra, § in Lycia, " they fell into the great line of the Egyptian corn-trade, and found a corn-ship of Alexandria bound for Italy ; and to this vessel Julius transferred his prisoners." ‖ After a very slow voyage, because of the strong

---

* Acts xxvi. 24-32.   † See Ramsay, St. Paul, p. 315 sq.
‡ Cfr. Acts xxvii. 3, 31, 43.
§ Instead of Myra, the Vulgate, the Codex Alexandrine and the Sinaitic have Lystra ; but Myra is the correct reading.
‖ Smith, New Testament History.

westerly winds which blew most of the time, they came over against Cnidus, a southwestern headland of Caria, and thence ran for the east and south coast of Crete, rounding the promontory of Salmone. Then they crept along the southern coast of Crete until they reached a place named Fair-Havens, now identified with a small bay a few miles east of Cape Matala.

As much precious time was spent at Fair-Havens waiting for favorable winds and as the season dangerous for navigation had already set in, for the great fasting day of the Atonement in September " was now past," a council was held to decide what was to be done. St. Paul as an experienced traveller was present and was for wintering in Fair-Havens; but naturally enough, the centurion followed the opposite view of the pilot and of the captain of the ship, and set sail as soon as a gently blowing south wind gave promise of better weather. Unfortunately there soon came a sudden change in the wind : it blew violently from the north, and, striking the ship, threatened to founder her in the open sea. This, however, was avoided by scudding before the wind to the southwest, and getting under the shelter of the small island of Cauda (now Gozzo).

Thence the ship was allowed to " drift with her head to the north, steadied by a bow sail, making leeway proportionate to the power of the wind and waves on her broadside." * During the whole time of this furious storm, the particulars of which are all so graphically and so accurately described in the sacred narrative, the presence of mind of St. Paul was admirable, and his advice of the greatest value both to the centurion and to his fellow-passengers. At length, after having been tossed about for fourteen days, the ship was wrecked off the coast of Malta at a spot to which local tradition has given the name of St. Paul's Bay, on the north-

* RAMSAY, St. Paul, p. 330.

eastern coast of the island ; and, as the Apostle had foretold, the whole company escaped safely to land.*

2. **Sojourn in the Island of Malta.** St. Paul's sojourn in the island of Malta, upon the shores of which he and his companions had been flung, proved a pleasant and useful one. From the first the inhabitants treated them with great kindness, and as time went on the miracles which God granted to His Apostle rendered Paul's influence very great, not only with the people and the centurion Julius, but also with Publius, the Roman governor of Malta, whose father he miraculously cured of a dangerous fever. That he availed himself of such favorable dispositions to preach the Gospel may naturally be presumed, but we have no positive information as to the success of his words ; we are simply told that at the close of his stay the inhabitants surrounded him and his companions with marks of honor, and gratefully supplied such things as were necessary for the voyage. †

3. **From Malta to Rome.** It was very early in the spring of 56 A.D. that, after a three months' sojourn in Malta, the centurion Julius and those entrusted to his charge set sail in another corn-ship of Alexandria, which had wintered in the island and was called the " Castor and Pollux." After tarrying three days in Syracuse they proceeded to Rhegium (now Reggio) in the Sicilian straits, and then through the Etruscan sea to Puteoli (now Puzzuoli), the most sheltered part of the bay of Naples and the port of the Alexandrian vessels. Here the passengers were landed, and, with the kind permission of the centurion, Paul and his companions, Luke and Aristarchus, enjoyed the company of several Christians of the place.

At the end of a week, during which the news of the

* Acts xxvii. For illustrations of the sacred narrative, see Jas. Smith, The Voyage and Shipwreck of St. Paul ; see also Fouard, Ramsay, and Vigouroux, Le Nouveau Testament et les Découvertes Archéologiques, livre III., chap. viii.

† Acts xxviii. 1-10.

Apostle's landing was sent to Rome, some 150 miles distant, Julius and his prisoners commenced their journey by land along the Appian Way. The Roman Christians, who had heard of St. Paul's approach, went to meet him, some of them, as far as the small town of " Appii Forum," about 43 miles from Rome, and others as far as the "Three Taverns," a hamlet 10 miles nearer the capital of the world. This twofold mark of respect and affection from the faithful of Rome greatly touched and encouraged the Apostle of the Gentiles, who soon afterwards entered the city which he had so long desired to contemplate (March 56, A.D.). *

* ACTS xxviii. 13-16.

SYNOPSIS OF CHAPTER XXVII.

THE LAST YEARS OF ST. PAUL.

I. FIRST ROMAN IMPRISONMENT:	1. The City of Rome described.
	2. Jews and Christians in Rome.
	3. St. Paul's Release after a Two Years' Imprisonment.

II. LAST JOURNEYS OF ST. PAUL:	1. In the West:	Visit to Great Britain universally rejected.
		Visit to Spain very probable.
	2. In the East:	Order of places visited, uncertain.
		Second arrest probably at Ephesus.

III. SECOND IMPRISONMENT AND DEATH:	1. Second Imprisonment:	Much more severe than the first.
		Acquittal in first trial.
		Sentence of death in second trial.
	2. Death of St. Paul:	Outside the city.
		Date of martyrdom (year and month).

IV. ST. PAUL'S PERSONAL APPEARANCE AND CHARACTER.	1. Personal Appearance of St. Paul
	2. Character of St. Paul.

315

CHAPTER XXVII.

§ 1. *First Roman Imprisonment.*

1. **The City of Rome Described.** At the time of St. Paul's arrival in Rome the great imperial city had already lost much of its republican simplicity, and was on the eve of still greater changes, not indeed as regards the main features of its ground, but as regards the general appearance of its private and public buildings. Now, as in bygone ages, the part of the city built in the plain watered by the Tiber was on a much lower level than either its quarters on the three detached hills (the Capitoline, the Palatine and the Aventine), which arose near the river, or those gradually built on the four ridges (the Cælian, the Esquiline, the Viminal and the Quirinal), which ascended beyond to the east and united together in the higher ground on which the prætorian camp was now situated. But since the capture of Corinth (146 B.C.), which supplied Rome with so many masterpieces of Grecian art, and especially since the civil war between Cæsar and Pompey (49 B.C.), when so many successful generals or greedy proconsuls and prætors brought home plunder and wealth, the city had rapidly lost much of its primitive, simple and unadorned appearance. Since Augustus, in particular, a new era had opened for imperial Rome: his example in erecting splendid public buildings had been closely imitated by his successors Tiberius and Claudius, and within a few years Nero, the Cæsar of the time, was to profit by the great fire under his reign to.

inaugurate those improvements and embellishments of the later emperors which made of Rome the finest city in the world.*

The population of Rome under Nero, though very variously estimated, amounted probably to one million, half of which only were free citizens. The great bulk of these—belonging to every nationality and religion—were poor and lived in crowded lodging-houses, while a small and most wealthy aristocracy dwelt in splendid palaces, attended by countless slaves. Indeed, it would have been difficult to imagine a greater contrast between the luxury of the few and the misery of the many, for in ancient Rome the extravagance of the wealthy classes did not even produce, as in a modern city, a general diffusion of work among the free population, because trade in its various branches, and also liberal professions, were entrusted to slaves.

2. **Jews and Christians in Rome.** Living in the midst of the Roman population, or rather settled mostly in the portion of the city now named the " Trastevere," or district beyond the Tiber, was a large Jewish community, the first beginnings of which went back at least to the year 63 B.C., when Pompey brought many captives from Judæa to grace his triumph. Soon manumitted, this Jewish element had grown rapidly in numbers and influence under the patronage of Julius Cæsar and of Augustus, and although the Jews had been expelled from Rome in 47 A.D., by an edict of Claudius, they had soon regained ground under Nero. They had no less than nine synagogues in the city, had secured the recognition and toleration of their peculiar customs to which here, as elsewhere, they showed themselves strictly faithful, and despite the popular hatred and contempt in which they were held, had greatly influenced in favor of a more reasonable creed and purer worship many men and women disgusted with heathenism. Finally their expectation of the

* Cfr. CONYBEARE and HOWSON, Life and Epistles of St. Paul, chap. xxiv.

very near coming of the Messias was also well known to their pagan fellow-citizens, and in so far concurred to prepare them for the glad tidings of salvation in Jesus.

It is quite natural to suppose that this announcement of the Gospel was made in Rome not long after the day of Pentecost, seeing that among those who witnessed the wonders of that great day, recorded in the second chapter of the book of the Acts, there were Roman strangers, both Jews and proselytes ; and we know for certain from St. Paul's Epistle to the Romans, * that for a considerable time before his arrival in Rome a large and flourishing Christian community existed in that city. It was also probably because the faithful had greatly multiplied in the Roman capital and had thereby occasioned some hostile movements on the part of the Jews against them, that Claudius published the edict above referred to, and of which Suetonius † says, " Judæos impulsore Chresto assidue tumultuantes Roma expulit." ‡

3. St. Paul's Release After a Two Years' Imprisonment. The centurion Julius, upon arriving at Rome, naturally delivered without delay Paul and the other prisoners to the prætorian prefect, who was at that time the illustrious Burrhus, and who showed to the Apostle all the indulgence a prisoner could receive. The Apostle was therefore allowed to dwell under military custody in his own hired house, with full permission to receive all that came to him. Without delay he availed himself of that liberty to have an interview with the chief of the Jews, to vindicate his reputation, and at the same time to call forcibly their attention to passages of Holy Writ, which told conclusively for the Messiahship of Jesus. The result of this conference was apparently not very successful, and we are not told whether any such was held between Paul and the Roman Jews dur-

---

* Cfr. ROM. i. 7, 8; xvi. 5 sq. † CLAUDIUS, chap. xxv.
‡ For the exact meaning of the word " Chrestus," see CRELIER, FOUARD, SANDAY, etc.

ing the "two whole years" which the Apostle spent awaiting the judgment of the emperor. During this time, also, he preached freely the Gospel to all comers, and wrote the two epistles to the Colossians and Ephesians, which so closely resemble each other ; that to the Philippians ; and finally the short but exquisitely delicate note to Philemon.

As the narrative of the book of the Acts ends with the mention of St. Paul's two years of imprisonment, it is difficult to say what became of him afterwards. Some have supposed that this period closed with St. Paul's trial and death, and have urged two principal arguments in support of that view : (1) the silence of the writer of the book of the Acts, who must have known of such a release if an actual fact, who, since he speaks of the two years' imprisonment, had a natural opportunity to mention also the vindication of the Apostle even at the tribunal of Cæsar, and who, indeed, should have mentioned it, because such an acquittal would have constituted a magnificent climax in the long series of instances which he gives of the favorable treatment accorded to St. Paul by the Roman authorities ; (2) the silence of all the apologetic writers of the end of the first and of the first part of the second centuries, who used every means to prove that the Christian religion was no enemy to state and society, and yet nowhere referred to a release of St. Paul, that is, to a striking argument in favor of their position, if such a release was known to have occurred.*

To these negative arguments—and scholars who deny St. Paul's liberation at this time have only such to offer—the great majority of scholars, Catholic and Protestant alike, reply by the positive testimonies of a tradition sufficiently early and explicit in favor of a successful termination of St. Paul's first imprisonment.† These same scholars appeal

---

* Cfr. MacGiffert, The Apostolic Age, p. 417 sq.

† Cfr., for instance, St. Clement of Rome, 1 Epist. to Corinthians, chap. v.; Muratori's Canon, in its account of the Acts of the Apostles; Eusebius, Ecclesiastical History, book II., chap. 22, etc.

also, and, according to our mind, rightly, to the Pastoral Epistles,* which contain many historical facts which cannot be placed before any portion of St. Paul's life previous to or during his first imprisonment; for even supposing, for argument's sake, that these epistles were not written by the Apostle to whom tradition ascribes them, yet their very early composition and ascription to St. Paul argue powerfully in favor of his release at this time. To these positive arguments it may be added here by way of confirmation that if it is strange—as every one must grant—that St. Luke should not have recorded St. Paul's release if it actually occurred, much more strange still must it appear that, if the Apostle was executed after his two years' imprisonment, the writer of the book of the Acts should not have mentioned the unsuccessful end of the trial and the death of his great hero. Again, as regards the silence of the early apologetic writers above referred to, it seems that the objection based on it loses sight of the fact that these apologists could not appeal to the release of St. Paul as an argument in favor of Christianity without giving ground for the retort that in the person of that very same Paul the cause of the new religion had been ultimately condemned after a more thorough examination of its principles and character : it is therefore possible to account satisfactorily for their silence otherwise than by denying a first release of the Apostle. Finally, it should be noticed that if we take into account the friendly testimony of Julius, the centurion, the favorable reports of Felix, the former, and of Festus, the actual, procurator of Judæa, the liberation of St. Paul appears much more likely than his execution at this time.†

* 1 and 2 to Timothy, Epistle to Titus.

† Cfr. FOUARD, St. Paul, Ses dernières Années, chap. v.; CONYBEARE and HOWSON, chap. xxvii.

§ 2. *Last Journeys of St. Paul.*

1. In the West. The greatest obscurity rests on the journeys undertaken by St. Paul between his first and second Roman imprisonment ; yet, as he had long cherished the project of evangelizing the West, it may well be supposed that not long after his release he carried this into effect. Some Protestant writers of this century have endeavored to prove that during these Western travels the Apostle went to England and implanted faith in that island, but, whatever the motives which suggested this supposition, it is beyond doubt that this visit, as Lightfoot puts it,* possesses "neither evidence nor probability," and in point of fact this journey to Great Britain is now universally given up. Not so with a voyage to Spain, which St. Paul had purposed to make after passing through Rome.† St. Clement of Rome, a writer of the first century, and perhaps one of the disciples of St. Paul,‡ refers probably to that voyage when he says that the Apostle "went to the extremity of the West,"§ and the Canon of Muratori, less than a century afterwards, speaks explicitly "of the departure of Paul from Rome into Spain." True there are no memorials of the missionary labors of the great Apostle in that country, but this should not surprise us, since, on the one hand, we have only a few facts in Spanish history referable to the period before the fourth century, and since, on the other hand, there is likewise no traditional trace of his work in other districts in which, however, he certainly labored. It has been surmised that his stay in Spain was of about two years, but in our utter lack of evidence in this regard it is better to refrain from conjecture.‖

2. In the East. Much obscurity surrounds likewise the last journeys of St. Paul in the East, although in connection

---

* St. Clement.   † Rom. xv. 24, 28.   ‡ Cfr. Philip. iv. 3.   § 1 Cor. v.
‖ Moule, On Romans, p. 23.

with them the Pastoral Epistles supply some useful data.
From Spain it does not seem that he would have any
special difficulty in reaching the churches he had formerly
founded in Greece, Macedonia, and Asia Minor, for there
was at that time " constant commercial intercourse between
the East and Massilia (the modern Marseilles) ; and Massilia
was in daily communication with the Iberic peninsula."[*]
He naturally redeemed the promise he had made soon to
visit Philippi ;[†] then, he might easily cross to Troas, where
he tells us that he left his cloak, books, and parchments,[‡]
and proceed to Ephesus, that great capital of proconsular
Asia, which he seems to have also visited when travelling
westward, as we learn from his words to Timothy, " I
desired thee to remain at Ephesus, when I went into Macedonia."[§]   When in Ephesus he would probably visit the
church of Colossa, according to his promise to Philemon.[‖]
From Colossa he might proceed to Miletus, where he left
Trophimus sick,[¶] and from Miletus sail to the island of
Crete, where he left Titus that he " should set in order the
things that are wanting." [**] In his epistle to Titus he mentions his resolve to winter in Nicopolis, probably the city of
that name in Epirus, in which case he would go to Corinth
and thence proceed to Nicopolis.[††]

Such are the principal Eastern cities and places which the
student of New Testament history may feel pretty sure
were visited by the great Apostle before his second Roman
imprisonment, but the order in which they have been described, although a plausible one, because founded on all
our available data, is to a very large extent conjectural. It
is also very likely that he went through many other places,
particularly of Asia Minor, but we have no means of determining which were those favored spots. The principal

---

* CONYBEARE and HOWSON, chap. xxvii.   † Cfr. PHILIP. ii. 24.
‡ 2 TIM. IV. 13.   § 1 TIM. i. 3.   ‖ PHIL. 22.
¶ 2 TIM. iv. 20.   ** TITUS i. 5.   †† TITUS iii. 12.

reason for admitting that Ephesus was the place of St. Paul's arrest is that Alexander, a coppersmith of that city, appears as the principal accuser of the Apostle after the magistrates had forwarded him to Rome.* Moreover, among the ruins of Ephesus a tower is still pointed out bearing the name of St. Paul's prison, and in which he is supposed to have been detained until he was sent to Rome ; but, of course, not much value can be ascribed to that tradition.

§ 3. *Second Imprisonment and Death.*

1. **Second Imprisonment of St. Paul.** We have, it is true, no positive information about the exact reason for which the great Apostle was again sent to Rome for trial. Yet it may be supposed with a fair amount of probability that when tried in Ephesus and when about to be condemned especially because teaching a religion whose tenets implied treason against Cæsar, he as a Roman citizen threw in an appeal from that inferior tribunal to that of Cæsar, and was in consequence again forwarded as a prisoner to the capital of the empire. †

It is naturally assumed that this second imprisonment was more severe than the first. A tradition which goes back only to the fifth century, and which is found for the first time in the interpolated Acts of the holy martyrs Processus and Martinianus, speaks of the Mamertine prison, at the foot of the Capitoline Hill, as the dungeon into which St. Paul was now thrown. This tradition is perhaps grounded on fact ; if so, it must be understood to refer to the upper part of that prison, for in it alone the Apostle, not yet entirely debarred from intercourse, could see the friends who had the courage to come and visit him.‡ However this may be, the excellent prætorian prefect Burrhus had died early in

---

* Cfr. Acts xix. 33, 34; 2 Tim. iv. 14, 15.   † Cfr. 2 Tim. i. 11, 12.
‡ 2 Tim. i. 15, 16.

62 A.D. and had been replaced by Tigellinus and Fenius Rufus ; the centurion Julius and the procurator Festus could no longer intervene in behalf of Paul, so that it is only natural to suppose that he was kept in close confinement, instead of being allowed, as formerly, to dwell in his own hired lodging and receive all comers.*

With the spring opened the regular term for trials, and as by this time accusers and documents had reached Rome St. Paul's case came up in due order before the imperial tribunal.   It is probable that at this preliminary trial he was brought before the emperor himself.   Nero still heard in person appeals in criminal causes, and in 2 Tim. (iv. 17) St. Paul says that he "was delivered out of the mouth of the lion," a metaphor which some years before had been applied to the Emperor Tiberius, when his death was made known to King Agrippa I., by his freedman Marsyas.† It is indeed wonderful that in this first trial the Apostle was not sentenced to death, for while a certain Alexander, a coppersmith, was now a most implacable prosecutor, Paul was in this, his sorriest need, deserted by all.   But if no man stood with him, as he tells us, the Lord stood by him, gave special power to his words, and delivered him out of the mouth of the lion.   The Apostle was remanded to his prison, and there waited for a second trial, which he rightly conjectured would lead to his execution.‡

However little we know for certain about St. Paul's first trial, we know still less concerning the second one, beyond the assured fact that it ended with his condemnation, and the probability that this time the emperor did not preside over the tribunal in person (as may be inferred from the words of St. CLEMENT of Rome, Corint. V.); all the rest, such as the grounds for condemnation, the quality of the accusers,

* Cfr. 2 TIM. i. 17; ii. 9.

† JOSEPHUS, Antiq. of the Jews, book XVIII., chap. vi., § 10.

‡ 2 TIM. iv. 14, 18.   For much useful legal information in reference to this first trial see LEWIN, vol. ii., pp. 377-381.

etc., is involved in deep obscurity. It may well be supposed, however, that the undaunted champion of Christ
openly professed his faith, protesting at the same time that
he had not violated any law found in the statute book ; *
but as a Christian he was probably pronounced guilty of
treason against Cæsar, and as a Roman citizen he was
sentenced to decapitation.

2. Death of St. Paul. The unanimous account of St.
Paul's death which has been handed down to us is that he
was beheaded outside Rome, on the road to Ostia, at a
place called Aquæ Salviæ, and now known as Tre Fontane
(the Three Fountains), about 2 miles from the city. On
the one hand, this account agrees well with the usage of
that time, viz., that the decapitation by the sword was
oftentimes inflicted at some distance from Rome on those
prisoners whose death might attract too much notice in the
capital. On the other hand, it seems to point to a date
when Nero's edict of a bloody persecution against the
Christians had not yet been published, rather than to a
time when that edict had been already carried into effect,
and when, consequently, the Apostle of the Gentiles would
probably have been beheaded within the walls by the centurion in charge of the execution. In so far, then, this
unanimous account offers a confirmation of what our
chronological calculations would naturally lead us to admit,
viz., that St. Paul's martyrdom occurred sometime before
the night of 19th of July, A.D. 64, on which began the burning of Rome, which soon occasioned Nero's ferocious edict
against the innocent followers of Christ.

This date is indeed a little earlier—by two or three years
—than the dates 66 or 67, usually mentioned in reference
to St. Paul's second trial and death, but it should be borne
in mind (1) that there is no year clearly defined by early
tradition on this point ; (2) that the divergence of three

* LEWIN, vol. ii., p. 400.

years between the date admitted here and the one more commonly received (67 A.D.) is to be referred to the fact that, with such Catholic scholars as Patrizi and Kellner, and other prominent writers of our day, we think that Festus was appointed governor of Judæa as early as 55 A.D. As to the month of June, in which since the fourth century the Western churches have celebrated the principal feast of St. Paul, together with that of St. Peter, it fits in well enough with what has been said above in connection with the holding of the trial of the Apostle in the spring of the year 64 A.D., and may therefore be retained, although some—among whom DUCHESNE, Les Origines Chrétiennes—have suspected that the 29th of June is simply an anniversary of the common translation of the relics of Peter and Paul which took place in 258 A.D.*

§ 4. St. Paul's Personal Appearance and Character.

1. **Personal Appearance.** It is impossible to describe with anything like fulness and accuracy the personal appearance of St. Paul, for our sources of information are both scanty and late. Yet as the passing descriptions of the great Apostle which have come down to us agree in several particulars, both with one another and with early pictures and mosaics, it cannot be denied that to some extent, at least, they give us correct data respecting St. Paul's countenance. † They all agree in speaking of his small stature, ‡ his long face with high forehead, aquiline nose, close and prominent eyebrows. Other features mentioned are partial baldness, gray beard, a clear complexion, and a

---

* Cfr. CEILLIER, Auteurs Sacrés, tome i., p. 219, footnote 9, TROCHON, Introduction, tome iii., p. 297, footnote 5 ; LEWIN, St. Paul, vol. ii., p. 405, footnote 163.

† The position assumed here is confirmed by the portrait of St. Paul on a very early medal discovered by Boldetti in the cemetery of Priscilla (see NORTHCOTE and BROWN-LOW, Roma Sotterranea).

‡ Cfr. 2 Cor. x. 10–14.

winning manner. * It may also be inferred from a passage
of the book of the Acts (xiv. 11) that there was in his face
a quick and animated expression, for we read that the inhabitants of Lystra, surmising Barnabas to be Jupiter, probably
from his majestic stature, took Paul as the eloquent and
active Mercury. Again, many scholars consider it probable
that the chronic and painful infirmity of which the Apostle
speaks repeatedly † was a severe inflammation of the eyes,
and appeal with great plausibility to several passages of
Holy Writ, such as Galat. vi. 11 ; iv. 15 ; Acts xxiii. 2–5, as
bearing them out. Indeed some, taking into account the
effects of ophthalmia in Eastern countries, go even so far as
to think that at times his eyes must have presented an un-
sightly and almost loathsome appearance. ‡

Finally, St. Paul ever wore the Jewish garb, and as this
resembled closely the Egyptian dress, it is not surprising
that, at the time of his arrest in Jerusalem, the tribune
Lysias should have supposed that he was that Egyptian
impostor who had hitherto foiled all pursuit.

2. **Character of St. Paul.** Of all the men mentioned
in the Bible, none has been more justly, more constantly
and more universally praised than the Apostle of the Gentiles. His character is made known to us in almost all
its aspects by the narrative of the book of the Acts and by
his own writings, and yet there is hardly one feature of it
which we would feel not to deserve our full admiration. Of
course, we can point out here only the principal traits of the
man, of the Christian, and of the Apostle.

Born in Tarsus of Jewish parentage, he was deeply attached to the city of his birth and to the race from which he
sprang;§ but this did not prevent him from prizing his right

---

* See FOUARD, St. Peter, chap. vii., p. 127, footnote 3 ; LEWIN, St. Paul, vol. ii.,
p. 410 sq.

† 1 COR. xv. 31 ; 2 COR. iv. 10 ; GALAT. iv. 13, 14.

‡ FOUARD, St. Peter, p. 126 ; LEWIN, St. Paul, vol. i., p. 186 sq.

§ ACTS xxi. 39.

of Roman citizenship and desiring to behold other cities besides his native place, and even besides Jerusalem, the metropolis of Judaism and of early Christianity. Frank, sincere, noble-minded, he could not help feeling indignant at the sight of everything low, insincere or selfish,* and with his keen sense of what was fair and just, he promptly resented anything that looked like a denial of justice † or an underhand interference with his rights. ‡ No one can help admiring his singleness of purpose, his strong will and his unflagging energy, so wonderfully combined with tact and courtesy. § Endowed with a deeply affectionate heart, he vividly appreciated whatever kindness and service were shown to him ; ‖ keenly felt the ingratitude or desertion of his friends or fellow-workers,¶ and evinced the liveliest interest and tenderest love for his faithful friends.** Finally, to a quick, penetrating and versatile mind was joined in him a wonderful power of adaptability to the most varied circumstances of time and place.

Of course all the precious natural qualities of mind and heart which may be noticed in Saul were raised to a higher order of perfection when, shaking off the yoke of Judaism with its exclusiveness and that of Pharisaism with its bigotry, he " put on Christ Jesus," the Redeemer of all nations. Furthermore, new virtues were implanted in his soul, and under the influence of divine grace, ever fruitful in him, †† developed into a Christian life the perfection of which can hardly be imagined, since it made of Paul so faithful a copy of Christ that he could write under the inspiration of the Holy Ghost : " Be ye followers of me, as I also am of Christ ; " ‡‡ and again : " I live, now not I, but Christ liveth in me."§§   Great indeed was his compassion

---

* Cfr. ACTS xiii. 8 sq.; xv. 38 sq.; GALAT. ii. 11 sq.   † ACTS xxiii. 1–3 ; xxv. 9–11.
‡ GALAT. ii. 3–5.   § GALAT. ii. 2 sq.; ACTS xxi. 39 sq.; xxvi. 24–29.
‖ 2 TIM. i. 16–18 ; ROM. xvi. 2.   ¶ 2 TIM. i. 15 ; iv. 9.
** PHILIP. ii. 27 ; ROM. xvi. 13, etc.   †† 1 COR. xv. 10.   ‡‡ 1 COR. xi. 1.
§§ GALAT. ii. 20.

for the poor, his forbearance towards his enemies, and his condescension towards the weak ; greater still were his humility, which made him look upon himself as less than the least of the believers, and his love of bodily mortification and of the cross, having constantly before his mind the uncertainty of salvation and the absolute necessity of union to Christ's sufferings here below to share in Christ's glory hereafter. But what was foremost in his thoughts and in his affections was the love of the Son of God, "Who had loved him and had given Himself up for him." It was this love of Christ which was the great stimulus of his entire life,[*] which caused him to challenge all creatures to be able to separate him from Christ, the supreme object of his affections,[†] to long for death in order to be forever with Christ;[‡] to be ready to die for the sake of His name ;[§] and finally, to exclaim : " If any one love not Our Lord Jesus Christ, let him be anathema !"[‖]

But it is especially when we consider St. Paul as an apostle that we are struck with admiration for his lofty character. Through the purest love for God and for souls[¶] he looks upon himself as under obligation to preach the Gospel to all : "to the Greeks and to the barbarians, to the wise and to the unwise," to the Jews and to the Gentiles. To fulfil this obligation he sacrifices every other purpose in life, gives up all that he has, and is ready to lay down his very life. For this same end he undertakes the most dangerous journeys by sea and by land, exposes himself to all kinds of persecutions, sufferings and privations, becomes " to the Jews a Jew, that he may gain the Jews," and "makes himself the servant of all, that he may gain the more," etc. He is full of the tenderest love for his weak converts,[**] knows how to encourage them either by praise or by reproach, brings down to the level of their intelligence the

---

[*] 2 Cor. v. 14.   [†] Rom. viii. 35–39 ; Philip. iii. 20.   [‡] Philip. i. 23.
[§] Acts xxi. 13.   [‖] 1 Cor. xvi. 22.   [¶] 2 Cor. xii. 14.   [**] Galat. iv. 19.

deepest mysteries which have been revealed to him, and for their sake does not fear to grapple with the most difficult problems of the day. His disinterestedness in pursuing the work of the ministry is probably greater than that of any apostolic teacher of the time, and his ambition to win hearts to the loving service of Christ is coextensive with the ends of the world. He is not satisfied with founding and organizing churches, but he watches over their spiritual interests even when a prisoner far from them, and knows how to urge them to carry out not only the precepts but also the counsels of the New Law. In a word, Paul was indeed "to Christ a vessel of election to carry His name before the Gentiles, and kings, and the children of Israel." *

* Acts ix. 15.

SYNOPSIS OF CHAPTER XXVIII.

LABORS OF ST. PETER AND ST. JAMES.

I. LABORS OF ST. PETER:

1. In Asia Minor (1 Pet. i. 1) and Probably in Corinth (1 Cor. i. 12; ix. 5).

2. In Rome:
   - Arrival of St. Peter in Rome.
   - St. Peter, bishop of Rome:
     - The fact,
     - Its bearing.
   - St. Peter and St. Mark:
     - The Gospel according to St. Mark.
     - The church of Alexandria.
   - Martyrdom of St. Peter (place and date).

3. St. Peter's Personal Appearance and Character.

II. ST. JAMES OF JERUSALEM:

1. The Christian Church of Jerusalem between 45 and 70 A.D.

2. Was James "the Brother of the Lord" identical with James "the Son of Alpheus"?

3. The position of St. James
   - in the eyes of the Jews (the Epistle of St. James).
   - in the eyes of the apostles and early Christians.

4. Martyrdom of St. James (Manner and Date).

331

CHAPTER XXVIII.

LABORS OF ST. PETER AND ST. JAMES.

§ 1. *Labors of St. Peter.*

1. In Asia Minor and Probably in Corinth. When we bear in mind the very prominent part ascribed to St. Peter in the preaching of Christianity by the opening chapters of the book of the Acts,* it seems strange indeed that afterwards only incidental notices of his labors should be found in this and the other inspired writings of the New Testament. This appears all the more surprising because all such incidental notices † clearly point to a fact which we would of course expect, viz., that the greatest consideration continued to surround his words and person. But whatever may be thought of the fragmentary character of these notices, it cannot be denied that they supply valuable though scanty details about the labors of the head of the Church during the long and eventful journeys of St. Paul which we have briefly described in the preceding chapters.

Thus from these sources of information we learn that, while St. Paul was pre-eminently the Apostle of the Gentiles, St. Peter was regarded as especially entrusted " with the gospel of the circumcision," ‡ and that he probably preached the glad tidings of salvation " to the children of Israel dispersed through Pontus, Galatia, Cappadocia, Asia, and Bithynia." § During his missionary labors he was, not

---

* ACTS i. 15; ii. 14; iii.-v.; viii. 14-20; ix. 32; xii. 17.
† ACTS xv. 7-12; GALAT. i. 18; ii. 7, 11-15; 1 COR. i. 12; ix. 5; 1 PETER i. 1.
‡ GALAT. i. 7, 8.   § 1 PETER i. 1.

unlikely, accompanied by his wife, who rendered to him those services which "the rest of the apostles and the brethren of the Lord" received from pious women who followed them with a view to contribute towards the spread of the Gospel by every means in their power, such as assisting the missionaries with their worldly goods, preaching to and baptizing women in the various cities which they traversed.*

Finally, from an allusion of St. Paul to Cephas' party, as a Corinthian faction distinct from those of Paul and Apollo, to whose preaching in Corinth these latter parties owed their origin, it has been inferred that the existence of Cephas' party pointed back likewise to the preaching of St. Peter in the capital of Achaia.† This inference is, indeed, rejected by many, yet it seems to be fairly probable, since St. Dionysius of Corinth, writing in the latter part of the second century, is quoted by Eusebius‡ as speaking of Peter and Paul as the founders of the Corinthian Church.

2. In Rome. It is hardly necessary in the present day to rehearse all the testimonies which go to prove that St. Peter went to Rome (*that is "the Babylon" spoken of in* 1 *Peter v.* 13) and labored there : to appeal, for instance, to the words of St. Clement of Rome (about 95 A.D.) in his Epistle to the Corinthians,§ to those of St. Ignatius Martyr a few years later in his Epistle to the Romans,‖ of St. Dionysius of Corinth,¶ of Clement of Alexandria,** of St. Irenæus,†† of Tertullian,‡‡ who all wrote before the end of the second century, and referred explicitly or implicitly to St. Peter's presence in the capital of the empire. All their testimonies, and countless others in the third and following centuries, have been tested over and over again by critics, by Catholics, Protestants, and Rationalists alike, and the

* 1 Cor. ix. 5. Cfr. Fouard, St. Peter, pp. 247, 248.   † 1 Cor. i. 12.
‡ Ecclesiastical Hist., book II., chap. xxv.   § Chaps. v., vi.
‖ Chap. iv.   ¶ Cfr. Eusebius, Eccles. Hist., book II., chap. xxv.
** Eusebius, book VI., chap. xiv.   †† Adv. Hæreses, book III., chap. i., § 1.
‡‡ De Præscriptione Hæreticorum, chaps. xxxii., xxxvi.

unequivocal verdict is that "in the light of such early and unanimous testimony it may be regarded as an established fact that Peter visited Rome." *

But while this most important point may be considered as settled, the same thing cannot be said of the question of the time when St. Peter reached the capital of the world, for the reference to this tradition is comparatively late and apparently discordant. It is only with Eusebius that we begin to hear of a date for the coming of Peter to Rome, and unfortunately his chronology is somewhat inconsistent, for, while in his *Chronicle* he admits that the apostle came to Rome in the third year of Caligula (March 15th, A.D. 39 to March 15th, A.D. 40), in his *Ecclesiastical History* † he puts St. Peter's arrival under Claudius (January 24th, A.D. 41, to October 13th, A.D. 54). Unfortunately, also, Lactantius— or whoever may be the author of the " De mortibus Persecutorum "—ascribes the arrival of the head of the Church under the reign of Nero, " after the apostles had preached already for twenty-five years." ‡ It is, indeed, true that the influence of St. Jerome, who, in his Latin revision of Eusebius' Chronicle, adopted the precise year 42 A.D.,§ the second year of Claudius, as the date of Peter's coming to Rome, has rendered this date extremely prevalent among subsequent ecclesiastical writers, yet it cannot be denied that for several centuries its accuracy has been questioned and rejected by many scholars, both within and without the Church.

Perhaps the most probable view regarding the arrival of St. Peter in the capital of the empire is the one which admits that he made two distinct visits to Rome, the first one either under Caligula or early under Claudius, the other one

---

* MacGiffert, p. 591.   Cfr., among other authorities, De Smedt, Dissertat. in primam ætatem; Fouard, St. Peter, appendix iv.
† Book II., chap. xiv.
‡ Cfr. Patrologia Lat., vol. vii., p. 195.
§ Cfr. also St. Jerome's De Viris Illustribus in Patr. Lat., vol. xxiii., p. 607.

under Nero. This opinion presents a plausible account of the fluctuations of ecclesiastical tradition concerning St. Peter's arrival in Rome and harmonizes well with the traditional length of twenty-five years of his Roman episcopate, traces of which go as far back as the end of the second century.[*] Again, it enables us to understand how the church of Rome had already assumed the form of a flourishing and well-organized community when St. Paul wrote his Epistle to the Romans ; why the Apostle of the Gentiles, who desired so much to see the capital of the empire, was, however, long deterred from going to and preaching in it " lest he should build upon another man's foundation "; why, in fact, he did not intend to preach, but simply to call there on his way to Spain.[†] Finally, the theory in question gives a natural explanation of the singular fact that the ancient martyrologies mention two distinct festivals in honor of the Chair of St. Peter, the former of which, marked for January 18th, was destined to commemorate the " Cathedra S. Petri qua primum Romæ sedit."

But whatever difficulties may be found in the way of determining the precise date of St. Peter's arrival in Rome, it remains beyond doubt that he visited that city and labored long therein, for only his prolonged leadership can account for the honor in which his memory was universally held by the Christians of Rome, and for the way in which his figure overshadowed that of the great Apostle of the Gentiles. Indeed, to admit that St. Peter ever set his foot in the Eternal City—as most Protestant writers actually do— otherwise than in virtue of the fulness of his apostolic power must ever appear a strange position to hold, and one arising from strong prejudices against the authority possessed by the Roman pontiffs to feed the whole flock of Christ as successors of St. Peter. If the prince of the apostles went to Rome at all, and especially if he long labored

---

[*] Cfr. DUCHESNE, Les Origines Chrétiennes, p. 73.   [†] ROM. XV. 20-24.

and died there, it must seem only reasonable to grant that
the Roman Church has the right to trace back the series of
her bishops to the one who was pre-eminently her first bishop,
to affirm that each of his successors holds an authority in-
herited from him, and finally to claim for itself that fulness
of power which Christ had entrusted to Peter, and "which
makes it a matter of necessity that every church should
agree with this Church on account of its pre-eminent authority." *

The precise form of teaching used by this first bishop of
Rome has been embodied and handed down to us in our
second canonical gospel, the writing of which, according to
a very ancient tradition recorded by Eusebius,† is the work
of Mark, the spiritual "son" of St. Peter.‡ In point of
fact the rapid, graphic, circumstantial, and eminently practical character of St. Mark's gospel commends it as an
original and faithful picture of the living word of Peter,
the former fisherman of Galilee and the personal witness
of the deeds of Christ, when addressing such men of action
as the Romans of his time. It is to this same disciple of
St. Peter that tradition ascribes the foundation of the great
Church of Alexandria in Egypt, and although the tradition
to that effect is found for the first time in the Ecclesiastical
History of Eusebius—that is, not earlier than the fourth
century—it should not be rejected at once, for it is beyond
doubt that this historian had at his disposal early and
complete lists of the Alexandrian bishops.§

That St. Peter suffered martyrdom in Rome is a fact no
less certain than his arrival in that great city, for the same
testimonies which tell in favor of the latter establish equally
well the former.   Tradition affirms also with no less cogency
that he suffered under Nero, and several particulars which

---

* St. Irenæus, Adv. Hæreses, book III., chap. iii., § 2.
          † Eccles. Hist., book III., chap. xxxix.   ‡ 1 Peter v. 13.
§ Cfr. Eccles. Hist., book II., chap. xxv.; book III., chaps. xiv., xxi.

have come down to us through the same channel place
it practically beyond doubt that he suffered in the great
Neronian persecution.   This is notably the case with the
traditional statement that he was crucified,* and more particularly still with the declaration that he was buried in
the Vatican,† for the imperial circus and gardens of the
Vatican were then the great scene of the butchery.   As
the great fire of Rome began about the middle of July
64 A.D., and as the bloody edict of persecution appeared
and was carried out very soon afterwards, it is probable
that St. Peter was one of the early victims of Nero, and
that he was put to death either before the end of 64 or in
the beginning of 65 A.D.—that is, only a few months after
the Apostle of the Gentiles.   This opinion is indeed somewhat at variance with the commonly received view that
the two apostles died on the same day—a view the preva-
lence of which is perhaps to be traced back to the influence
of St. Jerome,—but it harmonizes well with what was the
primitive tradition of the Church, viz., that Peter and Paul
" suffered martyrdom *about the same time.*" ‡

3. St. Peter's Personal Appearance and Character.

The earliest known representation of St. Peter's features is
that on a medal recently found in the cemetery of Domitilla,
and probably referable to the close of the first or the begin-
ing of the second century.   It is in close agreement with the
traditional representations in old Greek mosaics and other
early Christian pictures, and the features of the apostle are
so strongly characterized as to have all the appearance of a
portrait.   He has a broad forehead, rather coarse features,
an open and undaunted countenance, short gray hair and
short thick beard, both curled, full lips, and protruding eye-

* See TERTULLIAN, de Præscriptione Hæreticorum, chap. xxxvi.; ORIGEN, quoted by
EUSEBIUS, Eccles. Hist., book III., chap. i.

† See CAIUS of Rome, quoted by EUSEBIUS. Eccles. Hist., book II., chap. xxv.

‡ ST DIONYSIUS of Corinth, quoted approvingly by EUSEBIUS, Ecclesiastical History, book II., chap. xxv.   Cfr. 1 PETER iv. 12.

brows. This representation harmonizes also with the following descriptive portrait which Nicephorus, a Greek historian of the fifteenth century, gives of St. Peter, and which he probably took from some ancient picture of the apostle : " He was not fat, but pretty tall and upright ; had a fair and rather pale countenance. His hair and beard were thick, frizzled, and not long. His eyes were black, his eyebrows protuberant, his nose somewhat long and rather flat than sharp." *

It seems, therefore, that the personal appearance of the prince of the apostles contrasted much with, and was in some particulars inferior to, that of St. Paul ; and perhaps the same thing may be said in reference to his character when compared with that of the Apostle of the Gentiles. By nature, and indeed as by an almost necessary outcome of his primitive avocation in life, he was more self-reliant and less refined than St. Paul.† He was as good and sincere a man as his joint founder of the Roman Church, but was much less even-balanced and much more easily betrayed by the impression of the moment into rash words and deeds.‡ In him, then, much more than in the Doctor of the nations, natural dispositions needed to be corrected and elevated by the grace of the apostolate in order that he might remain to the end true to his faith and to his love for his Master ;§ and in point of fact it seems as if this pre-eminent grace of the apostolate had been less successful in perfecting nature in him than in St. Paul, for even long years after he had received the effusion of Pentecost and exercised his apostolic functions he was still "prone to vacillate and often mistaken as to the wisest plan to adopt." ‖

Be this as it may, it cannot be denied that the practical

---

* Ecclesiastical History, book II., chap. xxxvii.   † MATT. xxvi. 33, 35 ; xvi. 22, etc.
‡ MATT. xvii. 4 ; MARK ix. 5 ; JOHN xviii., 10, etc.
§ MATT. xxvi. 34, 69 sq.; LUKE xxii. 31 sq.   ‖ FOUARD, St. Paul, p. 77.

sense and prompt energy which characterized from the first the Galilean fisherman followed him when he took the helm of the Church, and that his habit of speaking quickly for his fellow-disciples proved later of great avail, when once converted he had to confirm his brethren by a prompt and unequivocal expression of the right belief.* Finally, his denials of the Son of God produced in his soul that deep humility which Christ had recommended to those in high station in His Church, and which shone forth in St. Peter's lowly acceptance of Paul's rebuke in Antioch, and more strikingly still in his care to make known in his preaching—recorded, as we have seen, in our second canonical Gospel—many details humiliating to himself.

§ 2. *St. James of Jerusalem.*

1. **The Christian Church of Jerusalem between 45 and 70 A.D.** While St. Peter and St. Paul were spreading the Gospel far and wide St. James presided over the destiny of the Christian church in Jerusalem. He had assumed this responsible and difficult charge soon after the death of " James the brother of John," who was put to death by Herod Agrippa I. in 44 A.D.; and for a long time one of his principal cares was to interest the members of the other Christian communities in the distressing poverty of the faithful who resided in the Holy City. † The great bulk of these consisted, naturally, of Jewish converts, who, more than anywhere else, found it hard to divest themselves of the notion that the Mosaic Law should be fully enforced upon the Gentiles who wished to embrace Christianity, and it must be confessed that in Jerusalem many things concurred to keep them in this frame of mind. The Temple, that magnificent house of Jehovah, upon which they had

* Cfr. LUKE xxii, 32 ; ACTS xv. 11.
† GALAT. ii. 10; 1 COR. xvi. 1-4; ACTS xxiv 17.

been used from their childhood to gaze with national pride, was still standing before their eyes with all the splendor of its architecture and all the pomp of its ceremonial. Its precincts, where was still found the wall of partition with its inscription, threatening instant death against every uncircumcised trespasser, continued to appear to them as sacred as before they had believed in the Messiahship of Jesus, and reminded them forcibly of the immense distance which they had been taught to set between the circumcised and the uncircumcised worshipper of Jehovah. That this Judaistic feeling, and all that it implied, redoubled in intensity when the great Jewish festivals brought into the capital of Judæa circumcised men from every quarter of the world, "with their offerings and vows," can be easily imagined. Thus, then, day after day, year after year, their veneration for the Mosaic worship and ordinances was kept alive, and it made them long for a state of things when all men should worship the great God of Israel in exactly the same manner and under the same conditions as the saintly ancestors of the chosen people. In Jerusalem, also, more than anywhere else, it was easy to remember that Christ Himself had received circumcision and submitted to Mosaic observances, and that, far from rejecting the Law, He had distinctly affirmed that He had not come to destroy the Law or the Prophets.* Finally, both the example of James "the brother of the Lord," who appeared to all a living model of faithfulness to the Law, and the opposite conduct of Paul, who was reported to teach men utter disregard for it, were calculated, each in its own way, to attach the Jewish Christians of Jerusalem to Mosaic social and religious practices.†

It is probably because of its Judaistic appearance that, after the short storm it underwent under Herod Agrippa I., the Christian community of Jerusalem enjoyed long years of freedom from persecution, even while the Jewish leaders

* Matt. v. 17.   † Cfr. Acts xxi. 20-24.

were most bent on bringing about the condemnation and death of St. Paul. It is also likely enough that this long period of peace, joined to the apparent lack of severance of Christianity from Judaism in the Holy City, contributed much to induce a large number of Jews to recognize Jesus as the Messias.*

While the church of Jerusalem shared so much in the religious feelings of the Jews of the time—and continued to do so up to the ruin of the city by Titus in 70 A.D.—it seems that a large number, if not the bulk, of its members, bearing in mind the prophetic words of the Saviour concerning the future ruin of both Temple and city, persevered in their wish that war with Rome should be avoided, despite the well-nigh unbearable injustice and tyranny of Gessius Florus, the second successor of the procurator Festus. In point of fact numbers of them withdrew to Pella shortly before Jerusalem was invested by the Roman forces under Titus.

2. Was James "the Brother of the Lord" Idenical with James "the Son of Alpheus"? It is difficult in the present day to determine whether James "the brother of the Lord," who ruled over the Christians of Jerusalem after 44 A.D., is identical with the apostle James called "the son of Alpheus" in the sacred narrative.† On the one hand, many able scholars urge in favor of the identity (1) how natural it is to suppose that St. Luke, after having recognized only two James, viz., the son of Zebedee and the son of Alpheus, up to the twelfth chapter of the book of the Acts, and, having in that chapter recorded the death of one of them (James the son of Zebedee), should go on in the same and following chapters to speak of " James," meaning thereby the other James already mentioned by him, and not a different James not yet introduced

---

* Cfr. Hegesippus, quoted in Eusebius, Ecclesiastical History, book II., chap. xxiii
† Cfr. Matt. x. 3 ; Mark iii. 18 ; Luke vi. 15 ; Acts i. 13.

to his readers ; (2) that the more probable meaning of St. Paul's words in Galat. i. 19, "But other of the apostles I saw none, saving James, the brother of the Lord," is that the James in question is identical with the son of Alpheus, since here St. Paul speaks of the twelve primitive apostles, from whom he disclaims to have received commission to preach the Gospel ; (3) that the great authority ascribed to James the brother of the Lord among, or even, as we are told, over, apostles * points to one of the primitive apostles, and consequently to one who is to be identified with James the son of Alpheus.†

On the other hand, such Catholic scholars as the Bollandist Henschein, R. Simon, Danko, Schegg, de Smedt, etc., maintain with the current notion of the Greek Church, and with what seems to have been the primitive tradition in this regard, that James the Lord's brother is different from James, the son of Alpheus. They readily admit that the brother of the Lord was an apostle, but only in the same sense as Barnabas or Paul, and appeal to several passages of Holy Writ where the brethren of Jesus are clearly distinguished from the primitive apostles as proving that James, one of the former, should not be identified with one of the latter.‡

Perhaps this second position (to which St. Jerome himself rallied when advanced in years, though he had strenuously defended the first in his youth) is more probable.

3. The Position of St. James in the Eyes of both Jews and Christians. Few Christian bishops ever enjoyed a more general esteem and admiration from their contemporaries than the first bishop of Jerusalem. The Jews, who witnessed day after day his long prayers on his knees in the sanctuary of Jehovah, and knew that in everything

---

* Acts xii. 17 ; xv. 13 ; xxi. 18.
  † Cfr., also GALAT. ii. 9, where James the Lord's brother is placed before Cephas and John.
  ‡ Cfr., for instance, ACTS i. 13, 14 ; MATT. xii. 47 ; JOHN vii. 5.

he gave to his followers the example of a scrupulous obser-
vance of the Mosaic Law, gradually looked upon him as one
of the glories of Judaism, and surnamed him " the Just."*
It is not, therefore, to be wondered at that, profiting by the
great respect which surrounded him in the Holy City, and
which was, of course, noticed by those of the Jewish race
who came to Jerusalem for the yearly festivals, that the
Lord's brother should have addressed " to the twelve tribes
scattered abroad " the catholic epistle ascribed to him.

Nor did he enjoy less authority in the eyes of the apostles and in those of the early Christians. His fellow-
apostles ever saw in him a near relative of Jesus, one who had
been favored with a special apparition of the Lord,[†] and who,
although personally a most strict observer of the Jewish Law,
had clearly realized the divine plan that the Gentiles should
be admitted into the Church without being required to submit to circumcision and to most of what it implied.[‡] Hence
they ever felt that despite his differences from them in outward conduct he was inwardly with them in all essential
points of belief and worship, that he was the man the most
suited to be the head of the church of Jerusalem, then so
entirely Jewish, and, finally, that he was one of the very
" pillars " of primitive Christianity.[§] As to the early Christians of Jerusalem, they had naturally the deepest veneration for the saintly head of the Church, for the man whose
relationship with the Messias was well known, and whose
personal influence in the Holy City secured for them a long
period of peace on the part of the Jewish authorities.

4. **Martyrdom of St. James.** In spite, or rather on
account, of his great popularity in Jerusalem James " the
Just" was sentenced to death in consequence of what
seems to have been a combination of the Pharisees and the
Sadducees. On the one hand, these latter hated a man

---

* Cfr. HEGESIPPUS, in EUSEBIUS, Eccles. History, book II., chap. xxiii.
† I. COR. XV. 7.　　　‡ ACTS XV. 13 sq.; GALAT. ii. 9.　　　§ GALAT. ii. 9.

whose whole influence was exerted in favor of Pharisaic
customs and beliefs and whose daily life was a silent cen-
sure of their own worldly conduct ; on the other hand,
many of the Pharisees, while unable to find fault with his
manner of carrying out the Mosaic Law, were jealous of his
authority, and, especially as he perseveringly made use of it
to discourage their cherished project of a national uprising
against Rome, they watched for an opportunity to put him
to death.   At length, as the successor of Festus delayed
much to reach Palestine, and as Ananus, the new high
priest appointed by Agrippa II., was a Sadducee well known
for his unscrupulousness, this was seized upon as a favorable opportunity to bring about a condemnation by the
union of both Pharisees and Sadducees against James, the
more so because once the sentence was passed it might
freely be carried out without waiting for its ratification by
the procurator, still far away in Alexandria.   The Sanhedrim was therefore gathered by Ananus and the charge of
breaking the Law distinctly set forth against James and
some others : the issue of the trial was of course a sentence
of death.   Even after all these forms of justice the Jewish
leaders did not dare to carry out directly their sentence
against James "the Just," but had recourse to a scheme
calculated, as they thought, to divide the multitude about
his fate.   They got him to ascend the pinnacle of the Temple and bade him to declare himself openly against Jesus.
What they expected happened   James proclaimed generously his faith in Christ, and in consequence his enemies,
simulating a righteous indignation against words so offensive
to Jewish prejudice, hurled him from the eminence and
then stoned him.

Such was probably the manner in which St. James'
martyrdom was brought about in 62 or 63 A.D.*

---

* Cfr. HEGESIPPUS' and JOSEPHUS' accounts of the death of James, quoted in EUSE-
BIUS, Ecclesiastical History, book II., chap. xxiii.   See also PHILIP SCHAFF, Hist. of
the Apostolic Church, p. 381, footnote 2.

SYNOPSIS OF CHAPTER XXIX.

LABORS OF ST. JOHN. CONDITION OF THE CHURCH AT HIS DEATH.

I. LABORS OF ST. JOHN:

1. First Residence at Ephesus:
   - Why and how questioned in our century?
   - Conclusive arguments in its favor.
   - Its probable motives and duration.
2. Banishment to and Sojourn in the Island of Patmos.
3. Second Residence at Ephesus (Legendary Incidents).
4. Death of St. John. His Character.

II. CONDITION OF THE CHURCH AT THE DEATH OF ST. JOHN:

1. The Church and the Roman Empire:
   - Territorial extension.
   - Legal status of Christians.
2. Internal Organization:
   - Conditions of membership.
   - Church officers and their support.
   - Public worship (relation to the Jewish worship).
   - Church discipline.
   - Bonds uniting the various churches.
3. Growing Influence of Christianity upon Public Morals.

345

CHAPTER XXIX.

LABORS OF ST. JOHN. CONDITION OF THE CHURCH AT HIS DEATH.

§ 1. *Labors of St. John.*

1. **First Residence at Ephesus.** The same silence of Holy Writ which surrounds the labors of St. Peter after the opening chapters of the book of the Acts may be noticed in connection with those of his fellow-apostle St. John, the beloved disciple of the Lord. We learn indeed from a passing reference to him in the Epistle to the Galatians (ii. 9) that he was in the Holy City at the time of the Council and was then considered with James and Peter as one of the pillars of the Church, but we are nowhere told in Holy Writ of the scene or precise nature of his labors after the Council of Jerusalem, and it is only through an old tradition that we know of his long residence at Ephesus, in which city also he would have written our fourth canonical gospel. This silence of the New Testament records, combined with that of St. Ignatius Martyr, has led many scholars—most belonging to the Rationalistic school—to suppose that this tradition, first mentioned by Irenæus,[*] originated in a wrong identification made by this ecclesiastical writer of a certain Asiatic presbyter John with the beloved apostle. This they seem the more authorized to suppose because in point of fact at least in one case recorded by

---

[*] Cfr. EUSEBIUS, Ecclesiastical History, book V., chap. xx.; ST. IRENÆUS, Adversus Hæreses, book II., chap. xxii., § 5; book III., chap. i., § 2; chap. iii., § 4.

Eusebius * St. Irenæus wrongly identified the presbyter John with the apostle of that name. †

Notwithstanding these and other no less plausible arguments, the tradition is too strong to be shaken. The testimony of Irenæus to St. John's residence in Asia derives a peculiar force from the fact that he was a pupil of St. Polycarp, a personal disciple of the beloved apostle, and is confirmed by the independent testimony of Polycrates, bishop of Hierapolis in the latter part of the second century, and of his contemporary Clement of Alexandria. To this external evidence it may be added that an internal study of the writings ascribed to St. John proves beyond doubt that in the latter part of the first century there lived in Asia Minor a personage "who had himself felt the direct influence of Jesus and who stamped his conceptions upon a large circle of disciples" ‡—a personage such as the apostle John, to whose presence in Ephesus tradition bears direct and explicit testimony.

But while the residence of the beloved disciple in the capital of proconsular Asia may well be considered as an unquestionable fact, its motives and duration still remain shrouded in the greatest obscurity. If, however, we bear in mind, on the one hand, the great political, commercial, and religious importance of Asia Minor, and, on the other hand, the early rise of heretical doctrines in the great churches which St. Paul had founded in that region, we shall probably have a correct view of the general conditions which induced St. John to take up his residence in Ephesus; but beyond this we cannot go, data failing us regarding the special circumstances of the time when he resolved to settle there. In point of fact, although in a general way it seems pretty clear that his sojourn in proconsular Asia

* Eccles. Hist., book III., chap. xxix.
† Cfr. Revue Biblique, January, 1898, p. 59 sq.
‡ MacGiffert, p. 607.

was a lengthened one, as required by his lasting influence upon its various Christian communities, we have no sure clew as to the precise date of his arrival at Ephesus. It is indeed taken for granted that, since St. Paul in his last epistle to Timothy, just written before his death, does not make, any more than in his other epistles to the Ephesians and Colossians, even the least reference to St. John, the beloved disciple did not appear in Ephesus before the death of the Apostle of the Gentiles: this, however, is but an argument *ex silentio*, and, furthermore, does not help us in determining positively the date when St. John began to reside in proconsular Asia. In like manner the end of his residence is uncertain unless we admit what Tertullian is the first to relate, viz., that in the persecution under Domitian the apostle was taken to Rome and thrown into a cauldron of boiling oil, which, however, did not hurt him ; for in this case John's first sojourn in Ephesus may have been of about fourteen or fifteen years.*

2. **Banishment to and Sojourn in the Island of Patmos.** It is also under Domitian that most of the early ecclesiastical writers who speak of the fact place the banishment of St. John to Patmos, one of the islands in the Ægean Sea. The aspect of this small, rocky, and barren spot agrees well with what we know of the custom of the period to send exiles to the most desolate islands. Of the apostle's sojourn there we have no record outside the statement often found in ecclesiastical writers that it was there that St. John wrote the inspired book of the Apocalypse. His banishment was brought to an end at the death of Domitian (A.D. 96), when Nerva, his successor, restored to liberty all those whom the tyrant had unjustly sent into exile.†

3. **Second Residence at Ephesus.** Of the life of St. John after his return to Ephesus we have only legendary

---

* TERTULLIAN, De Præscriptionibus, chap. xxxvi.
† Cfr. W CÆSAR, The Gospel of John, Its Authorship, 2d ed., p. 34 sq.

reports, which harmonize more or less happily with the character of the apostle. We briefly mention here the three which are best known and are probably grounded on fact.

The first one is recorded by Clement of Alexandria, who relates that after his return to the capital of proconsular Asia St. John, making a visitation tour to appoint bishops and organize churches, met in a town a young man to whom he felt himself strongly attracted and whom he specially commended to the bishop. The lad was first well instructed and next admitted to Baptism ; but by and by the bishop took less care of him, with the final result that the young man became the chief of a band of robbers. Great indeed was the grief of St. John when some time afterwards he revisited the town and learned what had happened. Then it was that the aged apostle hurried off to the place infested by the bandits, was taken by them to their chief, who, recognizing his old friend the apostle John, betook himself to flight. But the good shepherd pursued after him and succeeded in bringing about his conversion.*

A second legend which illustrates another feature of St. John's zeal is told by St. Irenæus,† who narrates that in his time " people were still living who had heard Polycarp relate that John, the disciple of the Lord, having entered a bath-house at Ephesus, and perceiving Cerinthus within, rushed out without bathing, saying : ' Let us fly lest even the bath-house fall upon us, since it contains Cerinthus, the enemy of truth.' "

The third legend is recorded by St. Jerome,‡ who tells us that when the aged apostle was no longer able to walk to the Christian assemblies he was wont to be carried thither, and that his address consisted every time in these simple and affectionate words: " Little children, love one

---

* CLEMENT of Alexandria, Quis Dives Salvabitur? chap. xlii.
† Adv. Hæres., book III., chap. iii., § 4.
‡ Comm. ad Galatas, vi. 10.

another." Wearied with this constant repetition of the
same lesson, his hearers asked him: " Master, why dost
thou always say this?" to which he answered: "Because
that is the Lord's command, and if this alone is done it is
enough."

4. **Death of St. John. His Character.** Despite the
rumor which circulated about the beloved disciple that he
was not to die, and of which we read in the last chapter of
our fourth gospel as of a misinterpretation of the words of
Jesus in his regard, St. John slept in the Lord and was
buried in Ephesus under the reign of Trajan (98–117 A.D.).
Of the various legends connected with his death and burial,
such as, for instance, that he did not actually die, but, like
Enoch, was translated without death, etc., the least that can
be said is that they are fanciful.   The age at which he died
has been variously estimated, some affirming that he lived
eighty-nine years, others one hundred, and others again one
hundred and twenty.   The exact circumstances of his
closing hours are of course unknown.

Of all the primitive apostles of Jesus, John was the best
loved by his Master, and none loved Him more in return
so that he is justly spoken of as the " apostle of love." From
beginning to end he was the sincere, loyal, and devoted
friend of Christ, and because of this he stood by Him at the
foot of the cross, and later rejoiced "at having been accounted worthy to suffer reproach for the name of Jesus." [*]
His was indeed a contemplative love, yet it never degener-
ated into that sentimentality which several, especially
painters, have wrongly conceived as one of the traits of the
apostle's character.   No doubt before the effusion of the
Holy Ghost on Pentecost some traces of jealousy, of personal ambition, and of wrathful feelings may be discovered
in him, and in so far prove that his nature needed perfecting, but they do not necessarily betray the weakness and

* ACTS V. 41.

fickleness of a feminine character. His courage in resisting
the Sanhedrists astonished the supreme judges of Israel no
less than that of Peter,* and his virile conduct during the
first fifteen years of Christianity caused all who knew him
best to look upon him as " one of the pillars " of the Church,
as they did upon James and Cephas.† His severe words
against heretics or unworthy Christians, his desire to be re-
united with Christ, his commendation of God's love towards
men, and the high value he sets upon brotherly love, together with countless other features noticeable in his writings, prove that he closely resembled St. Paul in his manner
of urging the truths of the Gospel upon his fellow-men ;
and it is well known that, like the Apostle of the Gentiles,
he led a life of perpetual celibacy, thus teaching by his own
example how to preserve one's heart undivided. Finally, to
John alone it was given to behold the Word of God in the
bosom of the eternal Father, to lean his head in restful love
upon the Sacred Heart of the Incarnate Word, and to take
the place of Christ Himself near His bereaved mother : and
these invaluable privileges clearly point to corresponding
high features in the apostle's character, such as lofty views,
delicate affection, and absolute trustiness. ‡

§ 2. *Condition of the Church at the Death of St. John.*

1. **The Church and the Roman Empire.** As we
have but a scanty and more or less reliable information
about tne scene and extent of the labors of almost every
other apostle besides Peter, James, John, and Paul, it is, of
course, impossible to give anything like an exact idea of the
territorial extension which the Christian Church had reached
at the death of St. John. It is beyond question, however,

---

* ACTS iv. 13, 19. † GALAT. ii. 9.
‡ For interesting details about John's character see WESTCOTT, Introduction to the
Study of the Gospels, chap. v.

that, like the mustard seed, to which it is compared in the Gospel, Christianity had, less than seventy years after the death of its Founder, taken deep roots in the Roman Empire, stretched forth its branches into almost all its provinces, and offered shelter to its various nationalities. Long, indeed, after Pentecost the early preachers of the Gospel had lingered in Jerusalem or its vicinity; but, once started to conquer the world to Christ, they rapidly founded great centres of Christian worship not only in western Asia, but also in southern Europe (Spain included) and in northern Africa.

Many things contributed towards this rapid and extensive diffusion of the glad tidings of salvation. There was, first of all, the enthusiasm of the early witnesses to Christ's words and deeds, an enthusiasm backed up by examples of heroic virtue and by stupendous miracles. Next, there was the wonderful unity which characterized the Roman rule over all the districts of the empire, and which, in many ways, prepared for their religious unity under the sceptre of Christ. Again, the feelings of countless souls, disgusted with heathenism and made acquainted with the worship of the true God and with the Messianic promises by the proselytism of the Jewish race, led them willingly to embrace the Christian religion, which offered a fulfilment of the Messianic predictions, and did away with the circumcision and other odious peculiarities of Judaism, while it preserved and perfected the monotheistic belief and the high morality of the Jews. Finally, there was the legal status of the Christians, who for long years appeared in the eyes of the Roman authorities throughout the empire simply as a Jewish sect, entitled, despite the opposition it met with from their fellow-Jews, to the same religious and civil toleration as the other worshippers of Jehovah. True the Jewish leaders were anxious to do away with this confusion, to show that Christianity was no mere sect of Judaism, and that, in its distinctive features, it was hostile to Cæsar ; in fact it was probably to their exertions, seconded by Nero's wife, Poppæa, who was a Jewish proselyte, that we must refer the final condemnation of St. Paul, together with those features of the Neronian edict of persecution which, representing the Christians as the enemies of the state, made of it a permanent law of the empire. Yet even this unjust decree, and especially its first sanguinary application in the circus and gardens of the Vatican, forced the existence of Christianity and its distinction from Judaism upon the attention of many, gave them an opportunity to admire the heroic courage of its martyrs, to inquire into and finally embrace its doctrine. Furthermore, a reaction set in even before Nero's death, the persecution abated, and for long years after the demise of the tyrant the Church enjoyed a period of peace, during which it made numbers of converts, some of whom belonged even to the family of the Emperor Diocletian.*

2. Internal Organization of the Church. Together with this rapid growth as to territory and membership, Christianity gradually and rapidly assumed its special internal organization. The conditions of admission into any of its distinct churches were of the simplest kind : it sufficed to believe "that Jesus Christ is the Son of God,"† to repent sincerely for one's sins, and to receive Christian Baptism, which was administered by immersion as far as circumstances of time, place, health, etc., allowed. It is also probable that usually when the head of a family was received into the Church all the persons of the household were admitted to membership, the adults by submitting freely to the same conditions as the head of the family, and the children by receiving Baptism, which made of them members of the Christian Church, just as circumcision had

---

* Cfr. P. ALLARD, Le Christianisme et l'Empire Romain, chap. i.
† ACTS viii. 37 ; 1 JOHN v. 1-5

made of children born under the Old Covenant members of the chosen people of God.*

Besides the men who founded any particular Church and were accordingly called its *apostles*,† each Christian community was placed practically from the beginning under the rule of special officers charged to watch sedulously over its various interests. ‡ Differently from the apostles— and apparently also from the " prophets " and " doctors " who exercised a general ministry resembling in many ways the apostolate §—the regular officers of a church were *appointed* over that special church and intrusted with all the administrative powers required by its peculiar circumstances. It seems probable that these pastors of the flock of Christ were bishops,‖ who governed particular churches with the help of deacons, and who had full power to raise others to the same dignity.¶ As the welfare of a Christian community depended so much on the prudence, integrity, and other moral qualities of these pastors, it is not surprising that high personal qualifications, such as those we find described in the Pastoral Epistles, should have been required in the of-

* Cfr. Acts x. 2, 44-48 ; xvi. 15, 30-33 ; xviii. 8 ; 1 Cor. i. 16 ; xvi. 15.

† Cfr. 1 Cor. ix. 1, 2.   ‡ Cfr. Acts xx. 28-31 ; xiv. 22 ; etc.

§ Cfr. Acts xiii. 1 ; Ephes. ii. 20 ; 1 Cor. xii. 28, etc.

‖ In connection with the government of individual churches during the apostolical age the following leading facts may be noticed :

(1) In his epistles to the Christian communities St. Paul addresses the whole Church, and when calling upon it to adopt any measures makes no mention of ecclesiastical officials.

(2) The hierarchical division he refers to in his Epistle to the Philippians (i. 1) comprises only bishops and deacons.

(3) The ecclesiastical officials spoken of in the Pastoral Epistles and in the book of the Acts seem to constitute a body of presbyters (1 Tim iv. 14), the importance of which appears at an early date in the church of Jerusalem (Acts xv. 2, 6, 22).

(4) Finally, the presbyters are at times called bishops and seem to enjoy the same powers (Acts xx. 17, 28).

These and other such data render it difficult for us to realize the elements of the hierarchy or their methods of government in the early Church, but they are just what we might expect in a period of formation such as was the apostolical age (cfr. Battifol, Revue Biblique, October, 1894 ; April, October, 1895 ; Weiszäcker, The Apostolic Age ; Jas. Hastings, Dictionary of the Bible, art. Bishop ; Church Government).

¶ Cfr. 1 Tim. iii. 1-10 ; Titus i. 5-11 ; Philip. i. 1 ; 1 Peter v. 1-5.

ficers of the early Church. It is indeed conceivable that, after the example of St. Paul, some of them worked at a trade for their own support, but they had certainly a right, founded on the Holy Scriptures of the Old Testament and on one of the sayings of the Lord,* to receive some help from the community to whose spiritual needs they ministered.†

One of the many duties of those Church officers was that of conducting the public worship, which, in the apostolical age, resembled closely that of the Jews. This resemblance was, of course, closest in Jerusalem, where the Christian community exhibited such a Jewish appearance, but it was also striking in the various towns and cities of the Roman empire. Thus, outside the extraordinary divine manifestations, such as prophesying, speaking with tongues, etc., of which we read in the religious meetings of the primitive Church, the public services comprised most likely the reading of a portion of Scripture, together with preaching, prayer, and singing of psalms.‡ Among the new features which could be noticed, we may mention here the public reading of the Apostolic Epistles, the giving of alms for the support of the brethren in need, and above all the celebration of the Holy Eucharist at the close of a common evening meal; to these may also be added the weekly celebration of the first day of the week (our Sunday), while of the great yearly festivals of the Jews two only seem to have been retained, viz., the Passover and Pentecost.

It was also the personal business of the heads of each particular church to watch over the good order of the Christian community outside the public meetings. Every moral abuse they had to reprove, and, as far as possible, they had

---

* I Cor. ix. 9, 13, 14.

† Cfr. I Tim. vi. 8, 9; 2 Tim. ii. 2-4; Gal. vi. 6. See also Allen, Christian Institutions, chap. iii.

‡ Cfr. I Tim. ii. 1 sq.; 2 Tim. ii. 15; Titus i. 9; ii. 7; I Cor. xiv. 16. Cfr. Weizsäcker, The Apostolic Age, vol. ii., p. 275 sq.

to ward off heresies, to put an end to dissensions or law suits between brethren, and even when necessary to cut off from their communion obstinate men of unsound faith or morals.* Other points of church discipline had also been authoritatively determined by the apostles before their death, as, for instance, the regulations concerning the selection of widows, deacons, and other church officers, the rules to be observed when accusations were laid to their charge, etc. That in these early days of Christianity the disciplinary power of the Church was at times vindicated by direct visitations from God for certain sins cannot well be denied;† but, of course, then as now, the ecclesiastical power of coercion was not a physical one, and had for its direct object the spiritual welfare of the culprit as well as of the community.

Finally, these same heads of a particular church did not look upon themselves as upon rulers altogether independent of those from whom they had received ordination ;‡ nor did they look upon the special church entrusted to their care otherwise than upon an integrant part of the flock of Christ and of the house of God. This last feeling was the natural outcome of that community of faith, hope, purpose, and interests which bound together so intimately all the early believers, and which manifested itself in many different ways, such as the welcoming of itinerant prophets and teachers, the exchange of apostolic or other important letters, the sending of official delegates to other communities whenever occasion offered, etc.§ To find the central authority established by Our Lord recognized and exercised we have, however, to wait until a somewhat later period.

Of course, when our canonical gospels made their way into general circulation, they contributed powerfully to keep up and increase the unity of mind and heart which

* Cfr. Acts xx. 28 sq.; 1 Tim. i. 3 ; v. 1 ; Titus i. 11 ; 1 Cor. v.-vi.
† Cfr. Acts v. 1 sq.; 1 Cor. v. 5.   ‡ 1 Tim. v. 17 sq.
§ Cfr. Acts xi. 27 ; 2 Cor. viii. 18, 23, 24 ; Colos. iv. 7-16 ; etc.

bound together the various churches; and this was also the result of the early persecutions and heresies which befell either the whole extent or individual parts of the mystical body of Christ.

3. **Growing Influence of Christianity upon Public Morals.** It is impossible in the present day to define the precise extent to which the rapid growth of Christianity during the apostolic age influenced directly the public morals of the time. Of course all those who sincerely embraced the faith came under the direct influence of the doctrinal and moral teachings of the Church, and in proportion to their efforts to tread in the footsteps of Christ and of His apostles contributed by their lives to raise the tone of society at large. A great change for the better was easily noticed in them—whether Jews or Gentiles, rich or poor, freedmen or slaves—after they had become Christians, and this, together with their perseverance in avoiding former occasions of sin, in practising the virtues befitting their station in life, was calculated to give a high idea of a religion which was capable of producing such results and to prove that its beliefs and its morality were conducive to the public good. It must have been, however, very slowly and indirectly that the spirit of the Gospel, so opposed to that of the pagan world, succeeded in effecting a noticeable difference in the public condition of morals, the more so because the bulk of Christians belonging to the lower ranks of society could have but little, if any, positive influence upon the leading classes. Yet it cannot be denied that Christian rules about marriage and family life were throughout that period incomparably more effective than the imperial decrees of Augustus on the same points; that Christianity, which caused so many men to look upon and deal with the poor and the slave as God's children and as members of one and the same mystical body of Christ, had done very much more than all the phi-

losophers of the time towards raising the dignity of human nature. It is also beyond doubt that the preaching of the Gospel had revealed to countless thousands the purifying power of suffering, the supremacy of conscience, the full value of the human soul, the blessedness of self-sacrifice, the pure joys of close union with God, etc., and thereby awakened in the depths of their hearts a holy enthusiasm for everything good, noble, and generous that would gradually force admiration and provoke imitation. Finally, if we contemplate what the new religion had already accomplished in the line of checking evil passions and of enabling men of all classes to practise heroic virtue, it must be admitted that the Church was destined to influence more and more powerfully public morals by a slow but sure undermining of the selfish views and degrading rites of paganism, and by "leavening," as it were, the whole of human society by the purity of its doctrine and by the grace of its sacraments: "The kingdom of heaven is like to leaven, which a woman took and hid in three measures of meal, until the whole was leavened." *

* MATT. xiii. 33.

CHRONOLOGICAL TABLE

ESTABLISHED ON THE NOW COMMONLY ADMITTED FACT
THAT THE BIRTH OF CHRIST TOOK PLACE SOME YEARS
BEFORE WHAT IS CALLED THE CHRISTIAN ERA.

Part First : The Gospel History.

Herod King of Judæa.....................................B.C. 37–4
Annunciation to Zachary...........................Oct., B.C. 6
Annunciation to Mary......................March–April, B.C. 5
Presentation of Jesus and Visit of the Magi.......February, B.C. 4
Return from Egypt.................................April, B.C. 4
Our Lord's Apparition among the Doctors..........April, A.D. 8
Preaching of John the Baptist.................Summer, A.D. 26
Baptism of Christ.............................January, A.D. 27
Beginning of Public Ministry...........February–April, A.D. 27
The Three Years' Public Ministry........April 27–April 30, A.D.
The Last Supper (Nisan 14th).......Thursday, April 6th, A.D. 30
Crucifixion and Death.................Friday, April 7th, A.D. 30
Resurrection..... ....Sunday, April 9th, A.D. 30
Ascension............. ....Thursday, May 18th, A.D. 30

Part Second : The Apostolical History.

A.D.

The Descent of the Holy Ghost on Pentecost Day...May 28th, 30
Death of St. Stephen...31 or 32
Conversion of Saul...31 or 32
St. Paul's First Visit to Jerusalem........................34 or 35
Death of Herod Agrippa I...................................44

ALPHABETIC INDEX.

CPSIA information can be obtained at www.ICGtesting.com
Printed in the USA
LVOW10s1910010114

367624LV00024B/971/P